Composition
at Virginia Tech

Written, Spoken, and Visual Composition

General Editor
Diana George
Director of Composition

Fifth Edition Author Team
Robin Allnutt, Jennifer Barton, Kelly Belanger, Sheila Carter-Tod
Katie Fallon, Diana George, Kaye Graham, Jennifer Hitchcock
Jennifer Lawrence, Tim Lockridge, Julie Mengert, Jennifer Mooney
Steve Oakey, Kelly Pender, Katy Powell, Suzanne Reisinger
Cheryl Ruggiero, Matthew Vollmer

Photo Editors
Diana George, Jennifer Lawrence, Cathy Skinner

Copy Editor
Ed Weathers

PEARSON
Custom
Publishing

Editor in Chief: Mark Loechel
Acquisitions Editor: Nancy Baudean
Development Editor: Rachel Snyder
Production Manager: Ed Perlmutter
Production Project Manager: Mirta Lind
Rights Editor: Jennifer Sczerbinski
Cover Designer: Eric Tamlin
Manufacturing Buyer: Mary Beth Cameron
Printer: Quebecor Taunton
Text Designer: Sara Arrand
Production and Composition: Sara Arrand, Berit Funke

Cover photographs by Richard Mallory Allnutt, © 2006.

PEARSON CUSTOM PUBLISHING
501 Boylston Street, Suite 900, Boston, MA 02116
A Pearson Education Company

Table of Contents

CHAPTER

3 Critical Thinking, Reading, and Writing   29

Acknowledgements

The English Department would like to acknowledge and give special thanks to Virginia Tech alumnus Richard Mallory Allnutt, seen here as photographed by Alexia Marie Garamfalvi, for the beautiful photograph featured on the front cover, as well as a number of photos in Chapter 7. Richard received part of his undergraduate education here at Virginia Tech, left us for Leicester University in England, then later returned to Tech for his MSc and PhD in Electrical Engineering. Richard now serves as both an Engineering Consultant by designing components for spacecraft antennae and as a freelance photographer. His photos are on covers of magazines such as *JazzTimes* and *Swing Journal,* and in a variety of international aviation magazines such as *Flypast, Aeroplane, Aircraft Illustrated, Combat Aircraft* and even the New Zealand journal *Classic Wings.* Richard also

Richard M. Allnutt

was the set photographer for the feature film *The Distance,* has shot promotional photography for Concord Records and HBO's *The Wire,* and was the production printer for *The Art in War* — a nationally acclaimed photography show on the war in Iraq. More of Richard's work can be viewed at http://www.rmallnutt.com. Thank you, Richard!

The writers of this book owe a profound debt of gratitude to the English Department, especially Chair Carolyn Rude; Tammy Shepherd, who was indispensable in coordinating our contacts with Pearson; Judy Grady, who handles our budget; and Sandra Davis who keeps our records straight.

This is the fifth edition of a highly successful project begun by Paul Heilker and his faculty and staff and carried on by Nancy Metz, Cheryl Ruggiero, Sheila Carter-Tod, and Shelli Fowler. To all who have come before us, we must say that we could not have written this text without your good work to guide us along the way.

Finally, *Composition at Virginia Tech* is successful because our Virginia Tech students are hardworking, talented, and patient. Our humble thanks to you. You make our days in the classroom some of the best.

Welcome from the Virginia Tech Composition Program

Welcome to Virginia Tech and to College Composition in the Department of English. This textbook was designed as a resource for you as you negotiate your way through writing assignments at VT and begin to adapt to the many different writing situations you will encounter as a student here.

Diana George is Professor of Rhetoric and Writing and Director of Composition at Virginia Tech

In Part I of this text, you will find an overview of your composition courses—1105, 1106, and H1204. Here, we present the goals and requirements of those courses. Composition in the English Department is shaped by the National Council of Writing Program Administrators' Outcomes Statement for First-Year Writing. This is a set of outcomes used in colleges and universities across the nation, and we are pleased to be able to introduce it to you in this edition of Composition at Virginia Tech.

Each of the chapters in Part II describes those outcomes in more detail. It is in this section of the text that you will find a fuller explanation for each of the terms in the Outcomes Statement. As well, you will encounter writing by Virginia Tech students and their teachers, discussion points, and exercises to engage you in the work of the course.

Part III shifts our focus to research. You will, of course, be doing library research and Internet searches, and your teacher will want to know that you can incorporate those sources into your own writing and cite sources properly. You will also be asked to do some fieldwork. Depending on your teacher, you might learn to do a short survey, to conduct an interview, or to take observation notes. The information you get from these types of sources is different from library information but just as useful. This section of the text will be especially useful for your work in 1106 or H1204.

Virginia Tech wants its students to have a working understanding of written, spoken, and visual language because there are many times when the written word alone is not the most effective means of communication. Think of how often you receive information through your radio or your iPod. As well, in our increasingly visual culture, the ability to read, analyze and produce visual texts has become as important as the ability to read, analyze, and produce written texts. Part IV, "Visual Literacy and Oral Presentation," will help equip you for working effectively with spoken and visual compositions.

Finally, we realize that in addition to making the transition into an academic environment that may require you to develop and negotiate your role as an effective communicator, you will also be moving into the larger context of Virginia Tech. Part V of this text was designed to show you where to go when you really need extra help.

Using The Brief Penguin Handbook

Throughout this book and the online companion website, you will also find references to *The Brief Penguin Handbook,* 2nd edition, by Lester Faigley. This handbook offers a fuller explanation of many of the concepts you have before you. As well, our Composition Companion Website offers exercises, videos of students and teachers talking about their work, and more resources that can help you in all of your work at Virginia Tech.

We recognize that "[l]earning to write is a complex process, both individual and social, that takes place over time with continued practice and informed guidance" (WPA outcomes). With this idea in mind, we welcome you to this text and this course sequence of English 1105/06 or H1204 with an acknowledgement and a promise. We acknowledge that composition in all its forms and for a range of situations is hard work. However, we promise to do what we can to support you in this work.

—The First-Year Composition Team

Diana George
  Professor of Rhetoric and Writing
  Director of Composition Studies

Sheila Carter-Tod
  Assistant Professor of Rhetoric and Writing
  Associate Director of Composition

Cheryl Ruggiero
  Instructor of English
  Assistant Director of Composition

Jennifer Lawrence
  Instructor of English
  Coordinator of The Writing Center

For more information on the Virginia Tech Composition Program, visit
http://www.composition.english.vt.edu/composition

"Writing is thinking."

Charles Steger
President of Virginia Tech

Message from the Chair

Carolyn Rude, Department of English

The Department of English values the first-year composition course. We recognize that writing is the foundation of the intellectual and professional lives of all Virginia Tech students, and we take our responsibility to you seriously. Writing well will mark you to professors and employers as smart and capable. Writing will help you think through issues and understand course material in any class.

Professor Carolyn Rude, Chair of the Department of English, seen here volunteering in the Writing Center.

The Virginia Tech custom textbook incorporates nationally recognized objectives for first-year composition. The book is organized around outcomes for first-year composition developed by the Council of Writing Program Administrators. The faculty in the English Department at Virginia Tech collaborate in writing. They have a shared understanding of the course and the methods of helping students develop as writers.

My favorite quality of the book is that it features the writing of Virginia Tech students: your voices, your issues, your inquiries, your insights. An exciting time in the year is the day when the department publicly recognizes the students whose essays are published here. Maybe you will be one of those writers in the next edition of the textbook, but all the students in the composition courses will be able to grow intellectually and in the ability to use language, visual as well as verbal, to express information and ideas.

Writing is hard work, especially when the issues are complex and the goals are ambitious. It's not always fun. But in the end, because people write, learning takes place, thinking and understanding deepen, knowledge is shared, important issues come to the attention of a group, decisions get made, policies are developed, priorities are negotiated, projects are funded, co-workers collaborate, and work gets done. All of these activities depend on writing. Virginia Tech aims to "invent the future," and the work completed in all of the disciplines will depend on writing if it is to make a difference.

In the Department of English, we welcome you to our courses. Please take advantage of the opportunities your composition courses offer you to develop your ability to think, to learn, and to express yourself convincingly.

PART I

Composition at Virginia Tech: An Overview

English 1105, 1106 and Honors 1204

The Virginia Tech Composition Program in the Department of English introduces you to the kinds of writing, thinking, and speaking that will be crucial to your success as a Virginia Tech student and to your success after you leave Virginia Tech. In First-Year English, we recognize that speaking and that understanding the uses of visual communication are both as crucial as writing in developing strong communication skills.

Your writing, perhaps more than any other single element, can distinguish you from others if you learn to write well. More importantly, it provides you with one of the most important tools you can carry into your professional and personal life. Writing well enables you to share your ideas and feelings in meaningful ways with your associates, friends, and family: it empowers you to make a difference in the lives of others through your thinking.

—Jerome A. Niles
Former Dean of the College of
Liberal Arts and Human Sciences

English 1105 (Introduction to College Composition: Critical Reading, Writing, and Thinking), English 1106 (Writing from Research), and English H1204 (Honors English) share a focus on the rhetorical dimensions of writing, speaking, and visual communication, but each is a separate course with distinctive assignments and goals.

English 1105 introduces you to college composition with an emphasis on analysis and critical thinking. English 1106 focuses on research methods, writing from sources, and producing longer and more complex compositions. Honors English (H1204) engages students in an advanced level of critical reading, writing, and thinking and also includes a research dimension.

All three of these courses include elements of spoken and visual language, and all focus on a specific theme chosen by your instructor.

Composition at Virginia Tech, then, is designed to achieve six key outcomes:

◆ A knowledge of composition's rhetorical dimensions

◆ An understanding of the uses of writing as a tool for critical thinking and reading

◆ An understanding of writing as a process

◆ A solid knowledge of the conventions of written, and spoken composition

◆ The ability to write from research and to develop different types of research projects

◆ An understanding of the many dimensions of visual communication

The first four of these outcomes are taken from the national Council of Writing Program Administrators' Outcomes for First-Year Composition.

1.1 ■ Council of Writing Program Administrators' Outcomes

Your instructors will use various methods to achieve the outcomes, but all the classes are unified by their emphasis on Rhetorical Knowledge; Critical Thinking, Reading, and Writing; Process; and Knowledge of Conventions.

Here is how the Council of Writing Program Administrators explains those outcomes.

Rhetorical Knowledge

By the end of first-year composition, students should

- Focus on a purpose
- Respond to the needs of different audiences
- Respond appropriately to different kinds of rhetorical situations
- Use conventions of format and structure appropriate to the rhetorical situation
- Adopt appropriate voice, tone, and level of formality
- Understand how genres shape reading and writing
- Write in several genres

Critical Thinking, Reading, and Writing

By the end of first-year composition, students should

- Use writing and reading for inquiry, learning, thinking, and communicating
- Understand a writing assignment as a series of tasks, including finding, evaluating, analyzing, and synthesizing appropriate primary and secondary source
- Integrate their own ideas with those of others
- Understand the relationships among language, knowledge, and power

Processes

By the end of first-year composition, students should

- Be aware that it usually takes multiple drafts to create and complete a successful text
- Develop flexible strategies for generating, revising, editing, and proofreading
- Understand writing as an open process that permits writers to use later invention and re-thinking to revise their work
- Understand the collaborative and social aspects of writing processes
- Learn to critique their own and others' works
- Learn to balance the advantages of relying on others with the responsibility of doing their part
- Use a variety of technologies to address a range of audiences

1

Knowledge of Conventions

By the end of first-year composition, students should

- Learn common formats for different kinds of texts
- Develop knowledge of genre conventions ranging from structure and paragraphing to tone and mechanics
- Practice appropriate means of documenting their work
- Control such surface features as syntax, grammar, punctuation, and spelling.

Adopted by the Council of Writing Program Administrators (WPA), April 2000

In Part II of this text we will take you through each of these. You will have an opportunity to read assignments written by Virginia Tech faculty and essays composed by Virginia Tech students.

1.2 ◼ Requirements for 1105 and 1106/H1204

◼ *English 1105 — Introduction to College Composition: Critical Reading, Writing, and Thinking*

This first course will introduce you to college-level composition. Even if you begin by writing about topics you know well, you will soon be writing about issues presented in readings or films or speeches, for example, that raise serious challenges.

In 1105, you will focus on a theme, but the theme is simply an avenue into composition assignments. An important lesson in 1105 is learning how to control your writing — knowing when a full-scale revision is necessary; knowing how to read for sentence- and word-level concerns; knowing when and how to proofread. You will be asked to brainstorm topics, to write drafts, to take revision very seriously. You might be asked to read each others' papers and give feedback — an important step in learning to respond to your audience.

You may find that 1105 presents you with assignments and challenges that are vastly different from those you completed in high school. You will be asked to question and think about the decisions you've made as you write and rewrite. You will be asked to identify and write for various audiences, and the type of paper you write will depend on whom you are writing for and what you expect your writing to accomplish.

Writing Requirements for 1105

- A *minimum* of 3 papers (a minimum of 15 pages total) for formal grading. (Each of these papers will also go through more than one draft before being given a grade.)

- A *minimum* of 20 pages of informal writing such as journal responses, discussion board postings, brainstorming, summaries, etc.

Oral Presentation Requirements for 1105

◆ *At least* one group presentation (though your instructor may include individual presentations as well)

Visual Requirements for 1105

◆ Analysis of visual materials. Visual materials include any form of visual communication — advertising, television, film, photography, painting, web design, product design, layout, street signs, landscape architecture, and more.

■ English 1106 — Writing from Research

As its name implies, English 1106 is an introduction to writing from research that you conduct on a topic determined by the course theme. In addition to learning how to find and cite sources from the library and the Internet, you will be introduced to different kinds of sources and to more than one research method. You will learn, for example, the difference between **primary and secondary sources,** and you will be introduced to **field methods** such as interviewing, conducting surveys, and other "in the field" types of research. As in all research writing, you must credit your sources using the appropriate form.

Writing Requirements for English 1106

◆ A *minimum* of 3 graded papers (a minimum of 20 pages total) written from sources. They will require more than one draft as you work with your teacher and your class to prepare them for the grade.

◆ A *minimum* of 20 pages of informal writing such as journal responses, discussion board postings, brainstorming, summaries, blogs, proposals, etc.

Oral Presentation Requirements for English 1106

◆ *At least* one individual presentation (though your teacher may include group presentations as well)

Visual Requirements for 1106

◆ *Writing* or oral presentations that use visual elements to enhance communication. You should learn how to use different kinds of visuals in your writing and your oral presentations.

■ English H1204 — Honors English

Honors English is open to all Virginia Tech students in the Honors Program and to students whose entrance scores indicate that they qualify for the course. Because it is an honors level course, you can expect to work both with close analysis and with research — both library and internet research and fieldwork. The reading in Honors 1204 will be chosen to deepen your critical reading, writing, and thinking skills and will focus on a specific theme or problem chosen by your instructor.

Writing Requirements for English H1204

◆ A *minimum* of 3 graded papers (a minimum of 20 pages total) written from sources. They will require more than one draft as you work with your teacher and your class to prepare them for the grade. At least one of these papers may ask for an extended analysis.

◆ A *minimum* of 20 pages of informal writing. This writing might be in the form of journal writing, blogs, proposals, etc.

Oral Presentation Requirements for English H1204

◆ At least one individual presentation.

Visual Requirements for H1204

◆ An understanding of visual analysis as well as an introduction to the uses of visuals in oral presentations and in written texts.

1.3 Course Themes

As we mentioned earlier, each course will focus on a theme chosen by individual instructors. Some of the themes from recent years are described below. Your teacher may chose one of these or another:

In each section of 1105 and 1106, your instructor will focus your work on a central theme or issue. The thematic focus allows you and your classmates to discuss issues that surround questions, ideas, movements, and concerns arising from specific topics.

◆ **Writing Through the Environment:** In this course, students examine human perspectives on the environment and human relationships with the nonhuman world. They read, discuss, and write about a variety of texts that explore the ways language and culture have shaped and continue to shape our conceptions of nature.

◆ **Writing Through Cross-Cultural Contact:** In this course, students explore how culture makes us who we are and what happens when we encounter people whose culture differs from our own. Students examine the diversity, richness, and beauty of cross-cultural contact — and the problems that cross-cultural contact can cause.

◆ **Writing Through Science and Technology:** In this course, students explore the problems, delights, and challenges created by recent developments in science and technology. The course examines various topics, such as cloning, genetic engineering, and the impact of computers on people's lives and on traditional concepts of intellectual property.

1

◆ **Writing Through Arts and Aesthetics:** In this course, students focus on aesthetic questions. How do we respond to art? How do human beings create art? Students explore the territories of art—in the past and in the present—and they look at the many ways art comforts the afflicted and afflicts the comfortable.

◆ **Writing Through the University Experience:** In this course, students explore the university itself as a text, one filled with energy, ideas, choices, conflicts, and obstacles. Students critically examine this complex text while they work toward a clearer sense of why they are here, what they want, and how best to achieve their goals.

1.4 ■ Evaluating your Work

What are teachers looking for in college writing? That has to be the question at the top of nearly every first-year student's list the first time a paper is turned in for a final grade. Your teacher will explain the specific demands of each assignment, and you should read every assignment very carefully.

In general, however, your grade will reflect both the goals of the course and the goals set for individual assignments:

◆ Audience awareness, including awareness of appropriate genre and structure, tone, voice, and style

◆ Evidence of critical thinking, reading, and writing; writing that reflects a high level of evaluation, analysis, and synthesis; fully developed ideas

◆ An awareness of purpose

◆ Clear focus

◆ Skillful integration of sources, including quotation, summary, paraphrase, and examples from visual/experimental texts

◆ Careful presentation of your material, including an attention to proofreading, language use, and an awareness of the visual dimension of your work

The final paper grade comes only after you have worked through several stages of composition. That likely means

◆ Writing more than one draft;

◆ Working well with your peers in group workshops;

◆ Having your work ready when it is due;

◆ Being willing to revise (not simply correct a few errors).

1

1.5 ■ What to Expect from this Book

This book is designed to lead you through the goals and outcomes of your First-Year English courses. Throughout the text you will find sample papers written by Virginia Tech students and assignments written by Virginia Tech instructors. You will also find exercises throughout each chapter meant to focus your attention on details important to the outcomes and to improving your writing. In addition, we have included cross-references to *The Brief Penguin Handbook,* where you will find more detailed discussion of all of these topics.

Of course, the textbook alone is only one important resource for learning to write well. To do your best, you'll want to take advantage of other resources just as crucial to your learning. In addition to this text and *The Brief Penguin Handbook,* those resources include your teachers, your peers from writing workshops, the Virginia Tech Writing Center, the library, and the Composition Text Companion Website.

PART II

Understanding and Working with the Outcomes

2

Rhetorical Knowledge

For many people, the word *rhetoric* is associated with empty or deceptive speech. You might have even heard someone say of a politician, "That speech was nothing but empty rhetoric." That isn't the way writing teachers use the word. Instead, when writing teachers talk about rhetorical knowledge, they are thinking of how writers decide what they are going to write, who it should be written for, what the consequences of their words might be, what form and tone the writing should take, and much more.

As you begin any writing task, you should ask basic questions—all of which constitute what we call "rhetorical knowledge." They might appear very simple, but they can lead to complex choices:

◆ What is your purpose?

◆ Who is your audience and what are the best ways to reach that audience?

◆ What impression do you want your audience to have about you as the writer?

◆ What about voice and style? If this is a very formal piece of writing, what will you do to signal that? If you want your reader to laugh, how will your language and style help make that likely?

◆ Are you writing in response to a particular situation or need? That is called the "rhetorical situation," and it can help you determine what you will write and how you will write it.

◆ What form—"genre"—will this composition take?

This chapter is designed to lead you through some of these questions so that you can begin to make appropriate choices and become a more effective writer.

2.1 ▮ Purpose

Before beginning, decide on a purpose for your writing. For example, do you want to *inform* your audience of a certain topic, *persuade* readers to think a certain way about a subject, *instruct* them, *entertain* them? Often, writing serves more than one purpose, but the primary purpose of your composition should come through clearly. Much academic writing, for example, is informative but also includes a persuasive undercurrent. You might want to entertain as well as convince.

It is very possible that your teacher will assign you a purpose in the same way that a newspaper editor assigns different kinds of stories to reporters. For example, if your teacher asks you to *analyze* or *explain* how a particular text or image works, your purpose is already spelled out for you. Or, you might be asked to *transcribe* and *report on* an interview you have conducted. Again, your purpose is assigned, and your job is to keep that purpose in mind as you write.

When you get any assignment, begin by noticing what the teacher is asking for and how that will determine the purpose of your text. Pay attention to words in the assignment that signal purpose—*summarize, describe, explain, analyze, narrate,* or *evaluate critically.* Each of these words indicates a very different kind of paper.

For more on Purpose, see *The Brief Penguin Handbook,* Chapter 1, section 1d.

EXERCISE

2.a Persuasive Project Assignment

The following assignment was written for English 1105 by Jennifer Barton, an Instructor of English at Virginia Tech. Read the assignment carefully and list all words in it that signal purpose:

Persuasive Project
Jennifer Barton, Instructor
English 1105

For this project, your goal is to persuade a specific audience to agree with a particular idea or to take a particular action. Your topic should be related in some way to topics we have been discussing in class, but is otherwise up to you. What do you want to see change?

Step 1: Determine your audience and purpose
Whom you write to affects what you say, and vice versa. If your purpose, for example, is to increase dining plan options for students, then students aren't going to be the best choice of audience. Although students might be the audience most sympathetic to your argument, they can't actually change the dining plan options. A better audience for such an argument might be the head of the dining services department.

Generally speaking, the more specific you can make your audience and purpose, the better your chances of successful persuasion.

Step 2: Choose an appropriate genre
What's the best genre to use to reach your specific audience? What genre will be the best tool for communicating your purpose? While a chatty editorial in the *Collegiate Times* might be an effective way of reaching students, for example, a formal letter might be a better way of reaching the head of dining services.

Step 3: Create the document
As part of your creation process, you should first develop some kind of an outline or blueprint to help you determine what kind of information you need to include, what kind of visual components might be useful, what organizational scheme will be most effective. Experiment with different possibilities.

Step 4: Analyze your document
In 3–4 pages, describe and then analyze the finished version of your persuasive document. Why did you make the rhetorical decisions that you made? What aspects of the document do you think are successful? What would you change if you could? Are you willing to present this document to your intended audience? Why or why not?

Notice that this assignment has four steps. How does the purpose change with each step? You might wish to discuss these steps with your classmates and compare how others identify the purpose or purposes of this assignment.

EXERCISE

2.b Reading Your Assignment

On a separate sheet of paper, list the words that signal the purpose of your current writing assignment.

2

2.2 Audience

Although in a writing class you may feel as though your audience is always your instructor, you may also find yourself writing to a number of different audiences in addition to your instructor. Some writing, for example, is primarily for you to read. That would be the case if your instructor asks you to begin your assignment by brainstorming, listing, writing out ideas or thoughts on a topic. You might also find yourself being asked to direct your writing to your classmates in an oral presentation or a peer review workshop. There are also times when an assignment reaches outside the classroom. You'll notice, for example, that the assignment in exercise 2.a asks students to identify an audience beyond the teacher or immediate classmates.

The more clearly you can envision an actual audience—people who you can imagine reading what you have written—the easier it will be for you to choose the appropriate language, level of formality, kinds of information you should include or exclude, and the form (or genre) for your assignment.

Chris Rossi, a first-year student at Virginia Tech, created the flyer reprinted here in response to Ms. Barton's assignment (reprinted in Exercise 2.a).

Chris Rossi is in General Engineering at Virginia Tech.

Do You Frequently Find Yourself In Some of These Similar Situations?

Maybe you should take a second look...

-Do you find yourself faced with new and exciting food choices?

-Do you frequently eat more food than an average meal or just snack to kill time?

-Do you frequently find yourself thinking you are "The King Of The WORLD"?

-Have you ever seen the world around you upside down?

ARE YOU MAKING THE BEST DECISIONS IN COLLEGE?

-Do you make up for lost sleep while in the middle of your most stimulating class?

-Is the last thing you see before you go to bed the sunrise or sunset?

Take a moment to stop and think about the decisions you have made since coming to Tech...

You Control Your Future

EXERCISE

2.c Reading for Audience

Examine the flyer carefully and answer the following questions:

- Who is the intended audience for the flyer? How do you know?

- What strategies (such as language, tone, visuals, etc.) has the student used to connect with this audience?

- How effective are Rossi's choices for reaching the audience he has in mind? What would you add or change?

EXERCISE

2.d Planning for Audience

As you work on determining the audience for your current assignment, use a separate sheet of paper to answer the following questions in as much detail as possible:

- Whom am I writing to or for? Who will read or listen to what I've written? (If possible, name specific people who might read this assignment.)

- What do they already know about my topic? What do they need to know?

- What are some strategies I can use to make them interested in my topic?

- What language would I not use?

- How formal or informal can I be?

- What can I say in my paper that will really connect to this audience?

Your answers to these questions will help you determine what you should say, how you should say it, and how you represent yourself in your writing. In other words, knowing your audience will also allow you to work consciously on the tone or style (voice) of your writing and will help you decide what you must say and what you should probably leave out. It will also help you decide on the type (or genre) of writing that will best suit the situation. For example, email works well with friends but is very bad for a formal business deal. As well, while you might be comfortable using IM language in an email message to friends, you would not use the same when writing to a teacher, a business associate, or someone you don't know well.

Once you identify your audience, what you need next is a way to appeal to that audience. In classical rhetoric, we have typically referred to these rhetorical appeals as *ethos, pathos,* and *logos.* Writers use *ethos* when they demonstrate to their audience that they are a credible and trustworthy writer or speaker. *Pathos* involves using emotion to move an audience. Writers employ *logos* when they make a convincing argument using empirical knowledge or reasoning.

2

EXERCISE	**2.e Rhetorical Appeals**

Look again at the flyer Chris Rossi produced in response to Ms. Barton's assignment. Which of these appeals comes through most predominantly? What details (language, image, font choice, design, etc.) can you name that create that rhetorical appeal? How?

For more discussion of Audience and Rhetorical Appeals, see *The Brief Penguin Handbook,* Chapter 1, section 1a–1c.

2.3 ■ Rhetorical Situation

Different situations and circumstances actually call for different kinds of rhetorical responses. We call those circumstances the writer's *rhetorical situation.* For example, a funeral normally calls for a *eulogy,* a speech that praises the worth of the person who has passed away. Most people would say that it would be out of place to stand up and criticize the deceased or to deliver a comic bashing of the family. Instead, the typical rhetorical response in a funeral is to remember the deceased fondly, to comfort the living, and to leave the audience with a sense that the world mourns the loss of, but celebrates the life of, the person about to be buried.

Of course, the rhetorical situation cannot determine the exact response or the form of that response, but the situation does make a difference in what you are able to write or say and what form it should take.

Once Chris Rossi completed his flyer, he moved on to Step 4 of his assignment. He took time to step back and analyze his work. In his analysis (reprinted below), he explains why he chose this particular topic and genre and what decisions he made to connect with his audience.

ROSSI 1

Chris Rossi
Instructor: Jennifer Barton
English 1105
18 October, 2006

COLLEGE LIFE: ARE YOU IN CONTROL?

Once students step onto a college campus for the first time, for many it being the first time away from home, they leave mom and dad behind and begin to fend for themselves. A good college environment cushions the transition for many from living at home in a monitored and supervised living space to being completely on their own.

However in college, without any supervision at all, many students tend to make some poor choices as many find out they must learn from their own mistakes.

My flyer aims to persuade college students to simply pay attention to the decisions that they make in college. Many of the mistakes made by my peers tend to come from the simple fact that they don't stop and think about situations before they get involved in them. Then they simply do something at the spur of the moment. The first design feature I incorporated into my flyer was the border. With the slightly offset triangular style as well as a color scheme to match the famous school colors, it instantly grabs the reader's attention and moves it along the perimeter of the flyer. The border is also angular which helps draw the reader's eye from the left to the right and from the top to the bottom with the natural sloping edges. Once the reader sees the flyer, they notice the largest text, which is located at the top of the page in bright orange. This not only draws the reader to the topic of the flyer but also sets up the persuasive process. Immediately below the main tagline is a catch phrase in a slightly smaller font but still maintaining the school colors only this time maroon instead of orange.

Next in order to get my point across about making poor choices in college I found pictures that depict those very poor choices being made every day by students. These pictures are extremely important because they have to be humorous by slightly exaggerating the truth, but not taking it out of context or reality. Also the pictures needed to have a level of humor because any college student that sees a flyer that is completely serious or strictly business will automatically tune the message out. Thus I found pictures of young adults indulging in food, heavily drinking, and sleeping through class.

All students are well aware that many students in college become familiar with the party life or at least have heard stories or seen pictures of such events. Another well known fact of college life is that many freshmen feel overwhelmed with the numerous food choices that they face once they arrive. With fast food and just about every food imaginable on many universities, most students don't make the best of food choices. Finally the last issue is just getting adjusted to the living quarters of college in which many students feel the need to sleep all day and stay up all night. This defeats the purpose of coming to an institution of higher learning if one doesn't pay attention in class or doesn't even attend.

Along with each picture I placed a set of two rhetorical questions to get the reader thinking about the decisions they might have made in the past. The pictures along with the questions are placed going from top left to bottom right, which is the same direction a reader's eye would naturally follow. The questions are posted in a moderately sized font, for ease of reading. The writing is also simple and short so it can be read quickly and still get the message across. The idea for the flyer was originally intended to be handed out, however a larger amount of information is needed to properly convey a meaningful message. So I came up with the idea that the flyer could be placed inside of a bathroom stall, which are always used and the occupants have time to kill. With this prime location to get the message across 100 percent of the intended audience would be reached. Also with such benefits as repetition the reader soon may even begin to unconsciously assimilate the information in the back of their mind and when they need it, the information is there to aid their decision making.

In case the point was completely missed by the audience I had added the blurb to the side about making the right decisions while in college. This is also useful to help summarize my key ideas and points right before the conclusion of the flyer hits. The conclusion is actually broken up into two separate parts; the first part consists of the actual intended message, which was to try and persuade college students to just stop and step back to think about the life they lead and the decisions they have made since coming to college. Secondly the flyer is pulled together with humor to provide a positive outlook to the reader. The majority of poor decisions occur due to not think-ing about a situation or due to some other underlying cause. The catalyst of the excessive lifestyle may have the reader in a position which makes them believe there is nothing they can do, yet the flyer allows the reader to gain something positive. The reader will leave feeling empowered and if the flyer affects as few as one or two peo-ple then it has accomplished its purpose.

I would like to see if this flyer could actually be circulated among the bathroom stalls across the campus. It will have a positive impact, and if nothing else will make people think about what they have been doing since they stepped onto the Virginia Tech campus. All in all, the individual is the one with the final say in any act that they might commit, but if a few more people are enlightened about their decisions maybe it might turn some lives around.

EXERCISE	### 2.f Naming the Rhetorical Situation

1. In Chris Rossi's analysis, he identifies the rhetorical situation he is responding to with his flyer. What is that situation? With a group of your classmates, discuss other possible ways of responding to that situation besides creating a flyer.

2. Rossi identifies the persuasive element of his flyer. How effective is this flyer at persuading its readers? What, exactly, is the flyer asking readers to do?

3. Suggest revision to Rossi's flyer that would make his purpose clearer or more effective. What specific actions could the flyer ask its readers to take?

For more information on Rhetorical Analysis, see *The Brief Penguin Handbook,* Chapter 7, section 7a–7d.

2.4 ■ How Genres Shape Reading and Writing

Whether we realize it or not, when most of us look at a piece of writing, we pay attention to what genre, or type, of writing it is. We do the same for different types of music (classical vs. jazz), television shows (comedy vs. drama), or even meals (breakfast vs. dinner). As we identify a genre, we bring to our reading, listening, or dining experiences a host of expectations that we have learned to associate with that particular type of music, TV show, or meal. These expectations come from our schooling, families, culture, and the whole range of our experiences.

Our expectations as readers are shaped by our understanding of particular genres. So, for instance, we don't expect to take more than a minute or so to read a flyer, whereas we expect to invest significantly more time in reading a book. Even creative works of fiction and poetry are constrained and guided by genre expectations. When writers meet most of our expectations, the communication process is smoother and often more successful.

Of course, really innovative writers and artists sometimes play with genre conventions and purposely challenge our expectations. The result can be delightful; genre can be stretched and reinvented, though there are times when less experienced writers try to do the same and can't quite pull it off. Don't let that deter you, but do make sure you are paying attention to which genres might work for your assignments and which are simply out of place.

EXERCISE   **2.g Working with Genres**

1. You'll notice that, when Chris Rossi decided on how to complete his assignment, he made the decision to create a flyer. That flyer also included images. Why might this genre work best for Rossi's purpose?

2. What other genres might Rossi have used to create the same effect?

3. Identify, as best you can, the genre expectations you brought to this exercise. Who or what influenced you? In other words, what do you normally expect a warning message to students to look like? Would it necessarily be a flyer? What do you assume an analysis looks like? Does Rossi's paper conform to that? How do you know?

2.5 ■ Learning to Write in Several Genres

Earlier in this chapter, you've seen examples of Chris Rossi's writing in two genres. To begin with, he produced a type of writing known as a "flyer." He then wrote about the strategies he used in the flyer to influence his audience. This second composition is an example of a second, very different type of writing, an "analysis." To produce the flyer and to write the analysis, Rossi had to understand what readers will expect from writing in each of these very different genres.

If Rossi's own genre knowledge had been lacking (let's say he never really paid much attention to flyers before), he would probably have a hard time imagining what readers expect from a flyer. If his flyer violates readers' expectations too drastically, they may become confused or annoyed and stop reading. If they are patient or very curious, they may take the time to try and figure out just what is going on. But readers who would be willing spend hours reading a short poem (because we expect poetry to require more time to yield its layers of meaning), most likely won't take that kind of time to understand a flyer (which we expect to communicate more immediately).

In this case, Rossi's flyer demonstrates that he understands a lot about what readers expect from a flyer. His past experiences with the genre of "flyer" led him to draw upon many features we might expect to find in this genre: borders, taglines, repetition, pictures, easy-to-read fonts, short and simple sentences.

Let's consider Rossi's *analysis* of the flyer. The type of thinking, organizing, and language required in an analysis is somewhat different from what is called for to create a flyer. It is possible that Rossi might be able to create a perfectly persuasive flyer yet not be able to explain how he did it or what exactly makes the flyer effective or ineffective. Conversely, a writer who can write a terrific analysis of a flyer may lack the visual design skills to create an effective flyer.

Analytical writing requires breaking material into parts to look the parts as separate from the whole. This intellectual task is the focus of many college writing assignments because it is closely tied to critical thinking and to thoughtful problem solving across the disciplines. Engineers conduct accident analyses, economists produce financial analyses, psychotherapists analyze their clients' mental processes, law enforcement professionals conduct crime analyses, and so forth.

You are likely to be asked to produce several different kinds of compositions in your first-year courses and throughout college. You could be asked to write journal entries, reports, transcripts of interviews, film reviews, film or literary analyses, summaries, arguments, profiles, memoirs, and more. Some of that writing will also include visual composition. Much of it will be the basis for an oral presentation as well. Each form demands that you make different decisions about what you can (or cannot) present and how you will present it.

The reading and writing assignments in your first-year writing course provide you with experience working in several different genres. Just as important, these assignments heighten your rhetorical awareness when it comes to genre demands and conventions. This awareness is an important component of becoming a writer who has control of the material and the presentation of that material. As you become more adept at recognizing genre conventions and constraints, you will see how the writing you do in first-year composition anticipates similar genres in your advanced courses and in your professional writing.

EXERCISE

2.h Identifying Genre Features

In the Fall of 2006, Professor Katrina Powell assigned a "literacy narrative" to her 1105 students. That is a genre many students are not likely to encounter before college and one that is often assigned in first-year writing courses. Carefully read through this assignment. What is Professor Powell asking from her students that is different from a straight autobiography or personal experience essay?

> **English 1105: First-year Writing**
> **Fall 2006**
> **Katrina Powell**
> **Literacy Narrative Assignment Sheet**
>
> **Assignment:** So far this semester we've been discussing the ways that various aspects of the culture define literacy. We've also talked about how particular notions of literacy, and those who possess it, have certain kinds of power in our culture. We've debated what it means to be literate and who gets to decide what significance it holds.
>
> For this assignment, write a personal narrative that specifically explores and defines the ways that you have become literate. When did you first learn to read and write? Who taught you to read and write and what significance has that played in your subsequent education? Who has been involved in your literacy learning? Has your literacy learning always meant learning in "school"? If it has involved more than school, describe your experiences. What other literacies do you possess besides school literacy? How have those other literacies been significant to you? How has technology influenced your access to literacy? What visual or graphic ways could you represent your literacy learning? How do you think your literacies have affected the kind of student you are, the person you are, the kind of citizen you are?
>
> Finally, think about your literacies in conjunction with the culture. What kind of power do you hold with what you know? In what ways do you feel powerless because of literacy or knowledge of language? Is it possible to change? Do you want it to change? Why or why not?
>
> These are all questions to help you think about your own experiences. I encourage you to mold this assignment to fit your specific experiences and thoughts about literacy and language learning.
>
> **Length:** Your essay should be 3–5 pages, typed, double-spaced.

EXERCISE

2.i Reading and Writing the Literacy Narrative

1. Read the literacy narrative by Jeong-Ah Lee, written in the Fall of 2006 when she was a first-year Virginia Tech student in Professor Powell's English 1105 class. What do you imagine might be the rhetorical situation to which this text is a response? What seem to be the writer's main purposes? What are her audience(s)? How do you know?

2. What genre conventions do you recognize in the text? What, if anything, have you written in this genre before? What have you read in this genre? Which of these conventions are most and least familiar to you?

3. Identify another genre the writer might have used to achieve the same purposes for the same audience. What are the advantages and disadvantages of the two genres for appealing to the likely audience(s)?

4. Identify another genre the writer might use to communicate her purpose(s) to a different audience altogether. What audience do you have in mind? How would the writer need to adapt her persuasive appeals?

5. Imagine a piece of writing associated with a particular occupation or discipline that would call upon some of the same conventions or features represented in this piece of writing. For instance, which, if any, of the conventions you see here might also apply to a genre in which a teacher might write? A social worker? A scientist?

Jeong-Ah Lee is a Physics major at Virginia Tech.

LEE 1

Jeong-Ah Lee
Professor Katrina Powell
English 1105: Literacy Narrative
Fall 2006

THE STORY OF LITERACY IN ENGLISH

Every young child learns how to speak, read, and write from their parents or siblings at home. Since I was born to a Korean family, Korean was my first language. My story of literacy in Korean is like any literacy story. However, my story of literacy in English is filled with special challenges, like not being able to use it all the time in daily life.

I recall my mom would speak a few simple words aloud and clearly to me when I was very little so that I could repeat after her, because that is the way infants learn to speak. At the age of three or four, I would look at the wall where my mom put up a poster, which contained twenty-four Korean characters colorfully printed and imitate them right next to each letter.

After I learned how to read and write from kindergarten, I would practice reading Korean words by looking at the signs of stores or streets on a bus. Since buses usually went fast, most signs just passed me, so it was good to practice reading words because I had to figure out what they were before I passed them by. I also sometimes learned new words from the signs by myself. I could take a guess at what those words meant by the appearance of stores or stuff displayed inside. I even saw English signs too, but I had no idea how to read them because they did not teach English to young children at that time and my parents didn't speak English at all.

At elementary school in the first grade there was a vocabulary test every day. My teacher dictated about ten sentences for every test and students listened carefully to write them down. This is how I learned Korean without any difficulty. Everybody around me spoke Korean to me and I saw Korean everywhere.

Before entering middle school, most students started to learn English outside of school so that it would be easier for them to learn English since they had already studied it. As for me, I started to study English when I was in the 6th grade. My first English education was done by a Korean teacher. It was a private lesson with four kids. It was about $100 per month and we met three times a week, so it was not so expensive, but some other private lessons can be much more expensive depending on the teacher. We used to meet once a week at one of the kids' houses. Each class was for an hour. We studied English grammar for half an hour, read a textbook for about fifteen minutes, and watched an educational video of English conversation or played games for the rest of the time. There was no pressure of exams, but only fun.

From middle school to high school, there was an English class of three to four hours a week. Middle school textbooks normally contained four parts: vocabulary, one or two articles, grammar, and a short conversation. Students took notes with a red pen when their teacher explained grammar. They only studied for tests which were mostly about grammar and reading. Speaking and writing were rarely done because what we had on the test was reading and listening comprehension. English in high school was quite different from that in middle school. Since all high school students' goal was to get a great score at the national college entrance exam, they learned how to get to the right answer quickly.

My English education of high school was done pretty much the same as others except that I went to a special English academy known as 'hakwon' in Korean. There are a lot of special English academies in Korea. Few students go there to study English in depth. However, most of them only go to study to prepare for school exams because in Korea the higher GPA they have the better universities they can apply for. Like I mentioned before, school English classes are not about communication with each other. They only teach things needed for exams, which is not conversational

English. There is, of course, some special variety of hakwon for practical English. Teachers are native English speakers and they teach how to speak. I have never been to such hakwon because I did not need to speak English in my daily life, which was what most high school students thought since they only wanted to get into a good college. Accordingly, even though I had studied English for seven years, I could not speak it very well.

After high school, most students stop studying English unless they are English majors or have to take a special test such as TOEFL, Test Of English as a Foreign Language. As for me, majoring in Physics and wishing to study abroad, I attended a particular TOEFL hakwon for a month to prepare for the test. They taught how to solve TOEFL problems very technically. Though I might have improved my English skills of reading academic materials or listening to scientific lectures, I still could not express what I wanted to say in English. Then I had a thought that if I wanted to learn how to speak, I should talk to people in English. I searched for pen pal websites on line and sent emails to people from all over the world. Since English was considered as a global language, every person spoke English to me. I remember my first e-mails written in English were not even as good as those written by American kids, but I kept practicing although it took a long time to write even a short e-mail. One day looking in a dictionary, I found that I did not even know how to use simple basic words such as "take" or "have" in a proper way. I thought that it was because I did not study English for myself but for tests. I was interested only in getting a good enough score at the national college entrance exam. I think teaching to the test may be effective at the moment, but in the long run students will have a narrow knowledge which will not last for a long time.

Since learning to communicate with people in English through the Internet, I also have started meeting native speakers in person. It was quite different from talking to people online. Now I had to know how to listen well and pronounce words correctly. I was a little shocked at first that I could not understand what they were talking about because I was used to listening to very clear and comprehensible English given for listening tests. In real life, however, people speak differently. They have their own accent and the way of their speaking varies. However, this process of learning conversational English was not stressful at all because I was not forced to do it. I did not have to worry about making mistakes which would have caused a bad result on tests of school. I had a lot of fun and thought that was how babies learned new languages.

That was when I started to watch babies when they talked to their mother or people in public. They do not care about people around them. They focused only on expressing their feelings to people. They spoke loud and sometimes sang a song even though their pronunciation was not perfect. They kept trying unlike me. They asked questions anytime without any hesitation. I thought I should leave my ego behind and be like those babies to learn new language, and that way I could learn more and more.

2

I still have a hard time getting used to English, my second language, which is very different from Korean in that Korean does not use the English alphabet and its grammar and pronunciation are totally different. Korean language, Hangeul, has its own letters including 14 consonants and 10 vowels and it has neither "ph" nor "th" sounds. As for the grammar, we use a verb at the end of a sentence unlike English whose verb comes after a subject. The most difficult when speaking English is that I still think in Korean in my head first and then try to translate it in English. When I speak in Korean, for example, I can explain what I want to say in a different way if I cannot find the exact word. Speaking in English at the same situation, however, I try to remember the right word instead of describing what I want to say. It is simply because thinking in Korean is easier than in English so I do not have to pay attention to myself too much. Like Richard Rodriguez, a Mexican-American who was alienated from his own culture at a young age, felt that he was comfortable at home when his family members spoke Spanish to him and mentioned that their voices insisting that he belongs there, they are family members, related, and special to one another, I feel the same when I speak my own language. Since I learned how to communicate in English, I have had a lot of chances to meet various people with new experiences. The possibilities that I was given by English are infinite. They broadened my network with people from Koreans to people from all over the world and that was how I could finally come to America to study. Being literate in English has never been easy at all. It is still hard and challenging, but I will keep working on that because I believe that there will be more opportunities when I become skillfully bilingual. I could even work either in Korea or in America, for instance, as a physicist in America and an English teacher in Korea. I hope some day I will be able to help people to learn English and face that challenge together.

For more information on Analysis, see *The Brief Penguin Handbook,* Chapter 7. For a brief discussion of genres of writing that are commonly produced today, see the Introduction to *The Brief Penguin Handbook.*

2.6 ■ Further Exercises for Exploring Rhetorical Knowledge

The following exercises are meant to give you more opportunities to test your rhetorical knowledge. You can use them on your own, in class for discussion, or as a group project.

EXERCISES

Purpose:

Identify the variety of purposes that might exist for an essay that focuses on each of the following topics and write a potential thesis statement for each purpose.

- mountaintop removal mining
- stem cell research
- strategies adopted by the US in the Iraq War
- urban renewal

Audience:

1. Write a 1-page letter describing your most recent weekend to each of the following readers: your best friend from high school, your grandmother, your minister.

2. Describe (in stereotypical terms) the target audience for each of the following magazines in terms of education, career, food preferences, drink preferences, clothing style, music preferences, ideal vacation spot, and additional interests.

- *Rolling Stone*
- *Mother Earth News*
- *Martha Stewart Living*
- *National Geographic*
- *Cat Fancy*
- *Maxim*
- *Vanity Fair*
- *The New Yorker*

3. Consider which rhetorical appeal (ethos, pathos, logos) might work most effectively with regard to the following essay subjects and potential audiences:

- mountaintop removal mining
- stem cell research
- strategies adopted by the US in the Iraq War
- urban renewal

Considering Genre:

Provide definitions for the following list of genres. What do they have in common? How do they differ?

- journal entries
- reports
- film reviews
- film analyses
- summaries
- arguments
- profiles
- memoirs
- comics
- brochures
- plays
- short stories
- poems
- songs
- novels
- novellas

3

Critical Thinking, Reading, and Writing

Overview

critical. Inclined to judge severely and find
fault. 2. Characterized by careful, exact
evaluation and judgment: a critical reading.
3. Of, relating to, or characteristic of critics or
criticism: critical acclaim; a critical analysis of
Melville's writings. 4. Forming or having the
nature of a turning point; crucial or decisive: a
critical point in the campaign.
5a. Of or relating to a medical crisis: an illness
at the critical stage. b. Being or relating to a
grave physical condition especially of a
patient. 6. Indispensable; essential: a critical
element of the plan; a second income that is
critical to the family's well-being.
7. Being in or verging on a state of crisis or
emergency: a critical shortage of food.

Writing well and speaking effectively are skills that need to be continuously developed and refined. Meaningful communication is essential for success in graduate work and all professional careers.

—Karen P. DePauw
Vice Provost for
Graduate Studies and
Dean of the Graduate School

If you look at *The American Heritage Dictionary's* many definitions of the term *critical* (reprinted on page 29), you will get a good idea of why the goal of "critical reading, writing, and thinking" might seem like a slippery one to pin down. After all, if you accuse friends or family members of being "too critical," you mean they are simply finding fault without thinking very carefully. And, yet, when your teachers talk about "critical thinking," they mean the second definition: "Characterized by careful, exact evaluation and judgment." In other words, critical thinking, reading, and writing, means that you are paying close attention to a text so that you can make a fair and informed judgment.

One of the key outcomes for first-year composition is to read, write, and think critically. That means using writing both as a means of exploring and reflecting and as a means of evaluating or analyzing. This chapter is meant to introduce you to the possibilities open to you when you use writing as a critical thinking tool. We begin with writing as inquiry—using writing to explore what you know about a subject. Some teachers call this kind of writing, "writing for meaning."

3.1 ■ Critical Thinking—Writing as Inquiry; Writing to Reflect

Although critical thinking and writing are important tools for analysis, before you get to the analysis itself you'll need to work through what you are thinking about a topic, what confuses you, and what you can say and cannot say about a topic. When you engage in writing as inquiry, you are also engaged in critical thinking. You are, in effect, writing your way through an issue or finding substance in what you have read, watched, or carefully examined.

In the following essay, for Jen Mooney's H1204 class in Fall 2006, Virginia Tech student William Rowland begins with a picture that he took of his father, his uncle, and the family dog on a beach. In his essay, he does not begin with an argument or thesis but, instead, with an implied question or two: "Why did I even take this picture? Why does it seem meaningful to me?"

As he examines the detail of the picture, he also comes to meaning.

Before you read Rowland's essay, take time to carefully examine the assignment he was working from (reprinted here). The theme for Ms. Mooney's class was "Gender and Gender Roles," so you should notice that her assignment directs the students back to that theme.

Jen Mooney
English H1204, Fall 2006
Writing Assignment 1: Reflection

Task: Choose a personal photograph—it can be one from your childhood, or one taken last week—and reflect upon how the experience or images it captures address issues of gender, particularly as those issues provide insight into your own awareness of what it means to be a man or a woman, to be (in essence) you.

Perhaps the best way to begin the study of any subject is by exploring your own experiences with it. Chances are pretty good that you're either male or female, so even if you haven't studied gender issues in a classroom sense, you still have a high level of expertise in the subject—in fact, you were born with it!

For the first major writing assignment in ENGL H1204, you will be asked to plumb your own experiences with gender issues—to explore, explain, and even question what it means to you to be a man or a woman.

The essay we will read this unit—Melissa Dodd's "My Sister and Me on Grandma's Lap" (*Brief Penguin Handbook,* 99–102—see also the Companion Website with voice-over on this essay)—should give you some ideas about how a piece of reflective writing can be approached. In the case of Dodd's essay—as well as the one you will be creating—she writes specifically about the reflections inspired by a family photo of her when she was a child. Moreover, the essay also focuses on gender issues, so it speaks directly to the topic with which we are concerned this semester.

As you will be able to tell from this example, and as we will discuss in class, good reflective essays include both description and narration. They provide detailed information regarding who, what, why, when, and where. In an effort to bring the reader into the experience, to have him or her share it, you must remember that details matter. Anything that can spark the senses—the warmth of the color yellow, the sharp smell of vinegar, the roughness of a jacket sleeve, the tang of key lime pie—should find its way into the reflective essay. Additionally, although the Dodd essay does not do this, reflective writing often includes dialogue.

Beyond description and narration, though, there is one more component that you must be sure to integrate into your own writing: the actual reflection that gives the essay its name. In the end, you must be able to step back and analyze the experience captured by the photograph you have chosen: What did (does) it mean to you? How did (does) it make you feel? Did (does) it change the way you view being a man or a woman? If so, how? If not, why not? What lesson(s) did (does) it teach you about gender? How might the images reflected in the photograph have shaped your maturation with regard to gender roles?

Overall Goals:

- To introduce you to critical thinking and analysis by asking you to carefully examine your own experience with gender issues.

- To introduce you to the rhetorical strategies in visual images (visual texts).

Skills/Criteria:

The essay should demonstrate your ability to do the following:

- Develop a reflection that explains the causes underlying your own judgment of an experience/object/issue;

- Effectively describe the experience/object/issue in concrete language;

- Effectively describe your response to that experience/object/issue in concrete language;

- Explain the underlying causes of that response in concrete language;

- Effectively use experiential evidence to support a point or interpretation; and,

- Organize the essay in such a way that mirrors the development of reflection, among other skills.

Techniques To Be Used: narration, description, reflection/analysis, dialogue (optional)

Basic Specifications: 4–5 pages, no outside sources, title, page numbers, double spaced text, other MLA formatting as needed, inclusion of the photograph (embedded in the essay itself). See Dodd and Compton-Vaughan as examples.

EXERCISE **3.a Writing to Reflect**

1. Before you read Rowland's essay, look carefully at the photograph. On a separate sheet of paper, write a short response to it. In your response, simply explain what you see and how the picture strikes you.

2. Read Rowland's essay and mark the place in it where the writing turns from exploration or inquiry to a specific thesis, central argument, or reflection as Ms. Mooney explains it in her assignment.

William Rowland is in General Engineering at Virginia Tech.

William Rowland
Instructor: Jennifer Mooney
English 1204H
07 September 2006

SEASIDE DISCUSSION

I sat on the front porch with my knees braced against my elbows, looking through the viewfinder of my new digital camera. I had been taking pictures of the sunset, but I turned to the left and snapped this picture as soon as I saw the three figures through the camera. It wasn't an artsy shot—I didn't stop to look at F-stop, shutter speed, composition or color balance—I just wanted to snag the three males before the discussion died and they walked back towards the house.

My dad, on the right, is in pure vacation-mode. It happens for only one week of the year, and I was lucky to be able to see it. He is barefoot, wearing casual clothes, and clutching a paperback thriller in his right hand. With his left hand he is waving back towards the property on which I sat, no doubt discussing his new idea as to what we should do with the run-down beach house built by his great-grandfather. His chin is grainy and unshaven, and the remnants of his gray hair are controlled by the wind much more so than by a comb or a brush.

My uncle, standing to the left, had just jumped in the water after riding his bike over dusty and bumpy dirt roads on the way to his house. He had made this beach-island his permanent home, starting his own architecture firm and making a living designing vacation houses. Because our old beach shack is easily accessed by him, my uncle is unofficially in control of the property, which explains the physical aspect of the conversation they are having. My dad is expressing an idea, using his arm to point towards an area of the property, while my uncle listens, arms crossed, and weighs the idea against the many others he hears when our family spends a week on the island.

The dog—a stubborn and arthritic 12 year old border collie who responds to the name Macky—completes the male environment on the beachfront setting. While he doesn't contribute with words, his physical presence conveys a masculine feeling of control. His genetic herding instincts, combined with a lack of sheep in his life, have manifested themselves into the instinct to herd members of our family. He watches over his two-man "flock," eagerly anticipating their next moves and eyeing potential threats from the beach or the distant horizon, likely seagulls or whiny, small propeller airplanes. Like the beach house, Macky is a constant presence on the island.

Although I am removed from the scene, I can see myself in the middle of the conversation. I would have been standing upright and maintaining a straight or even firm facial expression. As ashamed as I am to admit it, my natural reaction to being in the testosterone-influenced situation would be considerably different than to a situation in which a female was present. Many people would call it being "fake," but everyone adapts, mostly on a subconscious level, to the social environment in which they are present. I wouldn't be actively thinking about how to make myself look taller, tougher, or smarter, but my posture would make it appear that I was. And since the conversation would have focused on our beloved beach house, my stoicism probably would have been very real. I would have been serious, concerned, thoughtful—all of those stereotypically masculine things.

This beach house, referred to by our family as the "Shack," is far from polished. Accessible only by a dirt road, it is not connected to the outside world by power or telephone cables. Water is drawn from a nearby well into a holding tank by a noisy gasoline-powered generator. The interior of the house is equally rustic. The wood is grainy and gray, and the walls lack insulation. Wind whistles through screened doors and windows at all hours of the day and well into the night. Closing the windows makes the house eerily quiet and surprisingly uncomfortable, so we sleep through the night with the wind-driven chorus around us. The only odor I can detect is the soft smell of oil-burning lamps as they provide small beacons of yellow light in the pitch-black night. It is never enough light to read by, only to make it to the outhouse without crashing into walls and furniture. Use of the house is enjoyed more by the males than the females of our extended family. Something about the back-to-basics, bare bones lifestyle reaches out to the same instinct that would have me act tough around my dad and uncle. While it has been enjoyed by many women over the years, the house was constructed by men and, in my opinion and based on my experiences, is more likely to be enjoyed by men. Yet the presence of women resonates in it: for years, during our annual excursions, they have brought warmth to this house, cooking huge meals for our extended families, providing clean sheets and linens, making the bare walls and floors seem more like home. Stereotypical? Yes, but true.

I can hear in my head the conversation held between my uncle and father (and through actions, the dog). My dad is concise and clear. He restates his points as he does when he talks to me, and he clears his throat often. To him, getting across his point becomes a top priority, and if you show a lack of interest in the conversation, or if your eyes wander to a neighboring house or even the powerful sunset occurring at the time of the picture, he will bring your attention back to him. My uncle, the youngest child of the family, is more passive in his communications. I believe his style of talking is more effective. Instead of commanding your attention, he draws it in with witty dialect and interesting stories. The family is made of story-tellers, none of whom lack exaggerations aimed at getting a few good laughs. If my mom, my aunt, my sister, or any other female relative had been present, the conversation would have taken a highly different tone. There would be more "I thinks" and "I feel likes," and less "I knows." There would also be more focus on emotion. Sentimental value and family heritage would have replaced money as a top priority in their discussion, which involves a future plan for the property on which they are standing.

The world would not function without balance, and neither would our family. The input of women and (for that matter) girls is vital when it comes to making important decisions at all stages in life. The conversation depicted by this photograph might have been productive and insightful, but it should not stand alone, without the input of women. Their voices and opinions—their "I thinks" and "I feel likes"—might just make the difference between whether the beach house (even with its outhouse, thin walls, and well-drawn water) survives to host future family gatherings, alive with memories of past ones; razed to make room for an ultra-modern, clean dwelling with the latest in electronic gadgetry; or simply sold outright to fund the purchase of new property already outfitted with a "proper" beach house. However, since the synthesis of all components of the image speaks to me in a clear masculine tone, it is doubtful that emotion, memories, or sentimentality will factor into the decision. In this situation, the whole is greater than the sum of its parts, as each masculine component comes together to represent a scene, a group of men on the edge of a cliff, that embraces the roots of masculinity and, by doing so, represents potential imbalance. Will our beach house survive?

Notice that when you write to reflect, you are looking back at what you know or a response you had and attempting to make sense of that knowledge. It is a backward look. In taking that look back, you are able to gather your thoughts, see what fits, what is still a puzzle, how you might connect ideas.

When you use writing as inquiry, you are starting with a real question: What can you say about this topic? How can you figure out difficult passages of an essay, short story, or poem? Sometimes, simply by writing what you are thinking at the moment, you can begin to see patterns or to clarify thoughts that were, at first, simply a puzzle.

EXERCISE

3.b Writing as Inquiry

Use your current assignment to practice writing as inquiry or exploration. Try simply writing what you know about the topic, what you'd like to find out, what you want to say in an essay about it, and how you can make that relevant to readers who don't know you well.

3.2 ▎ More on Reflection

Reflective writing is largely a reconsideration of lived experience. In the assignment below, students were asked to reflect on the importance of music in their lives. While it would be easy for the writer to list their favorite songs or albums and stop there, reflection requires them to consider why a particular piece of music carries importance. Through reflection, the past is reexamined — often leading a writer to new or previously unrealized conclusions. In the essay that follows this assignment, consider how Zack's reflection allowed him to connect a piece of music to his past and how he then uses that bridge to gain a stronger understanding of his experience.

Tim Lockridge
English 1105
Fall Semester, 2006
Writing Assignment #3: "My Music" Reflection

While conducting interviews for your group presentations, you've asked a question — "What is music about for you?" — and likely heard a number of varied responses. This assignment asks you to consider and write on the same question. And while I'll provide you with a written example of my own response to that question and will also offer a number of music-centered essays and responses as examples, you are free to choose the ultimate path of your essay.

Remember that your response will likely be a personal narrative and, as such, demand a specific rhetorical situation and strategy. Your essay should also have a clear, relevant, and interesting point. We encounter personal narratives everywhere, from the internet to novels to newspaper columns. How do writers use the personal narrative to convey a moment or message? How can you write a narrative that readers will find interesting?

Here are three suggestions that might help you with the writing process:

1. Brainstorming will be a particularly helpful activity for this assignment. What are some of your favorite songs? Artists? Do you connect either of these to your life, or to particular moments in your memory? Consider Nick Hornby's essays on music, and how he ties music — and observations on music — to his lived experience.

2. Again, consider your lived experience and how music has connected to it. Have you tried to play a musical instrument or taken lessons? Remember the Sedaris essay and consider how he connects guitar lessons to his notion of family and masculinity. How does music tie into your notions of family or friendship or self?

3. When writing, consider sensory details and the five senses. How can you place your reader in a moment? How can you, by moving beyond simply "telling" a story, make your reader feel a connection to the text?

Since this is a personal narrative, it demands compelling and concise prose. You should be particularly aware of sentence length and variety, and you should also be diligent and ruthless when editing your drafts.

As always, final papers should be at least five pages in length and double-spaced — in a professional looking 12 point font — with one-inch margins all around.

3

EXERCISE   ## 3.c Making Connections

1. Look again at the above assignment and circle key words that tell you what you need to do to complete this assignment. What is Mr. Lockridge asking his students to consider?

2. With a group of your classmates, try some brainstorming. Make a list of your favorite songs or albums and then try to find particular memories that connect to music. What role has music played in your life? How can you use music as a gateway for reflection?

3. Begin prewriting — writing as inquiry. Think about specific points in the past, and describe them with as much sensory detail as possible. Do these scenes point you toward a realization? Can you thread them through a larger theme? How might you structure an essay around the frame of your lived experience?

Computer Science major Zack Villaire (left) with his teacher, Tim Lockridge.

Zack Villaire
Instructor: Tim Lockridge
English 1105
11.13.06

SUMMERTIME

I always remember being tucked into bed by my father as a child. He would lull me to sleep with a slow, and soothing, rendition of Gershwin's Summertime and while I would never fall asleep during his song, the comfort of him sitting on the bed and the words "there's a nothing can harm you, with daddy and momma standing by" always gave me the security to turn off the lights and close my eyes. One particular night in August always sticks out in my mind. Not because he ended the lullaby short, but because when I woke up the next morning, he was gone.

Contrary to Gershwin's lyrics, the living wasn't so easy after my father disappeared. My younger brother was just born and to support the growing need for money, a place to stay, and someone to watch over us both while my mother worked late nights at either one of her many jobs, we moved across the country where family members were much closer and willing to lend a hand. My mother was strong; she juggled a world record number of problems in the air, and still managed to fill my childhood with good memories, including my first guitar.

The guitar was nothing special, your standard plastic, battery powered child's toy, but in my hands, it was a dream. I remember playing the guitar in front of the television, mimicking the commercial jingles, learning the theme songs to my favorite cartoons, and even writing some of my own "music." One weekend I was blasting out the tunes to the worshipped Saturday morning cartoons while my mother cleaned up from breakfast, when the doorbell rang, followed by a short but hard knock.

I could tell by the way my mother reacted that she had been expecting this company all morning. She walked over to the door drying her hands and by the time she opened the apartment door, I was standing behind her. The door opened, my mother and I stepped back, and the man standing outside said, "Hey sport, remember me?" My only response was a slow nod while my eyes remained fixed on the man that once sang me to sleep. Sensing my uneasiness, my mother asked him to come in and sit down while she poured a cup of coffee from the kitchen.

My staring had started to make him the uneasy one so he tried to start up a conversation. "What do you have there sport? Been playing at any concerts on that thing?" I had forgotten about my guitar still strapped over my shoulder and broke my stare to look down at it, but even after running my hands over the buttons preparing to play something, I only looked back up in silence. My mother returned with the coffee and sat down beside me. She explained that my father was here to visit my brother and me, and would like to take me out to lunch. I don't remember agreeing to these plans, but I do remember getting dressed, lacing up my shoes, and walking out the door with my father.

My silent responses never slowed him as question after question poured from his mouth the whole way to his car. When we got to his car, I hesitated, going off with a stranger frightened me, but through his coaxing I ended up inside. My father pulled out of the parking lot, lighting a cigarette and asking more questions. I just sat there in silence wondering when I would get back home to my guitar. At McDonald's I was able to concentrate on my chicken nuggets rather than his never-ending stream of questions. My father was starting to see how much of a mistake trying to visit really was, and once we had finished, planned on driving me straight home.

Instead of sitting in awkward silence, my father turned on the radio. Having never been exposed to anything but commercial and television songs, I sat up listening. My father must have noticed the great deal of interest I displayed in his music, so he turned it to one of his favorite stations and began to sing and whistle to the tune. The country sounds of Clay Walker and John Michael Montgomery were something that I had never experienced before; this music was the type my guitar was destined for. Feeling much more comfortable, I began to sing along with what chorus I could pick up, but when he asked me if I wanted to learn how to whistle, I still only answered with a nod.

It took the better part of an hour to get it down, but the final product coming through my lips didn't sound too bad. I was in love with this music, it made me want to jump and dance, and it especially made me want to play my guitar. We sat outside in the parking lot until dark, listening to the sounds of Clint Black, Faith Hill, and what I deemed to be my favorite, Garth Brooks. This was more than a sorry father trying to regain some strong part of his life; it was a child learning how to appreciate music.

The sun had set and my father knew it was about time to head back to the apartment. We walked inside to my anxious mother wondering where we had been all day and I jumped up into her arms explaining how Garth Brooks had put on a special concert just for me. She laughed and told me to get into bed.

Sitting under the covers with a flashlight, I quietly played on my guitar while I listened to the murmurs of conversation through the walls. I imagined myself playing with Garth Brooks at one of his concerts, being a guest of honor and all. The images in my mind were slowly putting me to sleep until I shook up to the sounds of yelling and a door slam. My brother began to cry in his crib, and my mother picked him up crying herself. Instead of the country sounds of a guitar, I nodded off to the memory of my father's lullaby and the thought of never hearing from or seeing him again.

The next morning was just like any other Sunday, maybe a bit more solemn, but I still had the memories and dreams of that country music playing through my head. Weeks went by and just like normal; I would sit in front of the television emulating the sounds with my guitar. The only difference was that the country music channel had become my station of choice rather than Saturday morning cartoons.

One day I decided to have a little performance of my own for my mother and Aunt Terri. I stood in front of the old ice chest while my audience sat on the couch. I began to play one of Garth's best songs, *The Dance.* My guitar sung, I was in heaven, but my audience was bursting with laughter. Apparently the ice chest had decided to grab me with one of its handles and snag on my pants. I became red in the face and pouted with embarrassment, but every time I tried to run, the ice chest just held on tighter, ripping my pants even more and of course renewing the laughter of my unappreciative audience.

I remember that day extremely well not because of the disaster concert, but because when I woke up late that night to a knock on the door, two state troopers told me that my mother was in the hospital and very sick.

They drove us to my grandparent's house in the next city and there we stayed for two years. I started first grade, learned to read and ride a bike, and still loved country music. My old plastic toy guitar days were over; I had received a miniature string guitar for my birthday and played it nonstop. My Aunt Terri was staying with my grandparents too. She and her husband, Clayton, had just had her second child and were trying to find a place of their own. I would put on concerts for them after I came home from school; my brother would play drums, her children would clap and pretend to sing, and she would always laugh and remind about losing my pants to a piece of furniture. School, country music, and family were the three things that absorbed my day, except the day when he showed up.

I was writing a story about Garth Brooks and me playing at a concert in Tennessee when the teacher called me up to her desk. The school counselor, Mrs. Sikes, was standing at the front door and wanted me to follow her. I didn't understand what was going on, but it looked like I had no choice. On the way to her office, we stopped at my brother's kindergarten class and went to her office together. She opened the door and there sat the last man in the world I expected to see ever again.

We sat on his lap, talked about my mother, and tried to catch up. There were so many things I should have and wanted to say, but I only wanted to show him how much I appreciated him discovering country music for me and how much I wished to be like Garth Brooks and how one day I was going to play in real concerts. I never said a word. He pulled out his billfold, explained that he was living in California now, and how he had a wife, and two kids. He showed us picture after picture of his wife, their kids, and their dog. We saw a boy and a girl playing baseball and swimming in a pool. The girl liked to play with dolls, and the boy liked to play guitar. My father told us story after story of how wonderful these two kids were, how the boy was going to be a musician one day and how the girl looked just like her mother.

I remember I wanted to hit him, bite him, something to release all this anger and hatred that a normal child should never experience. In my mind I blamed him for

VILLAIRE 4

my mother being sick in the hospital, and blamed him for tearing my entire family apart, but I just sat on his lap, staring up in his face as if I wanted him to continue the stories. The school day was over, so he dropped us off at our grandparent's house, yet he refused to come in. I ran into my room crying, screaming, and yelling. I punched walls, threw things off my desk, and smashed my guitar into a million tiny pieces. My mother wasn't here to help me get over the feelings, my brother didn't understand, and my Aunt Terri knew exactly what was wrong, she just didn't know how to help.

I never listen to country music anymore. It reminds me of too many hurtful memories, some not even associated with my father. Fifteen years later and I still can feel the wind blowing at my hair as I experienced Garth Brooks with my father, I can still remember riding in the trooper's car, and I can still remember the splinters of the guitar stuck in my hand.

My children may never hear George Gershwin's famous lullaby, learn a musical instrument, or like country music. But I know that they will never feel the pain that my father inflicted on me, never have to stay with distant relatives because their parents aren't around, and never look at their father like he's the last stranger you ever want to see.

EXERCISE

3.d Analyzing the Reflection Essay

1. Zack tells a very personal story. It's easy for something personal to carry meaning with the writer, but it's more difficult to make something resonate with a reader. Look at Zack's essay and describe what makes it meaningful. Try underlining the sentences that specifically mention music. What role does music play in his story?

2. Point to places where you can see the reflection at work. Where does this essay become more than a simple memory? What strategies does the writer use to move through experience and toward meaning?

■ Reflecting on Your Own Writing

One of the most common assignments you will get in a writing class is to be asked to look back over the writing you have done throughout the term and reflect on how your writing has evolved, what changes you have made, and what changes you would like to make on these papers if you could write them one more time.

When you are asked to reflect on your own writing—either in a cover letter to a portfolio or a final writing about what you learned in the class, take time to look back at your assignments, the drafts you wrote, the decisions you made, and the responses your teacher gave you.

You can write a strong reflection—evaluating your own progress—by using a critical eye even on your own work. The weakest reflections are those that simply say, "I learned a lot in this class." The best reflections are specific. They point to decisions you made in your writing and in the revisions you made for final drafts.

3.3   Critical Reading (and Rereading)

While it's tempting to read a text for surface understanding alone, critical reading requires you to develop a certain familiarity with the material. You might already do this with your favorite movies, gaining a stronger understanding of the plot and a deeper connection to the characters with each additional viewing. Rereading also illuminates the things not immediately obvious, giving the reader a stronger grasp of nuance.

Take, for example, the poem below written by Virginia Tech MFA candidate Ennis McCrery. What would you need to do to read this poem critically?

Ennis McCrery is a candidate for the MFA in Creative Writing and a graduate teaching assistant in the Department of English at Virginia Tech.

Ennis McCrery

A THOUSAND BLENDED NOTES
—*after William Wordsworth*

In the backyard,
ivy ribbons the lilac hedge,
squeezing out the purpled
scent to strain through window
screens and settle, hushed
as television static about the house.
The dog, fat and lazy
from tasting winter stews,
tucks Easter's ham bone
beneath a heap of pine straw,
circles twice, and sleeps
in the shadow of leaves.
Creeping thyme
volunteers along the fence,
strings of toad eggs weave
iridescent in rain-filled flower pots,
and Daddy is dead again
amid grass and greenery.
My grief delicate and perfect
as the open-mouthed tulips lining
the front walk.

A THOUSAND BLENDED NOTES   *connection?*
—after William Wordsworth   *how?*

In the backyard,   → *setting*
(ivy) ribbons the (lilac) hedge,
<u>s</u>queezing out the purpled
<u>s</u>cent to strain through window   *alliteration*
<u>s</u>creens and settle, hushed
as television static about the house.
The dog, fat and lazy
<u>from</u> tasting <u>winter</u> stews,   *change in seasons*
tucks <u>Easter's</u> ham bone
beneath a heap of (pine straw,)
circles twice, and sleeps
in the shadow of (leaves)
<u>Creeping</u> (thyme)
<u>volunteers</u> along the fence,   *vivid verbs!*
strings of toad eggs <u>weave</u>
iridescent in rain-filled (flower pots,)
and Daddy is dead again   → *poem changed here!*
amid (grass) and (greenery.)
My grief delicate and perfect
(as) the open-mouthed (tulips) lining
the front walk.

simile: grief v. beauty? hmm...

Poetry, because of its brevity and density, begs to be read critically. In the illustration above, notice how active reading—underlining, circling, and annotating the text—has allowed the reader to realize and question some specific details.

A number of interesting details appear in this poem: a reference to William Wordsworth, a specific setting, an abundance of botanical imagery, and a shift in subject in the final lines. But notice how an active reading illuminates trends (the garden imagery appears more frequently in the poem's second half) and raises additional questions (how does William Wordsworth relate to this poem?). By investigating these patterns and questions, you—as the reader—have an opportunity to find your own place in the text, to apply the writer's words to your own life and experiences.

■ *So How Do You Read a Poem?*

Begin by reading it slowly, allowing the words to paint a picture in your mind. Look for the setting: here, it's the backyard, as the reader noted in the first line. The poem continues to offer a description of the backyard in the next four lines, and the reader has noted the use of alliteration (a repetition of sounds in the beginning of words). With the sixth line, however, we're introduced to the dog and to two different seasons—an emergence to Easter from winter—which helps us further visualize the scene. The poem started with a personification of ivy, and, after we move past the dog, the personification really kicks in: now the thyme creeps and volunteers along the fence. But a large change occurs with the line "and Daddy is dead again," which, after all the plant personification, feels jarring and unexpected. Here, five lines from the end, we're introduced to someone's dad—the first human we've seen in the poem. The poem quickly returns to lush, floral imagery, and the poem closes with a brief mention of the poet, whose grief, like a flower, is delicate and perfect.

Already, with our first reading, we've determined the poem's situation: it's spring, nature is blooming in the backyard, and the poet—noticing this—comes to a realization. We can gather this information from an initial reading, but stopping here would be like looking at the ocean and determining that it's simply the water between continents. While that observation is true, it misses many levels of function and nuance. You'll need to critically re-read the poem to acquire a fuller understanding of its subject and subtext. Use the following exercise as a place to start.

EXERCISE

3.e Critically Reading a Poem

1. We've determined that the poem takes place in Spring, specifically at Easter. How does the setting impact the poem's content?

2. The poet has noticed many things occurring in the backyard, yet her thoughts turn to her father and a realization about grief. How do these ideas work for or against each other? How does the poem prepare the reader for its ultimate realization?

3. Some of the verbs used suggest personification, or applying human characteristics to non-human things (for example, the thyme volunteers along the fence and the toad eggs weave). How does this change your perception of the poem's setting? Why might the writer want to do this?

4. The poem "turns" at the line "and Daddy is dead again." Why would the writer use "again" after a something as final as death? How would the poem change if "again" was removed?

5. This poem represents one of the most exciting moments in writing: when the act of describing one thing leads you to an unexpected conclusion. Try describing a place you know well, focusing on sensory details. Where might your writing lead you?

3.4 Writing a Critical Analysis

Critical analysis—no matter your major—will be important throughout your work at Virginia Tech. When you are asked to read and respond to a candidate's position statement, evaluate a lab technique, examine an architectural drawing for its strengths and weaknesses, or do a close reading of a piece of literature, art, or musical composition, you are engaging in critical analysis. In first-year composition, then, writing critical analysis is a key component in your education as a writer and thinker. That is one reason the Council of Writing Program Administrators lists "critical thinking, reading, and writing" as an important outcome of any composition program.

Establish the facts — Reread the text several times to establish the facts. You have to establish the literal meaning of any text before you can dive beneath its surface. You can't be an effective critical reader if you only read a text once. A civil engineer can't just eyeball a bridge and know whether unseen cracks have allowed water to degrade the underlying rebar. The engineer must return to the bridge with instruments, perhaps many times under varying conditions. In the same way, you have to go over a written text several times, with differing experiences to serve as diagnostic tools.

What do these words tell you? — You will likely know a lot more about the text than you first thought. Critical readers aren't looking for obscure symbols or codes that the author has deviously hidden in the text just to give teachers something to hold over students. Critical readers are looking for ways that the text means things to them, for information carried not only in individual words (though that's a good beginning), but also in the structures of sentences, the patterns of associated words, or of repetition. The meanings that you can discover by critical reading are not all the author's—they are partly yours.

In the assignment below, instructor Victoria LeCorre asks her students to critically analyze an advertisement. She refers to an essay her students read for the class—Susan Bordo's "Hunger as Ideology"—as one model for a thesis-driven analysis. Notice that she lists steps she would like her students to follow as they find their subjects and write their papers.

> **Writing an Ad Analysis,**
> **or Preparing to uncover hidden messages in your advertisements**
> **in a three-page, formal essay:**
>
> **1.** Reread Chapter 7 of this book on reading and writing about visuals. Concentrating on your advertisement, list the important details of the ad. (It would also be useful for you to review *The Brief Penguin Handbook* on "Composing in a Visual Era," pp. 1–26.)
>
> **2.** Examine your evidence carefully, isolating any patterns you notice. These may very well become the arguments for your body paragraphs.

3. Consider which one or two points from Bordo's article your advertisement best illustrates. You will weave her discussion in at appropriate points in your three-page analysis.

4. Write a preliminary outline or list of those details you are sure you want to cover in your paper.

5. Now begin writing a first draft. Your introductory paragraph will describe your advertisement as if your readers could not see it. Stay superficial. [Remember that writing an essay is like playing a game of cards whose rules include that you can only play each card once, so wait for the moment when it will have the most impact.] Explain where you found the ad (for example, in *Glamour*). You might also mention why you have chosen it. Then write a thesis similar to the following: "This advertisement's only function cannot be to sell X because it also manifests hidden purposes that reinforce claims made by Dr. Susan Bordo in 'Hunger as Ideology.'"

6. Add your body paragraphs. Each should further your argument, either referring to specific details of the ad or intersecting your argument with Bordo's.

7. Conclude. Reread your essay, quickly noting in the margins just what you've argued. Now take advantage of the momentum that you have created to reinforce your main points, and leave us with something vital to ponder. For example, this would be an appropriate place to write about the advertising world's reinforcement of society's desire to contain women, if that's a point you want to make.

8. Add a Works Cited page. At a minimum, it will contain an entry for your advertisement and another for Bordo's essay which was published in an anthology. Use MLA format for citations. Consult *The Brief Penguin Handbook* or go to the Composition Companion Website to find the Citation Generator listed in the Research Writing chapter.

9. Perform the logical paragraph test, using thesis and topic sentences. Read the paper aloud. If any sentences sound wordy, streamline them. Check your verbs, making sure that they are sophisticated and precise. Proofread, proofread, and proofread! A mistake ridden paper will not be taken seriously, no matter how subtle the analysis it contains.

10. Write several drafts, concentrating on better demonstrating the validity of your thesis, choosing the most powerful evidence and order in which you expose it, writing clearly and precisely.

11. Conference with me.

Good luck, and have some fun!

You'll notice that Ms. LeCorre's assignment is very precise in the steps she wants her students to take while writing their analysis. Not every assignment will have this level of detail or direction, but you can begin thinking as a critical reader and writer and set up some steps of your own.

Electrical Engineering major John Kollar is shown
here with his instructor Victoria LeCorre.

3

EXERCISE **3.f Practicing Analysis**

John Kollar wrote the following ad analysis in response to Ms. LeCorre's assignment. Read it carefully. When you have finished your reading, discuss with a group
of your classmates where the paper specifically engages in critical analysis.

KOLLAR 1

John Kollar
Instructor: Victoria LeCorre
English 1105
7 November 2006

GENDER INEQUALITY —"THAT'S HOT"

A seductive tune starts to play, and from an illuminated opening we see a
woman in the doorway. The camera descends to Paris Hilton's high-heeled shoes as
she drops the fur coat she is wearing. Paris, now clad only in a skimpy, black swimsuit, then walks across the warehouse, goes over to the only object in it, a black car,
and begins to "wash" it. In the process she gets herself wet and sudsy and mounts
the car. Paris stares seductively into the camera as her hair flutters in the air, at least
when she is not swaying it back and forth. The camera then cuts to Paris's taking a
big bite out of her Carl Jr. Spicy Barbeque Burger. She then begins to lick her fingers in
a very alluring way and sprays water all over with a sexually positioned hose. Paris
slides down the car, and the screen fades black with the slogan "The Spicy BBQ
Burger, That's Hot" flashing upon it ("Paris"). Although its main intention is to sell Carl
Jr. Spicy Barbeque Burgers, the commercial fits certain analytical views held by Dr.
Susan Bordo towards both genders in her essay "Hunger as Ideology."

The Carl Jr. advertisement uses Hilton's sexual charm to appeal to men. To begin with, a sexual tone is set by the stripper-like tune that plays in the background throughout the entire ad. This sound causes the male consumer to pay attention, making him feel that a risqué show is about to be performed in his own living room by a very attractive woman. The man would then notice that Paris is wearing very little clothing, creating "a strong immediate impact, even shock value" (Faigley 26) especially due to the color of her black swimsuit. This color is thought of as bad and "dirty" ("Black"). According to Bordo's essay, this commercial is an example of Baudrillard's hyperreality in that because Hilton dresses and looks dirty, she is dirty. For the man, Hilton is "the created image that has the hold on our most vibrant, immediate sense of what is, of what matters, of what we must pursue for ourselves" (143). It also presents this impure girl trying to wash and make something clean, but the irony is not generally noticed by the man who is too busy watching Paris, the modern day Marilyn Monroe, crawl all over the black car. The camera works at an angle so as to expose Hilton on top of the car as she peers into the camera. Hilton is thus above her audience, making them feel dominated by her sexual power. The text at the end of the advertisement is in a very alluring font, reminding the viewer of Paris, even though she has disappeared from sight. The text also reinforces which product to buy by associating Paris's trademarked catchphrase, "That's Hot", with the food. Through the entire striptease, Paris is in the middle of almost every camera shot, creating a static effect (Faigley 19). This emphasizes that the main point of focus is on Paris. The male consumer, raring with excitement, then feels that he must meet the demand of the blonde goddess and buy a Carl Jr. Spicy Barbeque Burger in order to be sexually pleased.

The Carl Jr. ad is also targeted at the female consumer. When women view this wonderfully beautiful woman eating a Carl Jr. Spicy Barbeque Burger, they feel as if they would be sexually appealing and beautiful also by eating the Carl Jr. burger, but they know that they cannot indulge. Bordo explains this as follows: "When women are positively depicted as sensuously voracious about food, their hunger for food is employed solely as a metaphor for their sexual appetite" (138). Here, if a woman decided to indulge in eating the Carl Jr. Burger like Hilton, society would deem her as a slut. On the other hand, if a woman were to eat voraciously in a nonsexual way, her appetite would be viewed as disgusting and repulsive, causing the woman to lose either way. Because the female still wants to attract a man, and because a man is so infatuated with the sexual image portrayed in the commercial, it makes the woman feel that she could sexually please her partner if she gets this burger for him. This leaves women in the audience wanting to buy the Barbeque Burger in order to feel sexually appealing and wanted by their partners.

This seductive Carl Jr. commercial has the purpose of selling burgers but does so in a very subtle way by concentrating on creating food as a sexually desirable object. It is done by making an extremely popular and beautiful woman use her sexual appeal to associate it with the desire for food. Hilton makes the men watching feel overpowered by this appeal, and the women in the audience feel that they must provide this sexual appeal for their spouse. A woman can only do this by buying Carl Jr. food, making her become the object of desire of her loved one, and, in essence, serving him, furthering the gender inequality demonstrated in the advertisement.

Works Cited

"Black." Def. 4. Merriam-Webster Online. 2006. Merriam-Webster, Inc. 30 Oct 2006
http://www.m-w.com/dictionary/black

Bordo, Susan. "Hunger as Ideology". *Ways of Reading: An Anthology for Readers.* David Bartholomae and Anthony Petroski, eds. 5th ed. New York: Bedford/St. Martin's, 1999. 138-172.

Faigley, Lester. *The Brief Penguin Handbook.* New York: Pearson 2006.

"Paris Hilton's Extended Car Wash." Perf. Paris Hilton. 2006 IFILM, corp. 30 Oct 2006
http://www.ifilm.com/video/2671832?loomia_si=1

3.5 ■ Preparing to Write Analysis— Informal Writing Tasks

The following informal writing tasks are designed to lead you through the process of writing a critical analysis. You can use them with any assignment that asks for analysis. In a writing class, the text you analyze might be anything from a poem to an advertisement to a film to a public space and more. All of these are possible subjects for analysis.

■ Informal Writing Task 1:

Write a brief summary or description of the text you plan to analyze.

■ Informal Writing Task 2:

Develop and answer focusing questions to help you discover and perhaps narrow your topic.

- ◆ What patterns do you notice?
- ◆ What doesn't seem to fit?
- ◆ What details do you notice?
- ◆ What is the overall effect of the text, image, space, or object?
- ◆ What made it difficult or easy to read?
- ◆ What questions does it raise?
- ◆ Does the text take a position that you can identify?
- ◆ What rhetorical techniques does the text use?
- ◆ What conflicts do you see in the text?

■ *Informal Writing Task 3:*

Develop a working thesis. Most often, the thesis in an analysis essay answers a "how" question. To get started, you might try to answer questions like the following:

◆ How does the author use _____ to accomplish _____?

◆ How does a particular rhetorical technique affect the success of the text?

◆ How does the pattern you found contribute to meaning?

◆ How does the text demonstrate _____?

◆ How do you respond as a reader or viewer?

■ *Informal Writing Task 4:*

Find evidence that supports your response or thesis. List pieces of potential evidence that you think might support your thesis, including quotations. This detailed evidence will provide support for your argument.

Once you have compiled your evidence, you are ready to write a draft. You already have a good thesis, interpretation, or argument in mind and a good idea of what evidence you will use as support.

For additional information about drafting, see Chapter 4: Writing as a Process.

For more discussion of critical thinking and writing analysis, see *The Brief Penguin Handbook,* Section 3, pp. 71–105.

3.6 ◼ Further Exercises for Exploring Critical Thinking, Reading, and Writing

EXERCISES

1. You can practice what you have learned in this chapter by doing a critical reading of your own. Read the following poem by Tim Lockridge, an MFA candidate in the English Department at Virginia Tech. Review this chapter, focusing particularly on section 3.3 (Reading and Rereading). Circle images and words that you find interesting or potentially important. Annotate the poem in the way we have annotated the McCrery poem earlier in this chapter. Then write a 2–3 page critical analysis.

Tim Lockridge is an MFA student in Creative Writing and a graduate teaching assistant in the Department of English at Virginia Tech.

Tim Lockridge

THE YOUNG WIDOW

You bring one knee to the soft earth, muddy your black
dress, trace your hand against the polished wood until
he is lowered and it is done. Neck loose, shoulders slack,
you look up: the leaves slightly shaking, the clouds still.
You leave and return with gifts. A blue scarf to drape
across the headstone. Picture frames laid on limestone:
a ferris wheel, a wedding cake. These moments scrape
and break wounds too fresh. Soon dusk draws you home.
But how the sun scatters night, makes room for morning,
that is how he wants to reach you. Folded letters found
in the bottom of a drawer. Pressed petals spilling
from a book. Memory like the slow echo of sound:
The hum of radio, a song you haven't heard in years.
Boxes left to pack, the lives we live in souvenirs.

2. Or, you might choose to examine a particular advertisement or product design. For example, Camel cigarettes recently came out with new packaging aimed at women. How would you critically read this package design, knowing that it is aimed specifically at women?

4

Writing as a Process

Writing as a process embraces the idea that writing involves invention, planning, drafting, revising, editing, and proofreading — all of these stages often overlap in some way. In this chapter, we discuss in detail what each stage involves. Throughout this chapter, we have gone through a rather individual but exemplary model of student writing, an essay written by first-year composition student Daniel Lassiter. In order to give you an idea about how the process of composing a paper might unfold, we have also included various invention strategies Daniel used to generate ideas and claims for his paper.

4.1 ▪ What Is Invention?

Generating ideas for writing is one of the most difficult challenges that writers face. Blank pages and blinking cursors are intimidating no matter how long you've been writing. Many writers wonder what they could say about a subject that hasn't already been said. Others are stumped by how to actually begin writing once they have a topic. One way to begin solving both of these problems is to ask questions. What *don't* you know about your topic? What are the unknowns? What (or where) are the gaps in your knowledge? If your writing process is guided by these unknowns or gaps—that is, if it is a process of inquiry instead of reporting—then you're more likely to be invested in your work and to discover something new through it. How, though, do come up with guiding questions? Of course one way is to sit down and write out as many questions as you can about the topic. But if you don't know where the gaps in your knowledge are, then you might not be ready to make such a list. The following invention strategies can help you identify those gaps. Importantly, they can also help you narrow or refine an idea that you already have.

EXERCISE

4.a Finding What You Know

Use the 17 questions below to identify what you know and what you don't know about your topic. Some questions may not apply to your particular topic.

1. What does X mean?

2. What are the various features of X?

3. What are the component parts of X?

4. How is X made or done?

5. How should X be made or done?

6. What is the essential function of X?

7. What are the causes of X?

8. What are the consequences of X?

9. What are the types of X?

10. How is X like or unlike Y?

11. What is the present status of X?

12. What is the significance of X?

13. How did X happen?

14. What is my personal response to X?

15. What is my memory of X?

16. What is the value of X?

17. What case can be made for or against X?

■ *Freewriting*

Freewriting is writing quickly and with no regard for grammar, organization, or style for a short period of time, usually about 10–15 minutes. Write your topic, however broad or narrow it is, at the top of your paper or computer screen. Then simply start writing. Write whatever comes to your mind as long as it's at least tangentially related to the topic. Do not stop writing to think. Write no matter what. Once the time is up, read over what you've written. Underline the most interesting sentence or phrase you wrote. Write this sentence or phrase at the top of your page and do another freewrite. Freewriting is meant to start your thinking. You will find that you can use parts of what you write but, very likely, not all of it and sometimes not much of it. The importance of freewriting is that you can use it to find out what you know about a topic, what you want to say about it, and what you still need to find out. It gets you started, but it is never the end point.

■ *Brainstorming*

Write down key words or short phrases in list-form under your topic. If you get stuck, look at one of the items on the list to see if it triggers something new or if there's a general term (abstractions like "power," "education," "culture," or "knowledge" are good examples) that keeps popping up and needs some fleshing. Assume nothing is self-explanatory—at this stage stating the obvious is a great way to tap into unknown territory. When you're done, use your word processor's cut and paste features (or arrows or color coding if you have written on paper) to reorganize your terms and find relationships, contradictions, and gaps in your knowledge.

■ *Mapping and Clustering*

Mapping is like brainstorming but for more visually oriented writers. Rather than listing concepts, start by writing a central word in the middle of an unlined piece of paper. As related concepts, phrases, and words pop in your head, indicate them as branches, arrows, in bubbles, or however you like to cluster. Some branches will lead to dead ends, others won't. At the end of a successful cluster session, you can focus on the blossoming areas and draw arrows between concepts to show their relationships. You can also look to see which ideas turned into dead ends. These dead ends might indicate where the unknowns or gaps in your knowledge are.

Depending on your particular writing assignment, your next step might be to begin searching for answers to questions that arise as you develop your ideas. That might mean investigating your own feelings and experiences, or it might mean doing library or field research. Don't be disappointed if you aren't able to answer your question(s) in exactly the way that you anticipated. Writing as inquiry is unpredictable. But that's why it's rewarding, both for writers and readers.

For more on brainstorming methods, see *The Brief Penguin Handbook,* Chapter 15, sections a–f. Also, refer to the Composition Companion Website: www.pearsoncustom.com/vt_composition.

4.2 ▮ What Is Drafting?

▮ *Developing Your Thesis / Main Idea*

Once you have gone through the planning process, you should have a rough thesis or main idea. Please note that not every assignment you write will have a clear-cut "thesis." Instead, you may often simply have a main point or argument that you are trying to make. Once you have that main idea or thesis, you will use it as a building block to begin the drafting process.

First, you may be asking, "What is a thesis?" A thesis is your main idea/focus, the arguable point that you are trying to make; a thesis gives your essay a clear purpose, direction, and focus and is the point that you want to "prove" in your essay. A thesis statement gives your readers a "map" of the paper that is to come: it lets the reader know what you will discuss in your paper and why.

A strong thesis/main point should have the following qualities:

1. **A strong thesis is explicit and clear — it's easily located and is discernible as the central sentence in the text, using clear, specific words**

   To avoid vague constructions in your thesis/main idea, you should not place words such as "this/that" or "it" at the beginning of your thesis. For example, "This shows the concept of emotion…"

   Words like "thing," "fate," and "society" can also be problematic because they are often vague. They don't say anything concrete. Always make sure that your audience has a very clear idea of your connotation when using such words.

2. **A strong thesis takes a clear stand; a strong thesis argues for a specific way the reader might interpret or "see" that topic.**

   Make sure that your thesis is an *arguable* assertion, clearly taking a stand on an issue; the most common error to avoid here is to ensure that your thesis is not simple plot summary.

3. **A strong thesis is original, making a deeply analytic, complex claim that reveals surprising connections, rather than claims that are superficial, simplistic, and predictable.**

   A strong thesis will bring a new "voice" or perspective to the discussion; it will not simply reiterate what has been discussed at length in class and class discussions; you will instead find a new way in which to view the text, coming to a new and original claim.

4. **A strong thesis matches the paper content; the final thesis draft correlates with the supporting evidence and support structure of the final paper.**

   Oftentimes, after revising a paper, a student will have a paper that does not match his/her thesis: when changing any element in your essay, always make sure to go back and ensure that your final thesis does match your final essay.

5. A strong thesis has a subject that can be adequately explored in the assigned length (i.e., not too broad, not too narrow)

You don't want to choose a thesis that you cannot explore due to it either being too broad or too narrow to fit your assignment's paradigm.

6. A strong thesis focuses on ONE main idea (i.e., isn't contradictory and/or trying to do too many things)

Make sure your thesis does not have a "split" focus, where you are trying to explore more than is possible.

Please note, too, that as you write and develop your paper, you can change your thesis/main idea—perhaps your paper is going in a new and unexpected direction or you discover more information about your topic that changes your perspective/stance on your thesis. That's fine and quite common—just make sure that your final thesis does, indeed, match your final paper.

EXERCISE

4.b Formulating a Thesis

Work through the questions below as you formulate a thesis/main idea for your paper.

1. Analyze your primary and/or secondary sources. Look for controversy, interest, tension, ambiguity, complication, etc. Does the author contradict himself or herself—what is his/her purpose by doing so? What are the deeper, symbolic points/insinuations of the author's argument? Figuring out the "why" to a question will put you on the path to developing a working, and an analytic, thesis.

2. Now, write down three possible theses/main points for your assignment. Then, look over each one carefully: which choice most accurately portrays how you feel about this idea? What option will give you the richest possibility to write a fully developed and thorough essay?

3. Because your thesis/main idea should take an arguable stance, you will want to anticipate the counterarguments; thus, think about what might be said against it. Write down three counterarguments that someone could have about your main idea/thesis. Then, write how you will refute these counterclaims somewhere in your essay.

4

■ *Beginning to Pull Your Paper Together*

Once you have your preliminary thesis/main idea, you need to begin thinking about how you will organize your ideas. How will you go about organizing and structuring your essay?

The brainstorming activities discussed in the invention section should produce some specific words or phrases that can be organized according to related ideas and points that would support the main idea. A successful paper needs a main idea that makes a point about a topic.

An outline can show the relationship between ideas, and it can provide a tentative plan for your writing. Later, when you are writing, you may decide that you need to add more support or change the order of information you are using in the paper.

In the outline, group similar ideas that are logically connected. Paragraphs are often ordered to reflect a relationship between cause and effect, to indicate a time sequence, to provide a definition, or to suggest a solution to a problem. Your outline will be your guide to writing the paper. If a formal outline is not required, you may not need to follow the formal structure. However, if you are asked to write a formal outline, use the standard format:

I. Introduction (usually includes the thesis)

II. First main point or reason

    A. Supporting evidence

    B. Supporting evidence

        1. Example or detail

        2. Example or detail

III. Second main point or reason

    A. Supporting evidence

    B. Supporting evidence

        1. Example or detail

        2. Example or detail

IV. Conclusion

Your own outline may include more sections than this one, and they may be organized in a different manner, but this format will generally suffice for more formal outlines.

EXERCISE | **4.c Sketching out a Rough Outline**

Using the example outline above, as well as the ideas in the planning section of this chapter, sketch out a rough outline of your essay. Make sure to include the main ideas that you will incorporate into your introduction, the body of your essay, and your conclusion.

For more information on planning and drafting, refer to Chapters 3 and 4 in *The Brief Penguin Handbook*. Also, refer to the Composition Companion Website: www.pearsoncustom.com/vt_composition.

4.3 What Is Revising?

Revising literally means to "see again"—how can you see your paper again through a fresh critical perspective? The first items you should consider when revising are thesis, content, development, and organization.

Thesis/Main Idea

One of the first items to revise is your thesis—your main idea.

EXERCISE | **4.d Revising Your Thesis**

1. Write your thesis/main idea on a separate piece of paper—does your thesis relate to your paper?

2. What in your thesis explains what you want to argue or explain in your paper? How do you indicate the direction of your paper with this thesis?

3. What is your main focus? Does your thesis/main idea have only one main focus? If not, how could you make it more focused?

Focus and Audience

Once you have revised your thesis, see if you have a unified focus and if your paper has a clear sense of audience.

EXERCISE | **4.e Revising for Focus and Audience**

In a notebook or on a separate sheet of paper, respond to the following questions. They are meant to refine what you are writing and how you are presenting it to appeal to audience.

1. How do the parts of your paper fit together? Note down any section that you think your audience will be puzzled over or that you had difficulty finding a way into as you were writing.

2. Who will be reading your paper (in other words, who is the audience of this paper)? What do you know about this audience? How will this shape the way you write your paper?

3. What expectations will your audience have of your writing? In other words, why would someone want to read your paper?

4. What does your audience already know or think about your topic? With that in mind, what do you need to tell them through your writing? How can you go about doing this?

4

5. Thinking about how you answered the above questions, explain why your tone is appropriate (or not) for the audience you have in mind. What specific choices have you made with this audience in mind?

Purpose and Organization

You should also reflect how well your paper is organized to meet your purpose.

EXERCISE

4.f Revising for Purpose

Use the following questions to help you revise for purpose and organization.

1. What are your instructor's goals for this paper? How do you know? What specific language in the assignment indicates those goals? Does your paper meet those goals?

2. Review your assignment, and make any changes you need to clearly address those goals.

3. Has your paper done what you intended it to, either through "solving" or attempting to solve your thesis/main point of your paper? How have you accomplished that, or what do you still need to do to make sure you do accomplish it?

EXERCISE

4.g Revising for Organization

Once you have addressed the two questions above, you should reflect upon the organization of your paper. One technique to help assess the organization and flow of your paper is to read your paper aloud.

1. Read your paper aloud to a classmate or group of classmates (peer reader). Ask your peer reader to make notes on any sections in the paper that are choppy or have a disruptive flow. Once you have completed that review, talk with your reader(s) about possible effective transitions both between and within your paragraphs.

2. Now go through your essay and write down some notes on the topics of the various paragraphs, or make a list of the topic sentences of each major paragraph of the paper. When you examine the list, is there another, perhaps better, way you could organize your paper? Are there any areas of the paper that should be moved to make your paper flow better?

Development

A strong paper will have clearly and thoroughly explored and developed points to support your thesis.

EXERCISE **4.h Developing your Ideas**

1. Closely examine each paragraph in your paper. On average, how long is each paragraph? After noting the length of each paragraph, do you have paragraphs that seem longer or shorter than others? If so, work on cutting down and trimming the long paragraphs or adding information to the shorter paragraphs (perhaps you need to add more source material, whether from a primary or secondary source).

2. Read through each paragraph/section of your paper. On a separate piece of paper, write the main idea/focus of each paragraph in a sentence or two. After examining this list, does each paragraph relate to the overall focus and/or thesis of your paper? If not, either eliminate the paragraph or develop it to make it flow better with your paper.

What About Sources?

Another issue in development includes examining any quotations you may have in your essay. Remember, an effective quotation will have a lead-in sentence and a follow-up interpretive comment where you explore the quotation in relation to your thesis and main idea.

EXERCISE **4.i Checking Sources**

1. Read through your paper, and circle each quotation in your essay. Does each quotation have a lead-in sentence? How effective are your lead-in sentences?

2. Do you relate each quotation back to your thesis/main idea? How effectively have you explored each quotation?

3. Does each quotation have a correctly formatted citation?

EXERCISE **4.j A Checklist for English 1106 and H1204—Research**

1. Are your primary/secondary sources effectively integrated into your paper (e.g., you smoothly integrate fieldwork into your research paper as well as a scientific article you read on your topic)?

2. Do you have a lead-in sentence to your quotations that introduces the source(s) to the audience, where you include the author and title of each work?

3. Are summaries and paraphrases correctly and appropriately cited?

4. Do you have a Works Cited page, where you cite every work you included in your essay?

4.4 ■ Working with Readers' Comments

One challenge for every writer is how to respond to readers' comments. In writing classes you will, of course, get feedback from your instructor, but you are very likely to also get feedback from classmates in peer workshops. Don't underestimate the importance of these comments. Your peers can be a vast source of information and help as you write your paper, so peer workshopping is an integral part in the revision process.

Below, then, is a typical workshopping sheet that an instructor may use in your composition course. If your instructor does not use this sheet in class, feel free to use it as your own writing exercise.

■ *The Peer Workshop*

When you exchange papers with classmates for a reading, you are participating in a peer workshop. You can use the following list to make the most of that workshop session:

1. Identify the paper's thesis or main argument: Is it specific but not so specific that the writer can't say much beyond it? If it is too broad (tries to argue too much), how would you suggest the writer refine that central argument? Work with your group members to help the writer come to a position that is focused, interesting, and that follows the expectations of the assignment.

2. How convinced are you after you have read the paper? What evidence or support or examples would make the paper stronger and easier to follow?

3. Are quotations used to support what is being argued in the paper, or do the quotes begin to take over? If they begin to take over or don't seem relevant, how would you suggest the writer revise? Check, as well, to see if the writer has followed the citation form your teacher has asked you to follow for this assignment.

4. Is the essay easy to follow? This is a question about organization. Are there parts of the paper that seem somehow out of place or that might be more effective earlier or later in the paper? Mark those and discuss them with the writer.

5. You aren't the proofreader, but if you notice obvious proofreading problems, mark them. Be sure, however, that if you mark an error, it actually is an error. There is no room for guessing when you are working with someone else's paper.

6. After you have finished reading, write a short response to the paper that tells the writer what works and what doesn't.

Notice how the questions deal mainly with issues of revision; grammar and mechanics only take up a portion of the workshopping.

■ Instructor Feedback

Some of you may also have your papers collected and commented upon by your instructors; these comments most likely pertain to revision (or "global") issues. Always make sure to read through your instructor's comments carefully, making the necessary changes that he or she recommends.

If you have questions about a comment, take your questions straight to the teacher.

If you are working in groups for peer review, share the comments with your group and see if they can help you make the revision suggested.

If you need additional help addressing the instructor's questions and comments, take your paper to the Writing Center — 340 Shanks. Make sure you take your assignment sheet and the instructor's comments with you.

EXERCISE

4.k Reading and Responding to Feedback

1. Take a draft that your instructor has just commented on. First, circle every comment that your teacher made.

2. Next, go through the comments you have circled. What patterns do you begin to see?

3. After noticing the patterns in your writing and your teacher's comments, how can you begin to work on these issues? Look through the prompts in this chapter, as well as throughout this book, to see how you can begin developing these areas.

4. Write down three goals, based on your instructor's comments, that you have as you begin writing the final draft of your assignment.

■ A Final Thought on Revising

The information above underscores the importance of not writing a paper the night before it is due. A well-written, effective paper involves many steps and stages, which are highlighted above. It is also important to note that there is not one "right" way to revise a paper. You may have different strategies to go about revising and writing your papers; use the way you find most effective. Remember to also use all of the help at your disposal: your instructor, your peers, and the Writing Center.

4.5 ■ What Is the Difference Between Editing and Proofreading?

■ *Editing*

Editing involves working on the finer details toward the end of the writing process. Some of the elements in editing pertain to spelling, grammar, and punctuation. It is useful to read your work aloud and have a hard copy of your paper to work from when editing your work. Finding problems and mistakes in your writing from the computer screen can seem elusive sometimes when trying to read at the sentence-level. What you may find when you edit at the sentence-level is just how unconscious writing can be.

When editing your paper, choose one or two agendas to review. If you have difficulties with comma splices or semicolon usage, then pick these grammatical issues to review as starting points in the editing process. Importantly, during this editing stage, you should also assess and improve the important stylistic and syntactical elements in your writing.

4

EXERCISE

4.1 Editing

Here are some questions and prompts that will help guide your editing.

1. Review repetitive language: what are the phrases and words you commonly use? Do you tend to overuse these words and phrases? Are these words and phrases really the most precise you can use to make your point more concise? Are there any long prepositional phrases you can cut to be more concise?

2. Examine the verb usage in your work — are the verbs in the correct tense? Check your writing for passive voice — look for "to be" verbs (is, was, etc.) followed by a verb ending with "ed." Replace passive voice with active voice whenever you can. Reword your sentences if necessary. Also, eliminate "to be" in general, as it is a weak verb form.

3. How is your sentence variety? Have you alternated long sentences with short ones? Is your use of sentence style effective for the reader?

4. Examine vagueness in your work. For instance, if many of your opening sentences begin with "It is" and "There are," then this is the opportunity to get rid of "vague" constructions to make your work more specific.

■ *Proofreading*

Proofreading is the next (and usually final) step you should undertake in your writing process. When you have errors such as inappropriate fonts, incorrect margins, and missing pages, it demonstrates a poor level of professionalism. Therefore, make sure to present your work in the most competent manner possible. Remember the pointers we discussed above — reading your paper aloud, annotating a printed copy of your work, etc. — to ensure that you do not submit a paper with a Works Cited page missing.

Please also refer to Chapter 5 in this book to help you with editing and proofreading issues in your work.

> For more on rewriting, editing, and proofreading, see Chapter 5 in *The Brief Penguin Handbook*. Also, refer to the Composition Companion Website: www.pearsoncustom.com/vt_composition.

4.6 ▮ Pulling It All Together

This chapter itself is a product of revision; multiple readers viewed copies of this chapter, and many discussions took place to shape the text as you currently see it. Every work undergoes a writing process — much like finding a voice in writing, finding your personal writing process becomes a journey of discovery and trial and error. This chapter has also explored the outcomes of writing as a process. What you do in the revision stage influences nearly every stage of your writing, so remember to go back to this chapter any time you are completing a paper.

Remember, too, sections of this chapter often overlap — you may be editing your work for semicolon errors, only to notice that your thesis still needs to be more specific. This is fine as long as you remember that writing is not necessarily a linear process. Not every student will have the same writing process or use all of the methods we or the student discuss, but we hope that you can apply some of the strategies above to develop your own writing experience to make it more rewarding and worthwhile.

4.7 ▮ One Student's Process

This final section illustrates the process that Daniel Lassiter, a student in one of Matthew Vollmer's sections of English 1105, used to develop his first paper.

Engineering Science and Mechanics major Daniel Lassiter (right) with his teacher Matthew Vollmer.

4

■ *STEP ONE: Daniel's Assignment*

Daniel began by reading the assignment sheet distributed by his teacher (Matthew Vollmer) to the class, a copy of which follows.

Stories that Ads Tell Assignment
Instructor: Matthew Vollmer

Your first paper assignment is designed to get you thinking about how narratives — specifically the narratives (or stories) evoked by advertisements — work; i.e., how they are constructed, how they motivate, how they create arguments that are both obvious and implicit, and how, ultimately, they influence and persuade.

We will focus on the study of print advertisements, specifically those that seem to target an audience whose members like to think of themselves as individuals — from those who set themselves apart from mainstream culture, to those who consider themselves downright deviant. No matter what the product — mp3 players, cell phones, cigarettes, beer, tampons, or SUVs — companies make use of particular symbols, images, and themes that encourage deviation from the norm. Your job is to investigate how one of these advertisements operates — on a rhetorical level.

Process

You will begin by searching print materials for an advertisement that promotes its product, in part, by associating that product with behavior, symbols, or images that could be defined as transgressive, deviant, risky, dangerous, or "edgy." Then you will write a paper describing the goals of this advertisement, and discuss how it works from a rhetorical perspective.

In order to guide you through the process of writing the analysis, we will analyze similar advertisements in class. You will bring your advertisement to class, where you will discuss it with small groups of your peers. You will ask questions like: what are the purposes of this ad? Who are the potential audiences? What's the rhetorical situation here? How is the ad making use of ethical, logical, and pathetic appeals? Why did the ad choose this image? These words?

Eventually, you will gather all of your writing about the advertisement in order to construct an essay that makes an argument about how the advertisement uses rhetoric to persuade. You will introduce the advertisement by describing or summarizing what's happening — or appears to be happening — on the page. You will then make some claim about what the goals of this advertisement seem to be, both explicitly and implicitly. Then, you will point to various aspects of the advertisement (text, imagery, symbolism, color, image composition, etc.) to support your claim.

■ *STEP TWO: Description of the Subject*

Daniel's next step, after finding an appropriate ad to analyze, was to type up a description of the ad. His teacher asked him (and the other students writing this paper) to identify what was happening in the ad, and to structure his description by identifying what a viewer might likely first notice, then move on to the other significant images, simply describing what things looked like and where they appeared on the page. Daniel was also asked to imagine that his audience was someone who had not and could not see this ad, in order to paint a more thorough description.

At this stage, it doesn't matter that Daniel's writing isn't fully developed—only that he pays attention to describing the various parts that compose the ad. As you can see, he takes time to discuss many facets of the advertisement and, in so doing, provides a comprehensive study of all the images and text .

Important 1: Showgirl—this looks like an early 1900s showgirl, with peacok feathers, high heels, bikini top with gold colored skin and clothing, playing poker. The 1900s dress suggests a time period where many people smoked and were ignorant about its health effects. Wealth because of the gold adornment and skin tone. Attractiveness because she is a showgirl, slim, and wearing very little.

Important 2: Ace cheat card—The cheating ace shows a lifestyle without regard to the rules and the smile she has makes her smug and cool in the act of cheating. Viewers also associate a fun, cool, adult lifestyle with those that play poker.

Important 3: Pleasureorbust.com—this is placed just over the surgeon general's warning implying that pleasure is more important than anything, even health. This phrase grabs viewers by appealing to their senses that smoking is all about pleasure and you don't need to think about anything else.

Additional:

Tiled background—usually associated with a commercial building, a public place with lots of people. Old earlier 1900s styling as well.

Casino chips—suggests money, gambling, card sharks, world series of poker, all involving slick and cool guys playing poker for large sums of money. Appeals to risk taking for a large gain.

Cigarette—in the midst of all this the lady is smoking while smiling and cheating. This combined with her dress brings viewers back to an earlier time period when many people smoked.

CAMEL casino logo—gold and flashy suggests high class and wealth with the cigarettes while saying nothing about the actual product.

Written text "here's 20 chips on me xoxo lola"—suggests that viewers will meet girls like the one displayed here if they were to gamble more. Provides more contact with viewers than just the eyes of the showgirl, she is now speaking directly to you and her name is Lola, not Catherine or Elizabeth but Lola. Associating certain types of women with gambling and with Camel cigarettes.

Surgeon General's Warning—obvious required health disclaimer.

■ STEP THREE: Refining the Analysis

Next, Daniel's teacher asked the class to answer a series of questions about their advertisements, in order to further explore how the text and images in the ad constructed meanings. Again, you can see that Daniel's writing isn't fully fleshed-out, and sometimes, he writes in incomplete sentences. But at this point, that's perfectly fine. He's still exploring and learning about his subject—refinement will come later.

1. In what ways does your ad attempt to gain the attention of its audience?

By placing an attractive showgirl wearing little on the page. By presenting chips on the page interesting those who gamble/ play cool/ want to gamble.

2. Which appeal is it making use of, and how? (By doing y, the ad accomplishes z.)

Ethos—credibility by name of cigarette (CAMEL)
Logos—smoke cigarettes become rich by gambling
Pathos—cigarettes provide pleasure

3. What is the audience for this ad? How do you know? (By studying x and y, one might conclude z.)

Younger people seeking attractive girls. Anyone who plays poker. Camel smokers.

4. What kinds of knowledge or experience does the ad assume its audience possesses?

Assumes you know Camel makes cigarettes
Assumes you know that presenting cards and chips = gambling for big bucks
Assumes you think you can get real money by playing online game

5. What associations might the audience make with the images in your ad? How and why are these associations important? How do they connect with the product? How might these associations motivate viewers to purchase the product?

Showgirl = early time period casino very popular b/c movie? = sex
Cards = cool by ESPN & movies making money by beating
Chips = $ big $ more effective than dollar bills

6. What kind of lifestyle do you think your advertisement tries to promote?

Risk taking   Casino life   Gambling   Vegas
Focused on pleasure

7. What kind of values?

money   wealth   superficiality   carelessness
cheating   attractiveness

8. What are the implied messages? The explicit messages?

Implied = cheating to gain $ is cool
Explicit = pleasure or bust, cheat, hazardous to health (warning)

9. What assumptions does the ad make about its audience? The values of its audience? The needs of its audience?

that they understand poker   been to casinos
like scantily clad women   want to gamble want to win money

10. What can you deduce about American culture in general by looking at this ad?

value naked women and $ no morals, scruples prudence
risk takers like casinos   independent

11. What is the overall effect of the ad? Does it disorient? Surprise? Confuse? Arouse? Startle? Mesmerize? Eroticize? Valorize? Aggrandize? Glorify?

Excitement b/c of big $

■ STEP FOUR: Constructing a Thesis

After considering the ways in which the Camel ad generated various suggestions and claims, Daniel began to formulate a thesis. He read over the exploratory writing he completed in class, and thought about the kinds of claims he could make about how the advertisement constructed meaning, both implicitly and explicitly. Finally, he composed four possible thesis statements and brought them to class, in order to workshop them with other students.

> *Americans believe they have many more material needs as compared to other nations.*
>
> *Capitalism creates transgressive behaviors in a society.*
>
> *American morality is damaged by the advertising industry.*
>
> *Transgressive advertisements are more effective in persuading customers than explicit product information.*

You may have noticed that all the above theses are well written—that is, on a sentence level, they make sense, and some actually represent complex and provocative claims about advertising. However, the theses are all extremely difficult to support, in part because they are making incredibly broad claims. It's next to impossible to adequately support a claim, for instance, that makes an assertion about *all* Americans. Neither is it possible, at least in a 3–4 page paper, to support a claim that attempts to evaluate capitalism *in general*.

■ STEP FIVE: Revising the Thesis

Eventually, Daniel focused his attention on making a claim about how the ad worked, specifically, and generated the following statement:

> *The showgirl presented in this ad represents an attempt to persuade viewers to choose pleasure over health.*

He then revised it again, in order to arrive at a statement that would preview all of the elements he wanted to discuss:

> *The prominent image of the showgirl, combined with text and other images, such as the cards, gambling chips, and cigarette, represents an attempt to persuade viewers to choose pleasure over health.*

■ STEP SIX: Writing the Paper

In writing his paper, Daniel had to make several key decisions about how to support his main argument. He decided to structure the essay by organizing it hierarchically; that is, turning his attention to the most prominent parts of the ad (those that supported his thesis the best), then moving towards less crucial, yet still relevant elements.

He also had to keep in mind that whatever he claimed about the ad had to be connected with its images and text. He quickly learned that he could not support claims about the intention of the company or the target audience, at least not without qualifying them.

For instance, here's a sentence that appeared in Daniel's rough draft:

> *The fact that Lola is cheating and remains smug and confident in her expression appeals to viewers who possess a strong sense of lawlessness and independence.*

Notice that this sentence suggests that Lola will appeal to those who possess a strong sense of lawlessness and independence — something Daniel might "feel" is true, but that he can't exactly prove — at least not without polling a number of people who fancy themselves independent. Therefore, he needs to qualify his claim. It turns out to be an easy revision; by changing "appeals" to "may appeal," Daniel can still make a forceful claim about how the ad "might" work, while acknowledging, however subtly, that not everyone in this category will respond the same way.

■ STEP SEVEN: The Final Paper

After reworking and reorganizing sentences and paragraphs, checking punctuation, qualifying claims, and making sure that he's revealed the logical connections between all his thought processes, Daniel turns his paper in. It might not be perfect, but because he's trusted the writing process, it's an effective draft, and one that makes a persuasive argument about the ad he's chosen to analyze.

Daniel Lassiter
Instructor: Matthew Vollmer
ENGL 1105
9/13/06

THE PURSUIT OF PLEASURE

"Why do you worry about something that can kill you in 10 years when there's so many things that can kill you today?"

— *Lord of War*, Directed by Andrew Niccol

The idea of prioritizing between the future and the present is a constant burden for virtually all people. Should more concern be placed on future security, predicting that in fact there will be a future, or should any and all immediate pleasures be pursued? In deciding where to draw the line for immediate pleasures there are many parties, in America especially, attempting to sway people for the sake of their profit. The image opposite (see Figure 1) is an advertisement for CAMEL products which attempts to do exactly that. The prominent image of the showgirl, combined with text and other images, such as the cards, gambling chips, and cigarette, represents an attempt to persuade viewers to choose pleasure over health.

The most prominent image expressing the importance of pleasure in the ad is the early 20th century dressed showgirl whose smug look is directed towards the viewer. She is very attractive and seductive in her high heels, bikini top, and semi-transparent skirt. She also has an ideal body shape and color tone as suggested by popular culture in the 21st century. This image blatantly appeals to men's sexuality and may suggest that men who smoke Camel cigarettes can participate, if only in their imagination, in the kind of lifestyle that includes the company of attractive and seductive women. More specifically, these deco-rated showgirls are nearly exclusive to Las Vegas, also known as the "entertainment capital of the world" or "Sin City." The idea that Las Vegas can be

Figure 1

connected to this advertisement quickly evokes countless pleasure and entertainment options located within the city and, in turn, urges consumers to experience a hedonis-tic lifestyle.

The character of Lola, outfitted in an early 20th century showgirl costume, reveals an important historical association. During this time period a great percentage of the population—at least those who could afford it—smoked cigarettes, partly for pleasure, and partly because they were unaware of the health risks. By glorifying this period in history, the ad may be attempting to evoke nostalgia for an era when peo-ple not only smoked for pleasure, but had no idea that cigarettes were the least bit dangerous.

This lady, "Lola," is also holding up a number of cards indicating she is participating in some sort of card game. By noticing the poker chips, large text displaying "Casino," and the ace under her leg (see Figure 2), from experience, one might assume she is playing a round of poker. This is an essential assumption for under-standing the advertisement that nearly all modern Americans would be able to quickly make. The mere word "poker" has the ability to conjure a number of images, including card sharks, cigars, alcohol, money, risk, illegal bets, dangerous gamblers, and sharply dressed casino patrons. The text "Here's 20 chips on me

Figure 2

XOXO Lola" provides additional ideas that attractive women such as "Lola" are plenti-ful in Casino settings and that in the presented lifestyle gorgeous women will hand out poker chips and kisses without a care. All of these associated images including

Lola are important in convincing viewers how pleasurable it is to be wealthy, lawless, and attractive.

Another explicit image is the ace of spades, located just under this woman's leg. The image suggests that Lola is cheating by using cards not handed to her. No doubt, with an ace of spades, her poker hand has definitely improved. The fact that she's cheating and remains smug and confident in her expression may appeal to viewers who have a strong sense of lawlessness and independence. Cheating as presented by popular media is displayed as exhilarating and pleasurable as long as you do not get caught. Therefore this transgressive behavior is promoted as positive and gratifying through the associations many people already have about cheating. From this single detail associations with all of the pleasures and appeals of cheating can be recognized and allegedly coincide with consuming CAMEL products.

The text displayed just under "Lola" reads "PLEASUREorBUST.com," (see Figure 3) directly instructing viewers to have fun at all costs. This text is supposedly part of the poker game which consumers can participate in but for this advertisement it explicitly states the purpose of all the images displayed here. This text is also located just on top of the surgeon general's warning about the health risks

Figure 3

linked to smoking cigarettes. This placement of the text—that is, the fact that it appears above the warning, ensuring the likelihood that readers will notice it—again serves to emphasize the importance of pleasure instead of health.

All of the explicit and implicit messages displayed throughout this ad hardly give accurate information about CAMEL cigarettes; however, they effectively communicate how much more important it is for individuals to follow their desires instead of making rational, informed choices. These persuasion tactics are critical for cigarette companies, especially at a time when most people understand the risks of smoking, thanks to antismoking ad campaigns, and the implementation of surgeon general's warnings on every cigarette carton and advertisement. Despite all of the antismoking promotions being presented CAMEL still draws on people's urgent sense of pleasure and gratification in this advertisement to overcome the negative associations. CAMEL states very clearly in this ad that your health is irrelevant if you are not blissfully ignorant and having as much pleasure as possible in this life.

4.8 ■ Further Exercises for Exploring Writing as a Process

EXERCISE

1. Select one of the following subjects and create a potential outline for an essay your teacher has asked you to produce:

- Successful study techniques for first-year VT students

- Making the transition from high school and hometown to VT and the Tech community

- Choosing a potential career

- Discussion of major artists in a particular genre of music [rock, country, rap, etc.] and their particular skills

- Your favorite film genre, your five favorite films within that genre, and why they're your favorites

2. Revise the following paragraph twice: the first time to improve the focus and organization; the second, to improve stylistic, grammatical and mechanical problems.

The coastal plane is one of Virginia's physiographic regions. Many of the state's most significant rivers have their head waters in this sub region, and Virginia's mulimillion dollar fishing industry dominates the sub region's economy. Two other sub-regions are the piedmont and the Blue Ridge. The Blue Ridge subregion is home to several of Virginia's most utilized Tourist attractions and is also the base of the state's apple economy. The Piedmont or the foot hills subregion is the states largest physiographic provence and with its massive chicken processing plants is crucial to Virginia's industrial agricultural economy. Two other Virginia subregions are the Ridge and Valley section and the Allegany-Cumberland Plataeu. The "Great Appalacian Plataeu", as the latter is often called contains all of the state's coal, oil and natural gas resources and thus pumps billions annually into the Virginia's economy. The Ridge and Valley Region, which is home to Virginia's largest public university, Virginia Tech, is the center of much of the state's information technology research and thus has the potential to become Virginia's most important economic sector.

4

5

Knowing the Conventions

"Knowing the Conventions" is the fourth and final goal in the WPA Outcomes Statement. That doesn't mean it is inconsequential. Indeed, for many readers, conventions matter a great deal. Conventions for composition refer to very obvious concerns like proofreading, citing sources, using the form appropriate for the paper you are writing, understanding which genres work in which circumstance, and more. In this chapter, we will cover conventions of proofreading, but we will also discuss other kinds of conventions—visual conventions, genre conventions, and style conventions.

5.1 What Are Conventions?

When we talk about *conventions* we are often talking of the established rules, standards, and methods that create order in virtually every facet of our lives. The term *conventions* also refers to expectations. We expect certain forms or ways of communicating in different situations. Most conventions have become so ingrained that we adhere to them without much thought. Think, for example, about how many times in the past few days you have adhered to the following accepted conventions:

- Stop when the light turns red.
- Hold the door open for the person entering the building behind you.
- Turn off your cell phone in the movie theater.
- Cover your mouth and nose when you cough.
- Respond with "you're welcome," when someone says "thank you."

Conventions also abound in the visual codes or signifiers designed to simplify our everyday activities:

But take the term "convention" and apply it to writing. How does it change? What does it become?

More often than not, when you hear the term *convention* in the writing classroom, you're likely to translate it into its adjectival form, either "conventional" or "unconventional." Unfortunately, in both cases, the descriptions can carry largely negative connotations: for the former, *ordinary, usual,* even *boring;* for the latter, *strange, eccentric,* even *weird.* And as a writer, where do you fall on this continuum between conventional and unconventional? Maybe you're determined to be neither.

When it comes to writing, it's sometimes easy to think of conventions not as helpful and simplifying but as restrictive, confining, and otherwise antithetical to the very idea of creativity. They're just entries in a lengthy list of DOS and DON'TS that totally stifles your ability to be yourself as a writer: *I can't use colloquialisms or dialect in my essay? I have to use Times New Roman, 12 pt.? I can't use "I"? I have to use MLA parenthetical documentation?*

How can you ever develop your voice as a writer when you have all of these rules restricting you?

In truth, because of their very nature, writing conventions can help you reach a broader audience as well as make that audience more receptive to the subject about which you write. Like the stop sign and the cell-phone-in-the-movie-theater rule, they help guide you and establish your presence as a contributor to an ongoing conversation or community of writers and thinkers. In essence, they do not silence you but instead strengthen and define your voice.

5.a Thinking About Conventions

With a group of your classmates, make a list of the conventions you have learned for writing school essays. Did you put your name in a specific place? Where did the title go? How long are typical essays in your English classes? List any expectation you can recall from teacher's instructions or from writing school papers for so long.

When you have completed your list, discuss with your group and the rest of the class which of these conventions can be broken without much concern. Which would you hesitate to break? What determines whether or not you feel free to break with convention in your assignments? What are you risking? What might you gain?

For further information on Designing and Presenting your material, see Chapter 15 in *The Brief Penguin Handbook,* 2nd Ed.

5

5.2 ■ Conventions of Formatting— Memos and Letters

Formatting refers to how materials are arranged on a page—how they appear visually to the reader or viewer. Commonsense formatting rules provide guidelines that every day help us to create documents that achieve a pleasing balance between text and graphics, make adequate use of white space, provide headings to direct the reader's attention, vary font sizes to suggest importance or relevance of material, and many other tasks. Formatting involves elements as complex as laying out text and visuals on a grid pattern and as simple as inserting enough paragraph breaks.

Formatting is crucial to every written document we write or receive. Good, logical formatting makes our lives easier, while bad formatting can waste our time and make not just reading but also the absorption of material infinitely more difficult. To reach an audience in an effective and reader-friendly manner, you should familiarize yourself with two of the most common types of document formatting: the **memo** and the **letter.**

■ *Formatting the Memo*

Whether or not you're aware of it, it is likely that every day you receive countless memos. Take, for instance, the email message you received from the chair of X campus organization to which you belong:

To: You
From: Chair of X Organization
Subject: Fundraising Subcommittee meeting
Date: 6 February 2007

Please mark your calendar for a special meeting of the sub-committee on fundraising: Tuesday, February 27, from 5–7 pm in GBJ. At this meeting, we will select a community event, brainstorm ideas for an advertising campaign, discuss relevant avenues for recruiting on campus, and begin sketching out ideas for posters and brochures. Be sure that you bring to this meeting your laptop, your organizational booklet, any sketches you have made for the posters, your sketchpad and pencils. In addition, if you can, bring a list that identifies 3 possible community events, summarizes them, gives relevant dates for them, and provides contact information for them. If you have any questions, please email me back or call me at X-1234. Thanks!

5

To: You
From: Chair of X Organization
Subject: Fundraising Subcommittee meeting
Date: 6 February 2007

Please mark your calendar for a special meeting of the sub-committee on fundraising: Tuesday, February 27, from 5-7 pm in GBJ.

At this meeting, we will select a community event, brainstorm ideas for an advertising campaign, discuss relevant avenues for recruiting on campus, and begin sketching out ideas for posters and brochures.

Be sure that you bring to this meeting
- your laptop,
- your organizational booklet,
- any sketches you have made for the posters,
- your sketchpad and pencils.

In addition, if you can, bring a list that
- identifies 3 possible community events,
- summarizes them,
- gives relevant dates for them, and
- provides contact information for them.

If you have any questions, please email me back or call me at X-1234. Thanks!

The *To, From, Date,* and *Subject* lines in the email above on the previous page are standard or conventional memo components, and they are embedded in some way in every email message you write. In the business world, memos generally are used for communicating within an organization (another convention). The only required element of a memo missing from an email is the designation "Memo," usually centered in all capitals at the top of the document.

The memo at top includes all the necessary information you need to know to prepare for the meeting. Additionally, you have the electronic message to which you can refer if you need to remind yourself what's going on and what to bring. But as a reader, how would you assess the formatting of the message? Is it easy to read? Is it easy to zero in on the different things you need to bring to or consider prior to the meeting? Consider an entirely different format for this message, at the bottom of page 78.

Perhaps your first impression is "Wow. That message is a *lot* longer than the first one!" And you're right: On the page, it seems longer. But the content is exactly the same, and what's more, the formatting is now much more **reader-friendly.** Simply put, due in large part to the way it is formatted, this version of the message is easier to read and therefore easier to absorb. Paragraph breaks give the eyes a rest and indicate where the message changes directions with regard to topics. And the bulleted lists identify in an easy-to-scan manner the variety of things you need to bring to the meeting, as well as the tasks you should perform.

(Hint: When you have a list of items you need to pass along, don't hide them in a paragraph but create bulleted or numbered lists!)

The differences in the two emails shown above indicate in a very visual manner why formatting conventions are so important to readers. Since most of what we write is intended for a reader, we should do everything we can to achieve reader-friendliness. A reader-friendly format goes a long way toward ensuring that your message is received positively.

The other most common form of correspondence with which you are likely familiar is the letter.

■ Formatting the Letter

Formal or business letters can be governed by a number of conventions. They can be written on letterhead—or not. They can be arranged in full-block format—or modified block.

But all formal letters share common features, illustrated on the following page.

5

123 Numbers Ln.   *return*
Harrodsburg, KY 11111   *address*
19 March 2006   *and date*

Ms. Ima Writer
214 Morning Glory Circle   *inside address*
Smithfield, VA 22222

Dear Ms. Writer: *salutation*

First paragraph of text. First paragraph of text. First paragraph
of text. First paragraph of text.

Second paragraph of text. Second paragraph of text. Second
paragraph of text. Second paragraph of text. Second   *body*
paragraph of text. Second paragraph of text. Second   *text*
paragraph of text. Second paragraph of text.

Third paragraph of text. Your letter can be 1, 2, or more
paragraphs, but paragraph breaks are vital!

Last paragraph of text. Last paragraph of text. Last paragraph
of text.

Sincerely,

                                    signature block—(Don't foget to sign it!)

Marcia Jo Brady

Although formal letters might include other lines of information — such as the Enclosure nota-tion (generally, "Enc."), which is placed 2 lines after the signature block and indicates that you are including something in addition to the letter — if you remember these key elements, then you'll be sure that you will be producing a letter that truly conforms to established formatting standards.

Of course, letters to friends and family members are a different matter entirely. You might like the look of the formal letter and decide to use that form in every letter you write. Most of us, however, allow ourselves to be informal and even playful when we are writing to people we know well about non-business or unofficial matters.

EXERCISE	**5.b Formatting Your Own Memos and Letters**

1. Look through your email and find a message you don't mind sharing with others. Take that message and revise it so that it is difficult to read because of the way it is formatted. Then, revise the formatting again to make it easier to read.

2. Write a letter to a friend or family member using the formal business format. (Again, make sure what you write is something you are willing to and that is appropriate to share.) When you have completed your letter (it need not be long), write a brief analysis of how the formal formatting changed the way your letter might be read or received by your close friend or family member.

For further information on letter conventions — especially Letters of Application — check out *The Brief Penguin Handbook,* 2nd Ed., pp. 134–138.

5.3 Other Formatting Conventions

In the world of professional writing, in particular, overlap exists between the concepts of formatting and organization, and each is dictated by genre. Such documents can be formatted as formal reports, arrangements that include covers, a table of contents, formal chapters, appendices, and the like. Such documents generally will take advantage of glossy paper, fancy color schemes, and photographs, among other eye-catching practices. For example, when a company produces for its stockholders an annual report, a document that discusses its status over the preceding year, it will most assuredly be in report format.

However, many formal documents are formatted as memos, and though many people believe that memos are supposed to be short documents, no longer than a page, they can actually be quite longer. In fact, you can produce a report in memo format — particularly when it is to be used "in house" or within an organization.

Regardless of whether what you write is set up as a report or as a memo, the genre often will determine what you include in the document.

For example, in a History, Sociology, or even an English course, you might be asked to prepare a **research proposal,** a document that sets forth your idea for an assignment (usually an end-of-the-term research project) and argues for its merits. Chances are good that in addition to an introduction and conclusion, this proposal might include such internal sections as

- ◆ Areas to be Studied: explains what facets of the subject you intend to cover in the final project.
- ◆ Methods of Research: discusses the research approach you might use.
- ◆ Qualifications: explains how you are qualified to write about this issue.

- ◆ Timetable: sets forth your intended schedule for completion of the project.
- ◆ Budget: estimates what possible expenditures you might confront (note: this section doesn't appear very often in a research proposal, but it can, depending upon the extent of the project itself.)

And if your proposal is approved, and you're working your way through the project it covers, you might have to produce one or more **progress reports** that will tell your teacher (and in the real world, your employer or client) about what you've accomplished — and what you still have left to do. Although this document is called a report, it likely will be formatted as a memo and include the following sections in order:

- ◆ Introduction
- ◆ Work Completed
- ◆ Work Scheduled
- ◆ Conclusion

Other genres call for specific formats as well. Visualize the formatting for a resume, newspaper article, web page, brochure, or even an essay formatted according to MLA guidelines. What sorts of things will you always find in each? Where are the headings? Where do you find the pagination (if it exists)? Formatting conventions often dictate a uniformity that makes each type of document especially reader-friendly.

That is not say that a writer can never successfully stray from formatting conventions. However, some conventions are more rules than mere guidelines. For example, when you're applying for an important first job, that's probably not the best time to experiment with formatting your resume and letter of application as a brochure. Or if you're creating a web site, it's probably best not to decide to do away with the tried-and-true convention of including navigation links on each page.

With formatting, much depends upon established conventions, but you must also consider the needs of your reader and the context. In your composition class, for example, your teacher (and fellow students!) will expect you to follow whatever established practices have been set forth for formatting your essay.

For further information on formats and designs, see Part Four of *The Brief Penguin Handbook,* 2nd Ed.

5.4 ■ Knowing How and When to Use and Cite Sources

Any time you write from sources, you are expected to tell your reader what the source is and how the reader might find that source. As with other features of good writing, source use and citation are governed by certain conventions.

At first glance, that might seem simple: Learn the citation practice, and use it. It would be simple if there were only one citation practice.

In your English classes, your teacher is likely to ask you to follow MLA or Chicago Manual of Style citation guidelines. These are the most commonly used in the humanities.

Your social science teachers — Psychology, Sociology, Political Science — may ask you to use APA style citations.

Your science teachers will ask for yet another citation — probably CSE (Council of Science Educators style sheet) — for your papers in their courses.

Each of these citation styles are covered in *The Brief Penguin Handbook* (pp. 243–378) so before you plan your citations, check with your teacher to find out which style sheet is appropriate.

Knowing when to use source references is a bit more complicated. In general, any time you are drawing from another source, you should tell your reader that. Even if you have gotten some of your ideas talking with friends or classmates, it is good practice to acknowledge their help in your paper. Published writers make a habit of including a note of acknowledgment at the end of their papers to honor those who have helped. You can do that, too, in an endnote or footnote.

EXERCISE | **5.c What Citation Convention to Use?**

Do a quick survey of your teachers for this term. Ask a teacher from each of the disciplines in your course schedule what citation form should be used for that discipline. Bring the results to class with you to discuss the different citation conventions and when to use each type.

You will find information on each one of these citation formats in your *The Brief Penguin Handbook,* 2nd Ed, Part Six.

5.5 ▌ Controlling Syntax, Grammar, Punctuation, and Spelling

In Chapter 4, we wrote about the difference between editing and proofreading your paper. When you make editing and proofreading decisions, you are following the conventions of syntax, grammar, punctuation, and spelling.

Effective communicators pay attention to error. That doesn't mean that they never make a mistake, but it does mean that they are careful to proofread so that they might catch as many errors as possible. You won't likely be getting to the actual proofreading stage until you are at the final stage of drafting of your paper, but you must get to that stage before you turn the paper in for evaluation.

It may be true that proofreading errors, as the Council of Writing Program Administrators notes, are "surface features," but that doesn't mean they are superficial or inconsequential. They are called surface features because they are the first things many readers see and respond to. That makes proofreading a crucial task.

If you are concerned about your own abilities to proofread and turn in clean copy, you might want to look over the list below and work on learning how to catch at least these common errors.

According to one study, the following are the twenty most common errors in student writing:

1. Missing comma after an introductory element
2. Vague pronoun reference
3. Missing comma in a compound sentence
4. Using the wrong word
5. Missing comma(s) with a nonrestrictive element
6. Wrong or missing verb ending
7. Wrong or missing preposition
8. Comma splice
9. Missing or misplaced possessive apostrophe
10. Unnecessary shift in tense
11. Unnecessary shift in pronoun
12. Sentence fragment
13. Wrong tense or verb form
14. Lack of subject-verb agreement
15. Missing comma in a series
16. Lack of agreement between pronoun and antecedent
17. Unnecessary comma(s) with a restrictive element
18. Fused sentence
19. Misplaced or dangling modifier
20. Its/It's confusion

EXERCISE   **5.d Catching those Errors**

Look over the list of twenty errors reprinted here. Choose 3 – 5 that you know you make or that you are likely to miss while you are proofreading. Look them up in *The Brief Penguin Handbook,* 2nd Ed., and focus on learning how to correct those errors. If the handbook is not clear enough, you can go to a number of on-line sources for help. Visit the Writing Center website http://www.composition.english.vt.edu/wc and visit the links page. You will find sites that help explain grammar errors or that help you learn how to cite sources.

5.6 ▤ Style: Strategy and Content— Words and Sentences

Obviously formatting and proofreading problems are issues of knowing the conventions. If you format a formal business letter to look like an inter-office memo, you are taking the chance that your readers won't take your letter as seriously as you want it to be taken.

Conventions also, however, refer to the choices we make in the style we choose.

▤ *Strategy and Content*

Several years ago, a police officer working on a master's degree at Virginia Tech was researching a health issue that affected police performance, or, as he put it, "fat cops and foot chases." He brought a draft to the Writing Center, saying, "My department told me to bring my paper here. They say it just isn't professional."

The writing coach discovered that the issue was not a matter of error but a conflict of styles. His professors wanted him to present his information in a conventional style developed over time to facilitate communication in their field, a style made up of patterns of evidence and abstraction. However, the writer had worked in the style that had made him a successful leader and instructor in his town's police force: he would define a concept and then tell a story to illustrate. Instead of abstraction, he liked action.

The writer and his professors were both right: action provides persuasive energy, while abstraction can make sense of evidence in a few powerful words. The police officer did learn to use his academic discipline's style—without giving up the added punch of a good story now and then. He learned that style has to do with strategy and content as well as word choice and sentence structure: his professors didn't just want him to use bigger words and longer sentences, as he had first thought; their style expectations were substantive, not superficial. However, he did also learn to use different shapes and sizes of sentences as well as different levels of vocabulary to accomplish his purposes.

You can see examples of strategy and content differences in the work of several student writers in this book. For the rest of this section, we'll be looking at some word and sentence matters that can help you to write with more power in any style.

▤ *Words and Sentences*

A first-year student some years ago assumed that to write in a university setting did indeed mean to use big words and long sentences. Here is an excerpt from his reflective paper draft about a traumatic experience:

> I ascertained that smoke could be seen ascending from the area of the
> sofa. I determined that a rapid exit would be the best course of action, so I
> advised my younger brother to precede me up the stairs with all due
> haste, noting as I accompanied him the emergence of flame throughout
> the length of the couch, ascending up the curtains.

His peer readers said they could not get into the story because of the big words and slow-moving sentences. One reader even thought the writer was using the inflated language for laughs, since the mismatch of subject and style was so extreme. The writer did not intend to create comedy—the fire was a horrifying event—so he revised to suit the subject matter and the reader's expectations for storytelling:

> Smoke billowed from the sofa. I yelled at my little brother: "Get out! Up the
> stairs now!" I stumbled after him as flames burst out, consuming the couch
> and licking up the curtains.

In his revision, the sentences are short to reflect quick actions. He deletes verbs about his thought process like *ascertained, determined,* and *advised* to focus on action verbs like *billowed, yelled, stumbled,* and *burst.* Without terms like *rapid exit* and *the best course of action* to slow things down, the concrete nouns *smoke, flames, stairs, couch,* and *curtains* stand out to provide vivid visual detail. This version definitely keeps readers engaged.

■ *Three Basic Style Principles*

The principles of sentence length and word choice that this writer used to revise his narrative can be applied to other genres as well. In any genre, three basic principles can add energy and power to whatever style of strategy and content is appropriate for your audience and purpose:

- ◆ Use specific, action verbs whenever possible.
- ◆ Choose specific, concrete nouns as often as possible.
- ◆ Vary sentence length in every paragraph.

> You'll find clear, detailed instruction for these style principles and many more in
> *The Brief Penguin Handbook,* Part 7: Effective Style and Language.

Below, you can see these principles applied in revisions by a Virginia Tech student.

Madeline McGuire, a student in a Virginia Tech English 1105 class, wrote this first draft of a paragraph as a ten-minute in-class exercise for her instructor Cheryl Ruggiero. In that short time, she drafted sentences that captured the two extremes of the subject that interested her: 17th century American Indians' violence in taking a woman captive and their kindness to her when she was distressed.

Madeline McGuire is an Engineering major at Virginia Tech.

There is not much information known about Indians in the 17th century. Mary Rowlandson's experience with the Indians was as a captive. She cried in front of the Indians because she feared death, but one of the Indians reassured her, "none will hurt you" (qtd. in Tompkins 112).

Tompkins, Jane. "'Indians': Textualism, Morality, and the Problem of History." *Critical Inquiry* 13.1 (1986): 101-119. JSTOR. 30 Oct. 2006 <http://links.jstor.org>.

■ Second Draft—Revising for Strategy and Content

In her second draft, Maddie revised her first sentence to add detail about the source of her information because her original first sentence had focused not on the material she was analyzing but on how little is known, which was not her topic. Her new first sentence acknowledged that little is known but went on to introduce a source that does provide some insight. She added more detail about what the Indians did, and then she provided an interpretive follow-up—which turned out to be her topic sentence—that related the evidence to her point: the irony in the two extremes of the Indians' behavior toward their captive. She also got a head start on sentence and word revision by replacing the wordy sentence "Mary Rowlandson's experience with the Indians was as a captive" with the subordinate clause "even though she was held as a captive." She was revising to make her point more clearly, and in the process she made the sentence stronger.

Although there is not much information known about the Indians in the 17th Century, a passage by Mary Rowlandson shares some insight. Her statement is controversial because even though she was held as a captive, she spoke of the kindness the Indians showed her. Rowlandson cried in front of the Indians because she thought "they would kill me" (qtd. in Tompkins 112). Upon seeing her tears, one of the Indians offered food to comfort her and assured her, "none will hurt you" (qtd. in Tompkins 112). It is ironic that the Indians would take a person captive and show that same person compassion through their hospitality.

Tompkins, Jane. "'Indians': Textualism, Morality, and the Problem of History." *Critical Inquiry* 13.1 (1986): 101-119. JSTOR. 30 Oct. 2006 <http://links.jstor.org>.

5

You can read more about composing topic sentences in *The Brief Penguin Handbook,* Chapter 4, section a.

■ *Third Draft—Revising for Word and Sentence Style*

In her third draft, Maddie revised the first sentence even more. She replaced the expletive "there is" and the wordy phrases it generated with the named agent "people today" and the stronger verb "know." Her new first sentence also did away with the redundant phrase "information known." She then replaced the general noun "passage" with the more specific noun "captivity narrative," and she replaced "controversial" with "contradictory," which was closer to the meaning she intended.

Although people today do not know much detail about the Indians in the 17th Century, a 1680 captivity narrative by Mary Rowlandson contains a passage that gives some insight. Her statement is contradictory because even though she was a captive, she spoke of the kindness the Indians showed her. Rowlandson cried in front of the Indians because she thought "they would kill me" (qtd. in Tompkins 112). Upon seeing her tears, one of the Indians offered food to comfort her and assured her, "none will hurt you" (qtd in Tompkins 112). It is ironic the Indians would take a person captive and show that same person compassion through their hospitality.

Tompkins, Jane. "'Indians': Textualism, Morality, and the Problem of History." *Critical Inquiry* 13.1 (1986): 101-119. JSTOR. 30 Oct. 2006 <http://links.jstor.org>.

You can read more about revising for word and sentence style in *The Brief Penguin Handbook,* Section 7. Sections Maddie used are as follows: expletives, Chapter 27 section c; named agents, Chapter 26 section c; action verbs, Chapter 26 section b; redundant phrases, Chapter 27 section a; wordy phrasing, Chapter 27 section b.

■ *Style Sheets*

Most publications, academic departments, and disciplines have developed expectations about the mechanics of style that they want every writer to use. Sometimes their guidelines are collected in manuals or style sheets that cover issues like capitalization of titles, abbreviations, acronyms, and documentation formats. You'll find documentation guides in *The Brief Penguin Handbook,* Section 6, for four styles: MLA, APA, CMS, and CSE. It's always a good idea to ask which style guide is required by the instructor of a class or the department or publication for which you're writing. Such style issues may seem minor to a student just beginning academic writing, but they are among the first things your university readers will notice.

EXERCISE

5.e Choosing Specific, Action Verbs

BE is not a bad verb — it's a marvelous word that we use to link identities. But in many instances, a more specific verb can carry more meaning and make your sentences more powerful. Though you wouldn't want to write without BE all the time, try the following exercise to make you more aware of the verb BE and how often you use it, as well as to discover the power of other verbs.

- Write a paragraph of at least eight sentences describing the place where you are right now with as much concrete detail as possible — sights, sounds, smells, textures.

- Do not use any form of BE: *am, is, are, was, were, being, been, to be.*

  - For example, instead of writing "There are a poster and a sign on the wall," you could write "A poster of Van Gogh's *Sunflowers* hangs on the wall next to a 'No Smoking' sign."

Reflect on your work: did you find it difficult to describe a static thing like a poster with an action verb? Did you use BE at least once without realizing it? If you shared your paragraph in an in-class workshop or on-line forum, did your readers find your scene easy to imagine?

EXERCISE

5.f Choosing Specific, Concrete Nouns and Noun Phrases

In the first example sentence from the preceding exercise, the noun *poster* is concrete — which is to say that it represents a thing accessible to physical senses — but it is not very specific. At the expense of adding a few words, the suggested revision names a particular, well-known image, "a poster of Van Gogh's *Sunflowers*," giving the reader a clear, specific picture.

Consider the following paragraph from an analytical essay.

> Masahiro Mori's theory of the "uncanny valley" suggests that humans are most afraid of what is almost human but not quite (qtd. in Bryant). Applying this theory, one could imagine that film viewers would be more frightened by a human-like robot than a machine-like one, for example. An animated corpse would be more chilling than a giant insect, and a ghost would be creepier than a non-human monster. The closer a thing is to seeming human without being human, the more it scares people.
>
> Bryant, Dave. "The Uncanny Valley." *Glimpses.* 13 February 2006
>   http://www.arclight.net/~pbd/nonfiction/uncanny-valley.html

Re-write the paragraph, substituting specific nouns for the underlined words and phrases. You could, for example, use a specific term for a human-like robot, or you could even name a well-known robotic character from popular films. Feel free to make other changes if you wish.

5

Reflect on your work: What images are called up for you by the sample phrases "a human-like robot" and "a ghost"? Are they specific or generic? Were you able to work through the choices that occurred to you and find specific examples that you yourself find chilling? What images do your own examples call up? If you shared your work in an in-class workshop or on-line forum, did your readers recognize the specifics you used?

EXERCISE

5.g Varying Sentence Length

1. Print out a substantial paragraph from one of your own essays for this or another course.

- Take two different colors of highlighters and block out each sentence in alternating colors.

- Look over the lengths of your sentences as revealed by the highlighting. If they're varied, you're already employing an important style tactic. If they're all quite similar, consider breaking up or combining sentences for emphasis.

- Read the paragraph aloud, exaggerating the ends and beginnings of sentences with your voice.

  - Can you read every sentence in a single breath, or do some sentences go on so long you must stop for air? Often, a breath stop suggests a need for a mental stop as well. Try dividing your sentence both for length and for emphasis.

  - Does your own voice keep you awake or put you to sleep? Try re-saying some of the longer sentences in a more conversational manner, and then write them down as you've spoken them. Use your voice to help you recognize the need for a more energetic sentence shape.

- Revise the paragraph by changing the length of at least one sentence.

2. Reflect on your work: Compare the original and revised paragraphs. Does the revision accomplish your original intention for the paragraph? If not, what has changed? If so, do you find the revision or the original more to your liking? Why?

5.7 ■ English as a Second (or Third or Fourth or Fifth) Language

If English is not your home language, you might find that you have challenges that many of your classmates do not experience. That is because you have acquired the conventions of your home language to a degree that you might not have acquired the conventions of a second, third, or fourth language.

Your most important resource for becoming comfortable with English is all around you: your classmates, your teachers, the films you watch, the magazines and newspapers you read, the Writing Center, and more.

Make it a practice to read a few pages of a magazine or newspaper every day. Read aloud and record yourself. Then listen to your voice. Ask friends and teachers if you can make recordings of them talking. Listen to phrasings and accents.

If you visit the Writing Center, you will improve most dramatically with regular appointments with the same writing coach throughout the term. Your writing coach will not proofread your paper, but a coach can help you spot your own errors and can help you develop ideas or restructure a paper as you are working through drafts.

Always let your teacher know if you are having trouble understanding assignments or classroom instruction.

> For more on the conventions of English if English is not your first language, see Part Ten of *The Brief Penguin Handbook*, 2nd. Edition.

5

PART III

A Focus on Research

6

Writing from Research

In addition to the four outcomes we have covered in Part II of this book, you will also be expected to come away from composition with tools for doing research and with some familiarity with oral and visual communication. Because research is a major part of your education throughout your career at Virginia Tech, English 1106 focuses primarily on an introduction to some of the kinds of research you will find useful in the next few years. This chapter will also be very useful if you are taking H1204.

6.1 Developing a Research Question

The first step in developing a research project is to come up with a specific question that will guide your research. Reflect on the course for which you're writing the paper. What topics discussed in class or in the readings have most interested you? Or perplexed you? Or angered you? Or saddened you? Or uplifted you? Develop a research question that is original that will keep you interested. You may have to develop such a question in stages. In fact, you may have to do some research to help you to develop and refine your research question.

In some cases your research question may be prompted by the readings and discussions you have had in class. Your teacher may assign you a specific research question with a specific goal in mind. Research prompted by your specific course or course theme will require specific questions and research methods. Whether you choose the topic or your topic is chosen for you, your challenge will be how to make this project and topic your own. Since a good deal is already written about most subjects, you will need to develop original questions concerning the topic. How do you make it clear that this is *your* question and *your* research?

You may be asked to conduct a project in your major field of study, research which is likely to be prompted by a capstone project or thesis. In that case, you'll want to know what the questions in the field are, what questions remain unaddressed or not fully addressed, what questions you might add, and more. If you are in an office or other work situation, research might be prompted by something that is happening in the company. Production might be down or employees might be unhappy about working conditions. The question and the research you do in response to that question will depend very much on local need.

No matter what your topic or study site, the methods and sources you use will be determined by your research question. Certain questions require particular methods and sources. In the following section, you will learn more about developing your question into a project that is manageable yet also original. In addition, you will learn how to develop research methods that most appropriately match the research questions you will be asking.

6.2 Developing a Manageable Topic

Developing a topic that is appropriate for the goals of your class requires much reading and thinking; that is, it takes time. Narrowing your topic to make it manageable within the time-frame and page constraints of your essay is one of the most difficult parts of this process. Like most writers and researchers, you might begin with a research question that is too broad, and through thorough reading, you can determine ways to narrow your research so that you are asking original questions about the topic.

EXERCISE | **6.a The First Steps**

Read your assignment carefully and answer the following questions:

- What theme or general topic have you been asked to explore?

- What research methods are you expected to use?

- What research methods does your research question require?

Next, begin preliminary research:

Find out what has been written on your subject already by doing a keyword search in the library's databases to get an idea of where books and articles on your topic are located in the library. Browsing these databases will give you an idea about the different ways scholars have approached the subject. Be sure to explore texts that give you broad and specific information about your topic. These texts may give you new ideas about how to approach or refine your research topic. A more thorough discussion of the different kinds of sources follows in the next sections about primary and secondary sections.

For more discussion on planning your research, see *The Brief Penguin Handbook*, Chapter 15, sections a–f. Also, refer to the Composition Companion Website: www.pearsoncustom.com/vt_composition.

6.3 ◼ Primary Sources

Primary sources are resources such as journals, diaries, records, interviews, experiments, surveys, observations, and other first-hand accounts and evidence that record, without analysis, the events or the topic you are writing about. Some primary sources can be found at the library, but you can also obtain primary sources for yourself by conducting fieldwork. Whether you are looking for a diary written by a nurse during the Civil War or you want to survey a group of Tech students living in the dormitories, by going out in the "field" you can find original research information yourself. "Fieldwork" is the kind of work completed when a researcher literally goes out into the "field." This term is used by scientists, biologists, and anthropologists who observe nature or cultures in their natural settings to understand plant growth or cultural habits. Social scientists who are interested in language use and development have borrowed the term fieldwork to describe the ways that they collect data about groups of people and how they learn or use language. Below is a description of the various kinds of primary sources and the ways you can generate them.

Court Records. County offices contain public records about land use, tax assessments, marriages, wills and estates, and court proceedings. These records might be useful if you are conducting a project about how certain land has tended to be used in a particular area of the state, or if you want to read transcripts from a particular court case. Like the library, county offices have staff who are very knowledgeable about the information stored there, and are usually very helpful in assisting you find information. Before you go to the office, however, it is helpful for you to familiarize yourself with your specific research questions and the information you might need to inform your project.

Archives. Historical documents and materials are contained in archives. Archives can be as small as a town's historical society's collection of old newspapers and genealogical records, and as big as the Washington D.C. National Archives, which contains significant historical documents such as past presidents' letters, commissioned photographs, oral histories, or slave narratives (See www.archives.gov for an overview of the National Archives' Collections). These historical repositories can be very helpful in finding original documents and photographs. Researchers appreciate the kinds of information that can be found in an archived collection. Sometimes documents that have never been viewed by the public can be found and can have an impact on the way a particular historical event is interpreted or viewed. Mostly though, the records located in archives are vast and require patient sifting through many files before useful information is found. As a researcher, spending time in court records and archives can reveal very interesting and very original information about your topic.

Interviews. Conducting interviews is a valuable way to find out information about a topic. You can interview professionals in your field in order to find an authoritative perspective on your major field of study. You can also interview a person who has direct experience with the situation you are researching. You might also interview fellow Tech students about their opinions on a given topic. When you conduct an interview, determine whether it is more appropriate to use a formal question-and-answer session, or an informal exchange of ideas, or something in between. Briefly explain your research project to your interviewee. Go to the interview with a prepared list of questions, but also be flexible as your interviewee may lead you in interesting directions that you might not anticipate. Ask for permission to tape record the interview to help you remember the conversation. If you ask open-ended questions, you are more likely to hear detailed answers than with yes/no questions. No matter which format you choose, take careful notes detailing both the questions and the answers. The goal of your interview is to gather information to help you with your research.

Surveys/Questionnaires. The goal of surveys and questionnaires is to collect the responses of a group of people. You may find it necessary in your research to find out a particular group's beliefs or attitudes. For example, if your research compares Virginia Tech's requirements to other colleges in Virginia, you might ask your fellow students the following questions:

◆ What required core classes do you find most useful at Virginia Tech?

◆ Who should be required to take a foreign language before graduation?

"What" and "who" questions are easy for respondents to answer quickly and accurately. A less valuable type of question to ask in a survey would be a "why" question. This is because "why" questions require answers to be a bit more thorough and planned. Respondents are less likely to give the proper attention to a "why" question for these reasons. Design your survey to be quick and to generate information that will help you as you write about your topic.

Correspondence. In addition to interviewing people, you might also use correspondence in your research. You may wish to consult an expert in your topic area or someone you know who is located out of town. By using email or written correspondence, you can quickly obtain information without traveling for an interview. Both types of correspondence will be useful to your research while contributing unique perspectives that you may not be able to find in a textbook. Depending on the nature of your correspondence and the questions you ask, the information you obtain can be considered just as formal as survey or interview information.

Observation. This is another valuable type of fieldwork that involves taking notes while observing others in their natural environments. Observations can range from a simple visit to a location to visiting a specific place over an extended period of time. Depending on your research question and topic, you will need to determine whether you need to observe a place over time or whether you can observe it once to get the information you need. You might also conduct impromptu interviews at your observation site to gain further perspective about the culture. Do you want to get a general idea of how people act in a given situation, or are you looking for more specific behavioral patterns?

Experiments. Experiments are usually activities or observations conducted in order to test a hypothesis. Specific kinds of experiments vary widely depending on discipline, ranging from "taste tests" between soft drinks to testing nuclear weapons. Experiments can also be quite simple. For example, you might wonder how many Virginia Tech students would bend down to pick up a quarter while walking to class. Your hypothesis might be that most students will ignore the quarter and keep walking. To test your hypothesis, you place a quarter on a busy sidewalk, and then sit a few feet away and observe. To ensure that your experiment is not biased, you might need to run your test for several hours a day, on several different days, and at different times of the day. Experiments can be useful ways to test theories; however, you must thoroughly think through possible experiments and make every effort to avoid bias.

Primary sources, depending on what they are, might also be found in the library. While you can conduct your own surveys, there are many researchers whose surveys, interviews, or observations are available in the library for your use. The following section describes the complex processes of finding information in the library, and the various kinds of sources you can find there, including primary sources.

EXERCISE   **6.b Identifying Primary Sources**

Once you have your topic, make a list of the possible primary sources you might use in your research. What would you hope to find with each of these sources?

6

6.4 Secondary Sources: Searching in the Library

As discussed in 6.2 (Developing a Manageable Topic), you will need to do quite a bit of reading to narrow your topic and to determine your specific research questions. Let's say, for example, that your topic is new treatments for autism. An article called "Cracking the Autism Puzzle" in *Popular Science* describes what researchers are learning about both genetic and environmental causes of autism. This is a great secondary source because it provides you with a quick overview of some important information: the names of the researchers, the labs at which they are working, and overviews of their projects. But the author of the article, Joshua Tompkins, is a journalist, not one of the scientists directly involved in the research. This means you have found a useful secondary source that you can now use to find primary sources. Search for articles by the scientists themselves, and you should be able to find relevant studies that they have published.

At Virginia Tech, you have valuable and convenient online information available to you. The University Libraries' website at <http://www.lib.vt.edu> will help you learn to use the resources available at Virginia Tech. In addition, the 45-minute tour of the library can be very useful in providing you an introduction to the resources there and how to find them. No pre-registration is required and tour schedules can be found at <http://www.lib.vt.edu/help/instruct/toursked.html>. You will be given a quiz after the tour, which the library staff will return to the instructor. You will also attend a library session through your class in which a librarian will teach you how to navigate the library website, how to search Addison (Tech's online catalogue) to find books and journal titles based on found article citations, and how to search article databases to locate articles on your topic. Here you can access the essential information resources, including Addison, and over 200 databases for finding articles by topic. Information about services, staff, collections, and policies is also available on the library website. The librarians at Tech's libraries are one of your most valuable sources of information. If you have any questions about how to get your research started, consult with one of them and they will be happy to help you. Almost every research project you do at Virginia Tech will require that you consult scholarly sources—books, articles, and websites written or created by professors, scientists, or other researchers who have extensive knowledge about a particular subject.

■ Searching Virginia Tech's Databases

Databases, which catalogue articles, can be accessed via the Virginia Tech library website. If you are trying to search these databases while off campus, you will need to provide your user information in order to gain access to the subscription-only materials. Some of the databases are general interest databases, which means that they catalogue articles from newspapers, magazines, and a limited number of scholarly journals. They are good places to begin looking for information. Once you have refined your topic, you may also want to search the subject databases, which catalogue articles from more specialized scholarly and technical journals. It is important to understand the difference between scholarly journals and more popular journals or magazines. Each contains valuable information. Popular journals, which usually are widely published and popular with mass audiences, can provide you with useful introductory and background information to help you understand a topic more broadly. Scholarly journals, which usually are written and published by academic researchers, contain more specialized information that will be useful to you as you begin to narrow your topic and develop research questions that are original to you.

To search for articles in general interest databases,

1. Go the library homepage: http://www.lib.vt.edu.
2. Under "Find," click Articles/Databases.
3. Choose "General interest databases."
4. Choose a specific database. "Expanded Academic" and "InfoTrac One File" are both good choices.
5. You can, if you choose, limit your search to "articles with text," which means the search will return only those articles that you can access online. You can also limit to "refereed publications," which will restrict your search to academic journals—i.e., articles that have been reviewed by other experts.

Not all of the articles listed in the database can be accessed through that database. To find these articles, you will need to note the journal title, volume and issue number, and date. You will then need to search for that journal on Addison.

Some of the sources you may find through database searches are not actually articles, but book reviews. Book reviews are useful for helping you decide if a particular book is of interest to your research, but should not be used as though they were articles. If you want to search specifically for book reviews, you can try the Book Review Digest, one of the online databases.

■ *Searching Addison*

Addison is the Virginia Tech library system's online catalog, available on the library's homepage. Library catalogs, as opposed to databases, don't list article titles. You can search Addison for books, journals, government documents, and other monographs. Addison is searchable by keyword, title, author, subject, or call number.

■ *Searching the Reference Collection*

Newman Library houses a special collection of books that may be accessed during your visit to the library. Some examples of sources found in this collection are atlases, almanacs, encyclopedias, dictionaries, and biographical references. These are general resources that are a great place to begin your research. Since these books are not available to be checked out, be sure to allow yourself ample time to look through them and take change to make copies if needed.

■ *Using Interlibrary Loan*

If the source you need cannot be accessed through Virginia Tech's online databases or by visiting the library, you might be able to have the source sent to you via interlibrary loan, or ILLiad. Some sources may be delivered in days; others may take several weeks. From the library homepage, click on the ILLiad link under "Services" and follow the instructions.

■ *Using Bibliographies*

You may find other helpful sources by browsing the bibliographies and works-cited pages of the sources you've already found. These sources might provide you with useful background material, give you a good idea of what work has already been done on your subject, or give you ideas for new directions in which to take your own research.

6.5 ■ Evaluating Sources

Because the strength of your argument will depend greatly on the quality of the sources you use, you should thoughtfully evaluate all of your sources. Below is a list of some of the kinds of questions you should ask about any source you find.

What are the author's qualifications?

For example, does the author hold an advanced degree in a relevant field? Is the author a scholar or a journalist? Is the author affiliated with a university, industry, business, or organization? What else has the author published? Is the author frequently cited by experts in the field?

What are the publisher's credentials?

Consider what kind of publication the text is—a book, an article in a peer-reviewed academic journal, a newspaper article, a television documentary, a magazine article, a webpage. Who is the audience for the publication? What is the reputation of the publisher? When was the text published?

How credible is the content?

Given what you know about the author, publisher, and audience, analyze the content of the source. Think about the purpose of the text. Is it to persuade, inform, entertain? What kind of evidence is presented? Does the text use mostly primary or secondary sources? Are sources cited or acknowledged? What biases are apparent in the text? What biases might you expect, based on the author and publisher? How well does the information in this source fit with the information in your other sources? What is the style of the language?

Is the source appropriate for your project?

As your research progresses, consider the source within the context of your project. How does the source relate to your other sources? What does it contribute to your understanding of your topic? Will using this source strengthen your argument?

6.6 ■ Writing a Critical Analysis of a Secondary Source

Whether you are taking English 1105 or 1106, your instructor might ask you to conduct a critical analysis paper on a secondary source and to write your findings in a formal paper. A critical analysis is similar to a rhetorical analysis, where you ask specific questions about how the source is written. In the sample that follows, the student used the following questions as a guide, analyzing the published source thoroughly and carefully, drawing specific conclusions about its rhetorical aim.

Critical Analysis of a Secondary Source Assignment
Katrina Powell
English 1105

For this paper you should choose an academic article in your major. In your analysis, examine how the author handles sources, makes an argument and establishes authority. Your analysis should address the following questions, but make sure you write it in the form of an essay. Don't let the questions dominate the structure of your paper.

1. Describe the text. Assume your reader is unfamiliar with it. Provide relevant information but don't spend too much time summarizing. What is the general topic? Is the subject a controversial one? What is the overall main point?

2. Identify the types of appeals the author uses, carefully examining the balance of ethos, pathos, and logos. How does the author develop the ideas of the text? Description? Definition? Comparison? Analogy? Cause and Effect?

3. Who is the author and how does that affect the rhetoric used? What is the tone of the text? Do you react on an emotional level?

4. What kinds of reasoning does the author use and why? How are the arguments arranged?

5. How is the author trying to manipulate the audience and complete his or her goal(s)? What is the specific audience for this text and what indicators are in the text that suggest this audience? What values might this audience hold? Who might a secondary audience be?

6. What is the goal/purpose/exigency of the text? To explain? Inform? Anger? Persuade? Amuse? Motivate? Sadden? Ridicule?

7. What vocabulary/definitions does the author assume the audience knows? How do these assumptions drive the overall argument?

8. When, where, and how is the text delivered? How does media play a role in its delivery?

9. What are specific figures of speech, metaphors, overall structures that work toward the overall goal of the text? Does the author use humor, parody, or sarcasm to make a point?

10. How do form and content work together in this text? Does the author use dialogue or quotations? To what end?

As you write your analysis, remember to read between the lines. What are the subtle messages the author/creator attempts to get across and how does this happen? Attend to the text's overall complexity and spend some time evaluating its overall rhetorical effectiveness (i.e., does it work?).

In the following analysis first-year Virginia Tech student Brittany O'Mara asks similar questions of her source. Her paper is a formal analysis of a source, but you can ask similar questions of all your sources to be sure that they meet your criteria as you conduct your research.

Virginia Tech Accounting and Information Systems major Brittany O'Mara

Brittany O'Mara
Professor Katrina Powell
English 1105
Fall 2006

A CRITICAL ANALYSIS OF "AMERICA'S RAILROAD DEPRECIATION DEBATE, 1907 TO 1913: A STUDY OF DIVERGENCE IN EARLY 20TH CENTURY ACCOUNTING STANDARDS."

In the article in the Accounting Historians Journal titled "America's Railroad Depreciation Debate 1907 to 1913: A Study of Divergence in Early 20th Century Accounting Standards" by Jan Heier, he discusses the different views on this heavily debated subject. Rather than making an argument by taking a specific standpoint in the debate he cleverly states "This paper tracks the debate over these depreciation issues from their inception in 1907 to their final disposition by the Supreme Court in 1913" (Heier 90). That is exactly what the article did. Heier told the story of the Railroad Depreciation debate.

The Railroad Depreciation Debate was a battle against betterment accounting and depreciation accounting. It was fought by the Interstate Commerce Commission (ICC) and the railroads. Causing this debate was the ICC's decision to regulate the railroad's accounting practices by enforcing a form of accounting which they thought would be more efficient at accurately calculating the income of the railroads, known as depreciation accounting. This process was done by subtracting a depreciation expense each year from a new expense account and then using the money to pay for the replacement of new railroad equipment when it came time. The ICC's view was that this was more accurate yearly because the equipment is used throughout the years and it subtracts costs each year rather than the previous form of subtracting it right when the new equipment was needed. This previous form is called betterment accounting which meant the cost of betterments (replacement/repairs of equipment) was subtracted from the income at the time of the replacement. The difference between these two forms of accounting is that it takes more work to perform depreciation accounting than betterment accounting because you now had to calculate the degree of wear for the equipment in order to subtract a specific percent from the expense account. The railroads demanded to remain using betterment accounting; however, the ICC had other plans.

To incorporate all sides of this debate the author used newspaper articles and statements rather than including his own opinion. Heier informs us "Though each source has its own biases, taken together, they give a sense of the passion on both sides of America's great railroad depreciation debate" (90). It was interesting that the author chose to show a variety of views on the debate rather than taking a side. Never once in the article did the author seem to be on a specific side. There was equal amount of support from the railroad's point of view, the ICC's side, and people who changed their views over time. This helped to show all aspects of the debate and how much it was talked about over the years until now in 2006, the year this article was published. But why would the author want to educate us rather than try to convince us?

From researching Jan Heier, an accounting professor from Auburn University Montgomery, it was obvious what his goal was. He aspired to teach about accounting history. In his Seminar in Accounting Theory class it begins with doing research in accounting, watching an accounting history video, and learning about the history and the development of accounting before teaching any actual accounting practices. His dissertation was titled "A Quantitative Study of Accounting Methods and Usage in Mid 19th Century Alabama and Mississippi," again relating to accounting in the past. To write his dissertation on such a topic it must have been one which was a primary concern and interest. His other works were also comprised of case studies relating to past accounting methods and the impacts on modern accounting. Not only did Heier

want to capture the passion of the two sides of the debate but he wanted to emphasize his own passion for accounting history through writing this article. This is the
reason why he does not argue on behalf of one side; it is the big picture that matters
to him. Since he cannot include his own opinions he chooses to use the articles from
the Wall Street Journal, the New York Times, the Railway Age Gazette, and the opinions of public accountants at the time of the debate to capture the overall idea.
Therefore the arguments are arranged in a fashion where two different ones are back
to back with a description of each making it hard for the reader to choose sides.

By using these articles and actual events out of history Heier grabs the attention
of people who are interested in history and journalism while mainly attracting
accountants. To make the interested believe what he is saying Heier uses much evidence to back everything up. The use of actual quotes and thoughts of people during
the debate makes you trust what he is saying. A prime example of this is when Heier
says, "The new act also gave the ICC the legal authority to set fair and reasonable rail
tariffs. To meet this new mandate, regulators were authorized to 'develop uniform
accounting rules, and to prescribe the forms of all accounts, records, and memoranda
to be kept by carriers'" [ICC, 1907b, p.139]. The law now empowered the ICC to have
rate setting as its primary mission" (Heier 92). He states a fact by simply incorporating the exact words from the ICC to let us know this is legitimate and not just something he infers or believes. This is how every item stated is proven. He may do this so
in the end he cannot be approached if someone disagrees with what he says.
Ultimately he is not saying anything himself he is just restating it using other's words.

If Heier does say anything at all the words may, seem, could, would, and possible appear which imply that he is suggesting something or is unsure. Generally I
would think that a writer should be certain about what they are saying and using
these words would bring down their argument but Heier's case is different. Since his
argument is not directly on the debate rather on the passion exemplified by the par-
ticipants he merely suggests things so that you can see the multiple sides of the dis-
pute. In this article it works efficiently to encompass the varying opinions.

Heier shows no emotion in writing this but it is obvious that he is avid about
the topic. The emotional aspect occurs just knowing how long this was debated and
the many people involved in this. The seriousness of this change in accounting practice got a lot of attention, meaning there must be some sort of emotional attachment.
It's awkward to have an emotional attachment to a specific type of accounting but this
is what the railroads had. Their willingness to fight and eventually take their objection
to the Supreme Court in 1913 shows fervor indicating emotion.

On the other side it's hard to understand and comprehend the passion in this
debate if you aren't an accountant or have some sort of accounting background. It is
an article obviously directed to accountants. If someone who had no idea about
accounting read this article it would sound as if Heier was just rambling on about the

same thing over and over again. He assumes that the reader will know the terms depreciation accounting, betterment accounting, and economic depreciation and is familiar with an income statement, balance sheet, and typical accounting proce-dures. If these terms sound foreign to you then reading the article would be a com-plete waste of time. I personally was unfamiliar with some of the phrases and had to research them. I even asked my grandfather, who is a CPA, if he was familiar with these terms and he said, "These terms are older so I don't remember them too well; I'm going to have to look them up." They must be pretty old considering he is seventy-one. So I may be a bit lenient in saying that this is directed towards account-ants in general maybe accountants who are also interested in the history like Heier. Since the author's goal is to inform us of the Railroad Depreciation Debate this may be his plan to teach more by requiring you to look up definitions yourself rather than including them essentially helping the reader to become more knowledgeable on the topic.

The setup of the article was successful at telling the story of the Railroad Depreciation Debate. It began with an abstract, led to an introduction, included a background, quite a few subtitles, and a conclusion. The article was structured in chronological order which is the case with many stories. It worked well to achieve the author's objective of enlightening the reader on the subject. If you were aware of the terms used then the article flowed well, and you were able to read about all the drama of the debate. By going straight through and just telling the story from begin-ning to end it helped the reader directly see what was happening.

Another way to help see what was happening was by including a table of Estimated Change in Railroad Financial Accounting Results (95) and a picture of "Note on ICC Accounting Change as Presented in the 1998 L&N Annual Report" (104). This helped show proof and data to demonstrate what was going on during the time. They both use exact data and information which again doesn't include Heier's own opinion but rather factual information. It is very useful to understand the change in money during the debate and the new orders during the debate.

Each claim made in the debate had an effect which was then published in a newspaper article and then put into the story. After one side in the debate said some-thing the other side would retaliate and it was published. For instance the section of the article titled "Theoretical Arguments" begins with an article from the Gazette [October 11, 1907, p. 90] by William Mahl where he protests that "This change will furnish the Commission with reliable data about the depreciation which has been car-ried into the operating expenses of the railroads will enable it to order adjustments suitable to each case if any such should be necessary" (Heier 105). Immediately after in Heier's article he states, "Even with the protests, Adams and the ICC issued more accounting regulations in January 1908" (Heier 105). Everything seemed to happen this way; people protest, the ICC does something to make them mad again, and the

6

cycle would continue. Heier was sure to include the cycle by the ICC and the railroads just so the reader was again able to see both sides.

At the end of the article Heier leaves you hanging. In the conclusion Heier said that his debate was only "round one" (120) and then says:

> The depreciation debate was again renewed in 1923 when the ICC ordered the depreciation of track right-of-way and way structures. This order set off another ten years of protest and litigation that would culminate in the ICC's canceling the orders in 1933 due to the economic depression. The final phase of the debate over betterment accounting would recommence in the mid-1950s with an attempt by Arthur Andersen to reinvigorate an economically moribund rail system through the convergence of railroad accounting practices with industry GAAP. (120)

This leaves you interested to hear more and want to know what happened with the new debate. This is another trick of Heier to get the reader to research and learn more about this debate instead so that they can learn more about the history.

The article "America's Railroad Depreciation Debate 1907 to 1913: A Study of Divergence in Early 20th Century Accounting Standards" is written to inform accountants about the history behind their work. Heier is a man who has two loves, accounting and history and he wants everyone to learn about it. In his writing it is obvious that he is trying to educate and get his point across in way that is trustworthy. His use of newspaper articles and quotes aids his goal by providing the evidence he needs to tell his story and supply sufficient reasoning. Heier is a man who is passionate about what he does and aims to spread his passion to others.

Works Cited

Heier, Jan. "America's Railroad Depreciation Debate, 1907 to 1913: A Study of Divergence in Early 20th Century Accounting Standards." *Accounting Historians Journal* 33 (2006): 89–124.

For more discussion on analyzing sources, see Chapter 18 in *The Brief Penguin Handbook*. Also, refer to the Composition Companion Website: www.pearsoncustom.com/vt_composition.

EXERCISE

6.c Reading the Source Analysis

1. Does this author's paper adequately summarize the article? What questions were left unanswered for you?

2. What is this author's general assessment of the article? Does she think the article is well-written? In what ways?

3. Does the author answer all the questions in the assignment prompt? What further questions could she address to make the paper more thorough?

4. If the author was in your workshop group, what advice would you give her about her essay?

6.7 The Annotated Bibliography

After carefully evaluating sources for credibility and relevance, you can move to the next phase of your project. Before beginning to draft research papers or research proposals, many scholars create an annotated bibliography that cites, summarizes, and briefly evaluates potential sources.

The information included in a working bibliography may vary from scholar to scholar, but all include a full citation of each source being considered. In addition, a working bibliography may be annotated to include a brief summary of the source and an evaluation of the source's potential value to your research project.

An annotated bibliography will help you keep track of, assess, and begin synthesizing outside sources for your final paper; rethink and perhaps revise your research question; and manage your time to keep your project on track. Creating an annotated bibliography will also help you to quickly assess whether you have a sufficient number of good, relevant sources for your paper.

EXERCISE   **6.d Writing Annotations**

Examine the following two sample entries from an annotated bibliography on the research question "What are the ethical considerations of fetal-tissue research?" What strengths and weaknesses do you see in these entries?

Lawton, Kim A. "Fetal-tissue Transplants Stir Controversy."
Christianity Today. 8 Mar. 1988: 52–53.

Lawton notes that nearly all the tissues used in research have come from elective abortions and that 92% of women having abortions said they would agree to donate their fetal remains to research since it would enable "some good to come out of their decision." She also points out a strange partnership between pro-lifers and feminists: both fear that if abortion becomes the accepted method of getting fetal tissue for research, women may be coerced into having abortions and later into more harmful procedures that would yield other beneficial tissues. Significantly, Lawton writes that if fetal tissue transplants were placed under the Organ Transplant Act, which forbids the sale of certain body parts for transplantation, there would be no potential for women to become commercially exploited "spare parts factories." Despite Lawton's obvious conservative and pro-life stance, this article is valuable for the unusual angles it offers on the issue—no other source so far has mentioned either the pro-lifer/feminist partnership or the Organ Transplant Act. Lawton also includes numerous quotations from fetal tissue transplant opponents without offering any statements from FTT proponents; while her treatment is thus a bit lopsided, I may find some good direct quotations I can use here. Finally, she unfortunately takes an unfair cheap shot at emotional appeal: scientists' desire for "fresh" tissues makes them take tissues from live fetuses, she implies. *InfoTrac Expanded Academic Database ASAP.*

6

Post, Stephen G. "Fetal Tissue Transplant:
The Right to Question Progress."*America* 5 Jan. 1991: 14–16.

Post writes that if medical research becomes dependent on electively aborted fetal tissue, an irreversible economic and institutional bond between abortion centers and biomedical science will have been established. He notes, however, that several people have argued that fetal tissue available from ectopic pregnancies, miscarriages, and stillbirths should be more than sufficient for research needs, but the possible chromosomal abnormalities of such tissues make them second-rate for research. Importantly, he points out that we just do not know what the ultimate impact of FTT on the incidence of elective abortion would be. He ends by questioning whether we the living should improve our quality of life at the expense of the unborn just because we can. The most in-depth and balanced of the many articles Post has published on FTT, this piece avoids finally coming down on one side or the other, but rather presents strong cases for both sides. I think his predictions of widespread civil disobedience or of our transforming FT donation into a civil duty are a bit far-fetched, but intriguing possibilities. This essay does, however, suffer from an unneeded tirade against "secular moral philosophers" as Post tries to cement FTT's status as a religious issue. *Medline.*

6.8 ■ The Proposal

Most research projects require some kind of proposal. The proposal is the document you use to demonstrate that you have a good project in mind and enough knowledge to complete it successfully. This is the document that will earn you the permission, funds, and resources to pursue your project. A research proposal details what you are writing about, how you are going to write about it, and why you are writing about it. Most research proposals include the following information:

◆ statement of purpose, audience, and tentative thesis

◆ brief summary or abstract of the project

◆ brief review of the literature

◆ rationale for the project indicating what is original about your approach

◆ description of research strategy and timetable for completion

Once you have gathered, evaluated, and chosen sources to use for your research project, and developed a clear proposal, you can begin the actual writing of the research paper. Remember to always have a clear understanding of the rhetorical situation (see Chapter 3: Critical Thinking, Reading, and Writing) before you begin to write. For an explanation of the writing process, refer to Chapter 4: Writing as a Process.

6.9 Summarizing, Paraphrasing, and Quoting

As you begin to draft your research paper, try to resist the urge to "sprint" through it; it would be a shame to have completed all the researching, evaluating, and planning only to produce a weak final product. It is important for you to consider the best ways to present supporting evidence in your paper. Summaries, paraphrases, and direct quotations are ways of incorporating material from sources into your writing.

A *summary* is a condensed version of another writer's text. It is always shorter than the original text. A good summary presents the original text's main ideas but eliminates all or most of the supporting details. It may reduce a paragraph to a single sentence or a chapter to a paragraph.

A *paraphrase* is a restatement of another writer's text in "your own words." A paraphrase presents the other writer's arguments, findings, and ideas in a passage approximately the same length as the original.

A *quotation* is an exact, word-for-word replication of another author's text.

It can be difficult to know when to use a summary or a paraphrase instead of a direct quote. As a general suggestion, consider using a direct quote when the other author's phrasing seems especially important or effective. Consider using a summary when it's important for your audience to understand the main point of the author's argument, but not necessarily the details. Use a paraphrase to convey a difficult or jargon-filled idea in terms your audience will understand.

Every summary, paraphrase, and quotation should include these five essential elements:

1. **An introductory or signal phrase.** This phrase should let the reader know that material from a source is coming next.

2. **The summary, paraphrase, or quotation itself.**

3. **A parenthetical citation.** In your English class, your instructor will probably require that you document your sources according to MLA style. See Chapter 21 of *The Brief Penguin Handbook* for information on MLA citation.

4. **A follow-up statement.** Make sure you follow each summary, paraphrase, or quotation with a few sentences that comment on the evidence. Do not assume that your reader will understand why you have included that piece of evidence. Make your reasons explicit with an analysis or an interpretation.

5. **An entry in your Works Cited list.** Again, see Chapter 21 in *The Brief Penguin Handbook* for a thorough discussion of how to list your sources according to MLA style.

In addition to information about MLA citation, *The Brief Penguin Handbook* includes a chapter on summarizing, paraphrasing, and quoting, and avoiding plagiarism. See Chapter 19 for an exciting continuation of this lesson.

For more information on the annotated bibliography and the purpose of documenting and incorporating sources in research papers, see *The Brief Penguin Handbook,* Chapter 18, section d, and Chapters 19 and 20. Also, refer to the Composition Companion Website: www.pearsoncustom.com/vt_composition.

6.10 █ Fieldwork Research Paper Examples

In both English 1105 and in 1106 you might be asked to conduct field research. The following assignment and sample paper were completed in English 1105 where students were asked to observe an event where people were using language in interesting ways, and then analyze that language use. As you read the assignment and the sample paper, think about the places you might be interested in observing and what you could find out about how people communicate.

Mini-ethnography Assignment
Professor Katrina Powell

"Ethnography is a qualitative research method that allows a researcher to gain a comprehensive view of the social interactions, behaviors, and beliefs of a community or social group. In other words, the goal of an ethnographer is to study, explore, and describe a group's culture" (Beverly Moss 155).

"Ethnographic research, another kind of qualitative descriptive research, examines entire environments, looking at subjects in context. This design derives primarily from phenomenology, anthropology, and sociology, which have argued for its importance as a research method to provide a window on culture" (Janice Lauer and John Asher 39).

All semester, we've been discussing what literacy means. We've debated the various definitions of literacy and we've compared that to our own experiences. As we begin to read Shirley Brice Heath's ethnography that studies the literacy in two Piedmont area communities, we will also conduct semi-ethnographic research in order to learn what some of the methodologies are and what studying a group or culture can reveal to us in terms of literacy.

Typically, an ethnography is a longitudinal study of a culture that "triangulates" multiple data sources such as observations, interviews, artifacts (writing), and surveys. Since we are learning about ethnography and literacy, you will conduct a "mini-ethnography" to learn through practice about conducting ethnological research—the kind of research many literacy scholars do. For this assignment, then, observe a particular literate event (we've discussed several options but feel free to discuss your ideas in class and/or with me). If you can, tape record the event and transcribe it so you can closely examine the language. Keep very detailed fieldnotes, describing everything that happens and your impressions/interpretations. As much as you can, prepare research questions before you observe; that is, go into your research with an idea of what you hope to find.

You will turn in your transcripts/fieldnotes, in addition to a "thick description" of what you find. In your description, or narrative analysis, draw some conclusions about what you saw. What are the patterns you saw or generalizations you can make about your data? How does what you observed and your impressions of what you observed fit into the theories of literacy we've discussed this semester? Does your study support or refute any of the discussions we've had? Be sure to include in your narrative the ways that you observed: were you an "objective" observer or were you a participant-observer? How did your presence alter the situation? How does your particular perspective affect the way you're analyzing the data?

Resources:

Bishop, Wendy. *Ethnographic Writing Research: Writing it down, Writing it up, and Reading it.* Portsmouth, NH: Boynton/Cook Publishers, 1999.

Moss, Beverly. "Ethnography and Composition: Studying Language at Home." In *Methods and Methodology in Composition Research,* eds. Gesa Kirsch and Patricia A. Sullivan. Carbondale: Southern Illinois University Press, 1992. 153–171.

Lauer, Janice, and John Asher. "Chapter 3: Ethnographies." In *Composition Research: Empirical Designs.* New York: Oxford University Press, 1988. 39–53.

Professor Powell's student, Brian Parrish wrote the following essay in response to her assignment. Brian is a major in Agricultural and Applied Economics.

PARRISH 1

Brian Parrish
Professor Katrina Powell
English 1105
12/6/06

"FIELD DAY OF THE PAST": LANGUAGE INTERPRETATION

On September 16, 2006 my girlfriend and I went to the Field Day of the Past Steam and Gas Show in Rockville, Virginia. I already knew that I was going to this when I went home that weekend so I decided to do my mini-ethnography on this event because I figured it would be different than what most other people would do. I will first explain what this event is and what it is all about because I figure that most people have never heard of it. It is a three day event that starts Friday and ends Sunday and runs from 8 in the morning and the exhibits close at 6 in the evening. Some of the exhibits include a rodeo, lawnmower racing, antique vehicles and tractors, and displays of old farm and construction equipment. The biggest thing that has grown there is all the companies from around the area come and set up exhibits showing their products. I normally go to the Steam and Gas Show to watch the tractor and truck pull that starts at 12 and normally ends around 1 or 2 in the morning. This show averages more people a day than the Virginia State Fair and it is becoming a very big event for the state.

I have been coming to this event since I was a little kid, so I have seen it grow and the crowd that comes to it is becoming more diverse all the time. When I was younger I would come to it with my grandpa and the only people there were older men that were involved with agriculture. Then as the event started to grow and it became more than just an antique tractor pull and expanded to a car show and fair rides then more people with more diversity started coming to the show. Now there is still a majority of agriculture based people there but it is becoming closer to there being more non-agriculture based people there.

I got there about twelve o'clock and went to sit down to watch one of my friends pull his tractor. They started out by shutting everything down and playing the national anthem. I believe this is a very important part of any kind of sporting event because it shows respect to our country through literacy. I noticed at an event like this everyone seems to be very patriotic and shows it by American flags being everywhere and people wearing clothes with them on it. Then there was some bad news: the announcer told the crowd that the normal announcer had died about a month ago. Many people knew him very well so they had a moment of silence to remember him. He was the reason that they started expanding this event and making it popular for a broader audience.

As I was walking around looking at all the exhibits of construction equipment I overheard a salesman for Carter Cat talking to a person about one of their bulldozers they had on show. So I decided to stop and take notes on how he did his sales job. He started out by shaking the man's hand and asking for his name, which was Matt. Then the salesman asked him what kind of business he was in and did he own any heavy equipment now. So Matt told him that he owned and ran a small demolition business where he cleared land and built ponds. Matt also told him that he owned a small Cat excavator and a Case bulldozer. Then the salesman asked if he was looking to get a new bulldozer and what brands he was looking at. Matt replied that he was interested in getting a new one because his old Case was getting a lot of hours on it and every time he turned around something was breaking on it and it wasn't reliable anymore. Matt continued by saying that he either was going to buy another Case or

Caterpillar. So then the salesman told him that he could show Matt the bulldozer and all the features of it. So they did this and Matt told him that he was going to look at some other brands so the salesman gave him some information packets on it and told him it was nice meeting him.

Then as I was walking around, I just noticed how the different age groups were looking at different types of stuff. Most of the real young children with their parents wanted to look at the animals. The animals there included just about all the domesticated livestock animals in the United States. Then the teenagers mostly looked at the cars and trucks that were there. They also liked to look at all the heavy machinery and the big exhibits that were at the event. Most of the older people stuck with watching the antique tractors pulling and looking at the old farm equipment. Tractor pulls are done by hooking a tractor up to a sled that you can adjust the amount of weight in and seeing how far it can pull down a 300 foot track. I thought it was cool to see how the age of the people affected what they were interested in looking at and watching.

So when I was back sitting down on the hill with my girlfriend watching the tractors pulling the sled I decided to ask an older gentleman that was beside me what interested him in watching these antique tractors. He was very nice and seemed easy to talk to. His name was Elton. So I asked if he had an agriculture background to make him interested in these tractors. So he told me that he had grown up on a beef cattle farm all his life and had recently turned it over to his son to run and he had retired from farming but still helps out when needed. So I asked him how it made him feel seeing all this old equipment being restored and still being used. Elton told me that it made him feel good that people cared about the heritage of these old tractors and how they showed an interest in keeping them around to show how stuff did have to be done when he was young. Seeing all this stuff made good childhood memories come back up and it also reminded him of his dad and grandpa. I really enjoyed having this conversation with Elton because I personally restore antique tractors but I never knew it affected people like it does.

After the tractors had finished pulling, then came the trucks. This includes street legal pickups, non street legal pickups, dump trucks, and tractor trailers. When the non street legal pickups pull many of them run on a circuit and pull for points because they have a champion at the end of the year. It amazes me that they actually have a fan base and people actually root for them just like in any other sport. The environment for these trucks pulling is very different than everything else because they are very loud and everyone likes watching them. The crowd starts getting rowdy by now because some of them have had a little too much to drink. This is supposed to be an alcohol free event, but we all know that never happens at a big event like this. So people tend to start getting all of each others' nerves.

I witnessed this first hand when the announcer tried to get the crowd into it when there was only one Ford pickup in the class and he was talking bad about them.

6

So there was this Ford fan beside me and he had too many drinks and when some-body came by talking bad about Fords he decided he was going to trip them for a joke. They did not take that too well and when the drunken man would not shut up the man ended up throwing him down the hill. So then I watched security drag them both out of there and give them a free ride in a police car.

I think that this ended up being a very good experience for me and I really enjoyed doing it. I thought it would be stupid before I did it but between listening to the salesman trying to say his equipment was better but not actually cutting down the other brand. Having the conversation with the old farmer and seeing how it really affected him and the older generation. Of course seeing a drunken man get beat up over a brand of pickup is always a funny sight. Then watching him try to explain to the security why it wasn't his fault and how he is not drunk but can barely stand up. It was very interesting to see how different types of people act.

EXERCISE

6.e Reading the Mini-Ethnography

1. How does the author describe the event he observed? Does he pay particular attention to the language used at this event?

2. What do you think of the picture the author included with his paper? Does he refer to it in his paper? How could the author strengthen the use of the photograph within his paper?

3. This paper is written in first-person point of view. What effect does that have on the reader? How would third-person point of view change your reading of the paper?

4. Who does the author interview for this paper? Does the interview add a compelling aspect to the paper? What further questions could the author ask of the interviewee to include in this paper?

5. What questions remain unanswered about the event that the author describes? What further details could he include to make his paper more thorough?

■ *Observation and Analysis of a Place*

The following assignment and student example were written for Virginia Tech Instructor Katie Fallon's English 1106 class. This fieldwork research paper asks students to analyze the ways people use a place.

Observation and Analysis of Place Assignment
Katie Fallon
English 1106

Choose one "public space" to investigate. Public spaces can include campus areas (Squires, libraries, gyms, the Duck Pond, etc.), parks (Heritage Park in Blacksburg, the Jefferson National Forest, the Huckleberry Trail, etc.), museums, cemeteries, and endless other possibilities. Your objective will be to write an analysis of the ways the place is used—how often is the place used, and by whom? What is it used for? What conclusions can you draw about the place and its users?

You should visit your place at least two or three times, preferably more. You will need to collect data through careful observations. You will also need to conduct at least two interviews; interviewees may include users of the place, persons in charge of maintaining or managing the place, or anyone you think will add something relevant to your essay. While it is not required, you may conduct a survey or distribute a questionnaire.

Virginia Tech instructor Katie Fallon with her student, Kristen Pevarski who is majoring in Biological Systems Engineering at Virginia Tech.

6

Kristen Pevarski
Instructor Katie Fallon
English 1106
21 September 2006

　　"Would you choose option number two or become a love slave to some inmate named Bubba?" This is one of many desperate attempts made by my Personal Health teacher to catch his students' attention. Once captured, he quickly loses this interest to other forms of entertainment my peers already brought with them to class. There are still students paying attention to the lecture but the majority is not. Indeed, lecture hall classes have become less about learning the information presented and more about getting through each class with as little involvement as possible.

15 Minutes until Class

The class before mine usually begins filing out about fifteen to twenty minutes before my class begins. One girl inches past a crowd of people on her tip toes, pivoting from side to side, trying to catch up with her fast companion. Another girl, dressed for the occasion of class, complete with a miniskirt and heels, promptly pulls out her cell phone investigating any missed calls, text messages, or possible new voice mails that may have been received while she was unable to respond. My class has its few anal retentive students, already lined up at the door waiting to file in and settle down. I unfortunately am one of them, grabbing my seat in the third row, third chair before anyone else with eyes on my spot could get it first. I usually lay down my bag and relax until class starts. The sound of chairs opening and the two main doors to Squires Colonial are loud in the background as we sit waiting for the class to start. My teacher typically saunters in about this time to set up his Power Point slides and to speak with his two GTA's about the lecture's proceedings. Just in case we were watching a movie, at least one of them needs to be perched above us ready to switch from his Power Points to the movie projector so time is not wasted. One girl walks in, grasping a cup of coffee from Au Bon Pain in her right hand and three books balanced on her left arm. She carefully maneuvers around some students talking to my professor while talking on her cell phone, her right ear touching her raised shoulder so as to wedge her LG phone inside, allowing her to hear her friend. Two friends are sitting in the front row arguing over an article in the Opinion section of the Collegiate Times. The girl is arguing that chivalry is gone while the guy listens. He watches the other kids walking in the lecture hall until it is his turn for a rebuttal of "It is woman's fault that chivalry is dead," another exciting discussion, another exciting class.

5 Minutes until Class

My teacher begins dimming the lights and turning on the projector. The blue screen turns on as a "please wait" sign appears while the applications are loading. He signals to his GTA in the back of the room with a nod and "Drug Awareness" with little bulletins suddenly appears on the screen. My teacher surveys the screen, nods his approval once again to the GTA, then begins extracting a large amount of notes and clear slides from his briefcase. He smiles at a couple of students walking in then proceeds past them to drink his Dasani water. This is usually the time my twin arrives to class, rushing past the group of kids still searching for a place to sit and throwing her bags down by our feet. Never one to be early, she makes it a habit to never stay in the classroom more than the class length of an hour and fifteen minutes. My sister says, "Why would I rush to get to class? If I do end up coming to class, I rarely take notes and even then my notes become more doodles than actual facts given to us by the teacher. Especially when you have a class in a lecture hall, it becomes the one that will be skipped if I didn't get my nap." One girl slides in past us, muttering, "Excuse me, sorry, excuse me, sorry…" It goes on until she finally reaches her seat in the middle of our aisle and settles in. Class is finally almost ready to begin.

Beginning of Class

The beginning of class is always an interesting time to see different students' activities. Some students, typically freshmen, come prepared to learn while other students come prepared to sleep. A group of four students open their three-ring binders. They carefully extract a large section of printed notes, neatly stapled together, and already hole-punched so as not to be lost on the way to class. They take out their highlighters and one pencil each. This is when our chairs live up to their full potential. Besides just being comfortable in the traditional Hokie maroon red, the side tables, carefully folded between the seats, are being taken out for support. Their notes are neatly placed on top of the table as their pencils are poised in their hands and their eyes are glued on the teacher. This is unusual as the majority of the class is setting up different forms of entertainment to keep them occupied. Amanda, another student in Personal Health, said, "I normally sleep, if there's anything important that I might miss, I know other people in the class that can give me the information so there really isn't any reason not to [sleep]." In the back of the room, one kid has out a notebook to write notes on while another is already engrossed in a Patricia Cornwell novel. There is an obvious rift between those students who are ready to learn and those students who are ready to distract themselves; however, those students who are ready to not pay attention far outnumber those who are going to pay attention.

The teacher smiles, then announces, "It's about time to start, and there are still many empty seats in the front of class." Not many people accept his offer; they still search for a seat in the back section of the lecture hall. The girls sitting in front of us have decided that each class period, they only print off one set of notes. Each week, one of them is going to have to pay attention and jot down his examples. Last week, the brunette took the notes and she's arguing that it's time for the blonde to take them. It's only fair. The blonde grabbed the notes and unfolded her table. The brunette smiled in triumph and took out the Collegiate Times. Unfortunately, taking diligent notes has become a chore and something that is either hardly done or done only to get out of it another time. My teacher begins his presentation poised on top of a semi-circular stage, created so it would face the whole lecture hall and not solely the section straight in front of him. His voice is magnified across the room by the small microphone attached to his shirt and resting on his hip. His voice booms across the room but is muffled by iPods and by the eight, four on each side of the room, rectangular sound buffers positioned on the two main walls. His words get lost as the whispers of socializing students create a constant murmur in the background. As Ben said of his lecture hall class, "I look forward to going to Personal Health every week. I get to see my friends and you also don't have to pay attention. You can just hang out and relax, catch up." This is true of many other students as well; they come to class to socialize rather than to learn. As the teacher removes the podium from the center of his stage, attention is becoming scarce and most people have already begun looking for other forms of entertainment to get them through the hour and fifteen minute lecture that has only just begun.

3 Minutes Past Beginning of Class

Besides not being ready to learn, many students thoughtlessly arrive after class has already begun. It is difficult to obtain the information when someone misses the beginning of class; however, retrieving the notes or writing down examples is the last thought on many students' minds. I begin to notice the two groups of kids wandering in the door. One of the two groups can be characterized as apathetic. This is the group that rarely cares about the information missed and rarely cares whether or not they are on time, let alone that people are watching them walk in. The door slams shut behind them as they walk to the front of the class and choose a seat there. One student's backpack is just thrown on the floor creating yet another loud noise to distract the rest of the class. The other group of kids is the ones who didn't want to be late. Maybe they wanted a good seat or maybe they did not want to miss the beginning of class, whatever the reason, they did not choose to be late. They had to walk across campus from their last class that got out ten minutes ago, they did not realize what time it was and had to run to class, whatever the reason, this group does not like to be noticed as they shuffle into the room. One girl carefully guides the door to close. She doesn't let it slam since that would create even more of a disturbance than her walking in late already has, so she decides to stealthily enter and quickly grab a seat. She peeks around the corner at the lecture hall then hangs an immediate left and walks as close to the wall as possible until she finds the closest seat. She sits down, her face red from either running to class or embarrassment and gets ready for another lecture. Hence, there are some students learning, but many students arrive late to lecture hall classes, not caring about the information missed.

Fifteen Minutes into Class

By this time, if a kid is going to pay attention, he or she already would have. If he or she is not going to pay attention, then he or she typically has already found something to occupy his or her time. There are some students, however, who manage to accomplish both tasks of distracting themselves and paying attention at the same time. The girl next to me is playing on her TI-83. Once she gets a score she feels worthy of, she passes it to her male companion to play, then lays her head back and focuses on the lecture. Another girl down the aisle from me is occasionally glancing at the teacher with her notes on the table and her cell phone in her hand. She is busily writing the second text message of the class to her friend. She is probably complaining about how boring the drug lecture is today and how she wants to leave, yet another continuation of her previous text message on the slow progress of class. Another group of kids in the back are sleeping while their friends are staring back and forth from each other to the sleeping kid, plotting things to do to him. Me, I have already begun my countdown till the end of class. I try to pay attention, but it's the same lecture I think everybody heard in grades 5–12 about drug use from their D.A.R.E. officer. I erase the sixty minutes to go on my paper and just stare off at the fifty-nine on my paper. This is just another attempt to make the class go by faster by breaking it into smaller sections. I have had a difficult time paying attention by this point in class; therefore, I have found something that will occupy my time. Giving up on listening to the lecture and finding other means of entertainment is common among students in lecture halls.

45 Minutes to Go

There are times when a majority of the class pays attention; although rare, this does happen. My teacher has won this short round and received the attention he had been seeking when he nods to the GTA in back and announces to the class that we are watching a movie. The girl text-messaging everyone on her contact list looks up to find out more while some of the kids in back sleeping opened their eyes long enough to find out whether it's worth staying up for. Most of the notes get shuffled to the side as people prepare to relax and stop focusing on schoolwork. The Power Point flashes on the screen then disappears to a black screen with a big "input 1" in the lower right corner. At the same time as when "input 2" appears on the screen, so does the words, "Sixty Minutes Special Report." My teacher explains the report is on health and the dangers of anorexia and this is one lady's perspective on why anorexia and bulimia are so wide-spread now. About a quarter of the kids previously occupied in something non-class related have already returned to their entertainment while most of the class is still debating whether or not this movie merits their attention. The decision is always made quickly so the movie has got to be interesting in the beginning. Therefore, there are times when the students pay attention to the class but this is an infrequent occurrence.

40 Minutes to Go

Again, there are times when the students pay attention to the information presented. The movie has succeeded at least for the past five minutes. The producers decided to show Victoria's Secret models parading across the screen in their lingerie which worked to grab back the male population inside Squires Colonial lecture hall. Intermittently, the report switches back to the models and other shots of women in the media in their underwear to grab back people's attention while they also focus on an older woman complaining about women's obsession with their appearance now. After almost every comment, a large number of the students laugh wondering where her comments are based. She does not exude the credibility she was hoping for and succeeded in turning the once-serious show into a comedy over her exaggerated remarks. The movie does seem to be getting the students' attention, though, good or bad. I'm paying attention.

30 Minutes to Go

Now that class is halfway through, people become restless. Even if students start paying attention to the lecture, this is only a short and infrequent occurrence. The movie is over and the students are returning to their normal habits during class. The girl down the aisle has taken out her cell phone once more to check her new text-message and to respond. A couple down the aisle from me is whispering into each other's ears giggling and planning their weekend's adventure. My sister has decided that instead of taking notes, she will write sarcastic remarks on the side of them. She also has taken up drawing in class; a good example of her artwork is the caricature of my teacher in the front of the classroom waving his arms around trying to be entertaining. Another girl down the aisle from me keeps switching which leg she is going to cross over the over. She tries her right over her left, then finds that uncomfortable and switches yet again to her left leg over her right. She is trying to find some way to keep comfortable in the tiny space allotted to her. While the blonde is doodling balloons on her paper, her friend has gotten to the Sudoku in the paper and is searching for a pencil. She stares at the ceiling as she reaches into her bag, feeling around for a pencil. She pulls out her writing utensil then frowns when she has pulled out a pen. Pens do not work for Sudokus so she reaches into her bag yet again, this time with a little more selectivity. She pulls out her second attempt and realizes that it is indeed a pencil. She returns her bag to the floor and silently and slowly folds the newspaper so that only the Sudoku is showing. This will occupy at least 15 minutes of class. The Collegiate Times has become quite a distraction for many of the students in my lecture hall. If they have already finished the Sudoku, the headlines are then read straight through until they have no choice but to put up the paper and pay attention to my teacher's lecture about drugs. Indeed, halfway through the class my teacher has failed to retain even half of the students' attention.

15 Minutes to Go

After the halfway mark, the next landmark in progression of the class is the fifteen minute to go mark. Many of the students, struggling to pay attention, begin losing the battle. At this time, if a student was not paying attention at the beginning of class, there is a strong probability that he or she will not be paying attention now. The boy across the aisle decided that his chair was too comfortable to resist. I have been watching his progression as he first slumped down, head resting on the back of his chair. As he tried to stay awake, his eyes slowly started closing and finally shut altogether. He's been sleeping for the past 15 minutes. I guess that was more entertaining than listening about the problems associated with heroin. The small gold clock on the wall has become a beacon for me and other students now. I look to it for hope of a quick end to the class, however improbable that might be. The minute hand reads twelve o'clock. The clock has started getting more attention than my professor. The students are becoming more and more restless as the clock ticks away the minutes, causing more attention to be taken away from my teacher and more attention towards the events happening after class.

5 Minutes to Go
When there are only five minutes to go, all the students become restless and only a handful still absorb what the teacher is trying to convey to us. The majority, however, are either starting to pack up their belongings or are still occupied in whatever has been entertaining them throughout class. My sister has begun a countdown of the minutes left till class ends; a 5-4-3-2-1-0 are written in small letters along the side of her page. She is slowly erasing each number as the tiny black second hand reaches the top and marks off another minute of class done. The boy sleeping across the aisle wakes up with a start. He jumps and then sits straight up. He looks around to make sure no one saw and then decides to sit back in his chair, giving up his search. A couple of girls behind him start giggling when they see him but he didn't spot them when he did his survey of the room. The girl reading the Collegiate Times, finished with the Sudoku now, has folded up the paper and laid it down into her bag. She now sits up and decides to try and make it through the last couple of minutes listening to the teacher. Maybe there are some important announcements that he'll skip to instead of the normal Power Point lecture. Undeniably, there are some students still paying attention but many are just paying attention to hear when they are dismissed.

3 Minutes to Go
Even at five minutes to go, there are still students sitting up straight listening intently at what the teacher is teaching. At three minutes to go, however, all of this is lost. Papers begin to shuffle as I hear almost the whole class, at the same time, filing away their notes for another class. My sister is intently staring at the three on her paper hoping somehow that her staring at it will magically make it become a zero and we can all leave to grab lunch. The teacher scans the room before realizing that most of the class has already packed up and is now just waiting for his go ahead to leave the room. Only a couple of people are still ready to take notes or even listening to him talking now. "Alright, I'll see you next Thursday." Class is ended.

Class is Over
Classes used to be about arriving and spending the time listening, taking notes, and focusing on the material. That has recently become a habit of the past for my Personal Health class. The days are gone when students have to pay attention to the

teacher. Whether the notes are online or taken from other students, class has become more about entertaining oneself to pass the time than trying to learn the information when it was first presented. Students become more and more apathetic and the information is becoming harder to convey. As the world moves closer to indifference we need to make a move towards more interaction in class and more interest in the information influencing our future careers.

Works Cited

Ben. Personal Interview. 20 Sep. 2006.
Kara. Personal Interview. 21 Sep. 2006.
Amanda. Personal Interview. 23 Sep. 2006.

EXERCISE

6.f Examining the Observation Report

1. Describe the rhetorical situation. What is the author's purpose? Who is her audience?

2. How could this paper's introduction be strengthened?

3. What do you think about the section headings? What do they contribute to your reading of the essay? What do they take away?

4. This paper is written in first-person point of view. What effect does that have on the reader? How would third-person point of view change your reading of the paper?

5. If the author was in your workshop group, what advice would you give her about her essay?

In the essay that follows, also written for Ms. Fallon's class, Virginia Tech student Michael Mauceri uses the same assignment to write a very different paper—one that also follows the assignment.

Instructor Katie Fallon with Michael Mauceri, an Architecture major at Virginia Tech.

Michael Mauceri
Instructor Katie Fallon
English 1106
23 September 2006

THE QUICK RIDE

The hum of the large engine rumbles along the street as Tom's Creek Blacksburg Transit takes off to the next check point. A few anxious students sigh in disbelief as they watch the greyhound look-alike bus soar off down the road. They would have reached the bus had it been a minute earlier since the BT always leaves on time. Most students who live off-campus need a form of free transportation in order to reach destinations such as campus. Throughout the day, Virginia Tech students dominate Tom's Creek BT. The bus provides a lending hand for students by supplying a free taxi to travel. The manners of students riding the bus change during the day when comparing the crowded moments of the afternoon to the calmness of the twilight hours. The talkative personality will find the urge to entertain and communicate while the reserved, soundless student chooses to listen and observe. Throughout different periods of the day, the characteristics of Tom's Creek BT influence the behaviors and actions of its various passengers.

Tom's Creek BT is unique not only by operating continuously, but also in the features that distinguish the vehicle from the original school buses. The bus runs a simple route circling the off-campus apartments from seven o'clock in the morning until nearly two o'clock the next day. There are nearly five Tom's Creek buses operating relentlessly amidst the day and night, separated by a mere ten minutes. Each BT bus can hold over fifty passengers; however, many bus drivers have to take the exception to stack in an extra five to ten students when afternoon hours pour out students from their classes. The BT bus is not the ordinary yellow banana every high school student can remember. The front windshield and grill is flat with large, bold text that is lit as a scoreboard, allowing a student to clearly recognize his or her bus from over fifty yards away. The seats inside the BT are bucket seats with soft, carpet-like covering that have a blend of red and grey. When a student enters the sliding door, a surprisingly nice area of space from side to side is noticed. Gigantic windows cover the side walls of the bus which are slightly tinted for a rider's convenience. The size of the windows can create a spacious feeling for the passengers by taking in more light. Students who begin to load up Tom's Creek BT after nine o'clock in the morning realize the perimeter seats are occupied. Therefore, the rounded, stainless steel railings become an essential support for students needing to stand. The railings are accommodated by helpful, plastic loops hanging above a traveler's shoulder. These loops act as a safety net for students holding tight as the bus comes to a sudden stop. The buses carry an extremely effective air-conditioning system positioned in the back.

6

The cool atmosphere provides passengers with a comfortable sense of room temperature that helps dealing with crowded packs of people. The features of Tom's Creek BT define a well-suited automobile for students seeking public transportation.

As the morning sun rises and early classes begin, the flow of students increasingly moves from the apartments to the bus stop. This popular area begins to overfill as girls and boys crowd the sidewalks with their backpacks and books in hand. Several students begin to chatter about the previous night's events while a solitary student anxiously flips open his cell phone to check the time for the bus's arrival. The echo of the bus's diesel engine is heard from around the corner of Patrick Henry Street, and most of the students begin to huddle around the part of the curb where they anticipate the bus door to open. Frantically, guys reach for their wallets to bring out their Hokie Passports which are used for free entry onto the bus. Many of the female students carry their passports in their purses, requiring a little more effort in showing the bus driver their identification as they dig through the female products overwhelming the purse. The bus drivers need to see the identification to prove a student's enrollment at Virginia Tech. However, students will observe a certain leniency as the bus drivers barely even look at their identification. The bus drivers have an embedded visual representation of these orange cards that allow students to quickly enter without really showing the details of their identification. With a mere glance, many bus drivers quickly click the green button tallying up each passenger as a student enters the bus. The bus stop represents a simple gathering of students who understand collectively that the amount of time to enter the bus will only require a split second.

The location of a student's apartment can influence the level of a person's patience for Tom's Creek BT. According to Ryan Holloway, a senior engineering student, "catching the bus is mostly a burden since I have to walk a long distance to my bus stop." Considering the stops for the BT are spread out on Patrick Henry Street, many of the students find themselves rushing to get to the nearest point in time. Holloway remarks, "It makes me mad when I rarely give myself enough time to get out a minute or two early from the apartment." He usually finds himself running in the trails of the bus as he watches the brake lights depart, knowing he missed the bus by thirty seconds. Despite Holloway's frustration with his location, he frequently demands the bus since he is "always saving money on gas" by using this form of public transportation.

Some students make an extra effort in reaching the bus on time because they cannot afford to miss a class. Keith Williams, a junior business major, states, "giving myself an extra five minutes to walk out to the bus stop allows me enough time to wait around for the bus rather than chasing it down." Williams uses the bus in order to get to his twelve o'clock classes. He assures these classes "require that everyone be there on time." He feels certain knowing that Tom's Creek BT brings him to his destination "always on time." Another assertive student, Amanda Kroll, needs to take the bus every day to get to her morning nine o'clock classes. She finds it crucial in being prepared to reach her bus stop twenty minutes before nine. Classes that require a student to arrive on time make a person such as Amanda eager to catch the bus without complaining. The students who find it necessary to make it to class promptly respect Tom's Creek BT as they acknowledge the bus's instant service.

Students clutter Tom's Creek buses by nine o'clock in the morning when campus is the main destination. As students pack together, some standing and others sitting, the entire bus feels weighed down. The face of every individual seems to be telling a similar story of how crammed one person can feel. Some passengers stare out the window, probably estimating how much longer the ride will be until they reach the ultimate relief. Many students attempt to study the last bit of information in their notebooks to pass the momentary ride. Then, there are the students drifting off into a slight nap as they have not yet awakened. These travelers, who seem to bobble their sleeping heads along the ride, are desperately hoping the trip will take them just a little further so they can keep their eyes closed.

The main stop on campus for the jammed, packed bus is at McBryde Hall. The routinely announced message plays consistent to an operator on the phone informing the riders that they are approaching McBryde Hall. The students begin to unclog the stuffed space, feeling release as they depart from the rear exit door. As the last student steps off the bus, a moment of silence and relief is witnessed by the bus driver. It is as if the load of the vehicle and the look of tired faces have caused the driver to drag the passengers all the way. The early morning rides are dominated with tired students, yet the arrival to campus sparks a little life for riders obligated to exit Tom's Creek BT.

As morning classes end, students scramble to catch the bus route back to the apartments.

Tom's Creek BT can be found in front of Burruss Hall and a second alternative route can be used next to Torgerson Hall. The buses begin to load up in the same crowded fashion of the morning routes. However, the environment and surroundings of the bus shine brighter as anxious students carry on more conversations with their neighbors than the silent morning ride. Many of the students feel that the same crowded place from the morning has become more tolerable as they can determine the short amount of time it will take to reach home. Students stand entirely too close for comfort, yet the shared realization that classes thus far have been completed ignites a sense of satisfaction.

The passengers begin to participate in the quick ride to their apartments. Within the first two minutes of the route home, the little yellow cord hanging as a clothes line is pulled by a student in the back. Immediately, the "stop requested" sign illuminates in red and the repeating message is heard from the speakers reminding the bus

6

driver that a stop has been requested. Several students turn their bodies and twirl their heads searching for the first person to depart. Being stuffed together, everyone feels linked. Immediate actions are taken collectively to move out of the way for a student trying to squeeze through to the exit door. Each stop has a time interval of about a minute, releasing more and more students. The spaces between people gradually increase and the last students standing seek nearby seats that have been evacuated. The student passengers who are left on the bus recognize the propaganda and advertisements along the top walls. Having fewer people and faces to observe, these signs such as PK's bar and grill and New Fitness Community Club become distractions for passengers trying to find something to contemplate. Eventually, a student reaches his or her stop and pulls the yellow cord in a gratifying manner. As a passenger departs from Tom's Creek BT, a round trip has been completed and a certain fulfillment has been reached by making it home safe and free of charge.

The evening hours bring a calmer atmosphere on the bus route of Tom's Creek BT. Most of the commuter students have finished their classes a few hours ago. The bus rides are mostly dominated by students who have night classes and non-student passengers such as customers from Kroger. Tom's Creek BT conveniently passes by Kroger shopping center which is also connected to the Math Emporium. At this time, the ride from campus moving towards Kroger rarely has a single passenger standing. The energy within the bus is less wired than the chaotic afternoon overwhelmed with students. An older man reads the newspaper as he awaits his stop further down the road, since the early stops include the student apartments. The evening conditions and surroundings inside the bus resemble a sort of peace as most of the passengers sit quietly. Some students who are sitting alone on the evening ride pass the short time by entertaining themselves with the contagious iPods. These sources of technology take away the quality of observing the bus at this hour. With the setting sun, the quick ride home is graceful and inspiring as many passengers ponder what has been accomplished in a day's work. The bus rides during the evening provide an escape for people to settle and reflect on the events of the day. With fewer passengers consuming most of the air, the twilight rides carry a lighter mood in which many travelers behave in a relaxing and insightful manner.

The passengers of the bus who are not student commuters make up a certain twist in the way people perceive and use the bus. Dean Ferguson, a Blacksburg resident for forty-three years, compares the bus to a "dependable tool" he has been using for years. He needs to take Tom's Creek BT to get some daily groceries "the wife demands." He enjoys taking the evening rides because "the afternoon rides are impossible to catch when students are packing the vehicle to the rim." Similar to many of the student commuters, Ferguson believes the afternoon situations are overwhelmingly congested. He finds the evening trip on the bus certainly "easier and less hectic," especially when he has more room to carry the groceries. Ferguson enjoys a lighter surrounding to effectively use Tom's Creek BT. He perceives the public place in a different way than most of the students who use the bus. He is not involved in the most crowded parts of the day; therefore, he can not relate to traveling shoulder to shoulder with someone he does not know.

Students riding the bus daily to campus contain various perceptions about the public surrounding. Kelly Harris, a sophomore commuter, views the bus ride as a time "when students really tend to keep to themselves since we really don't know anyone." The faces on the bus are always changing as new people choose to ride at different times. Keeping to themselves, a majority of the students riding the afternoon routes display timid qualities. Harris asserts, "Most of the students stare at one another, especially the guys and girls, yet hardly anything is ever said." The curiosity of each individual is always burning while the communication is rarely presented. The students may be missing out on an opportunity to meet someone new by riding Tom's Creek BT. Anthony Davis, a junior student, feels certain claustrophobia when catching the one o'clock bus to campus. Rarely finding a seat, Davis attempts to stand near the rear exit door "to be one of the first persons to get off the bus." The students who cannot stand riding cramped next to several bodies can feel restless and uncomfortable. Commuters such as Lindsey Jarrett feel "agitated" when they have to "breathe down one another's neck." Jarrett is bothered to share her space with a stranger who needs the bus for the same reasons. Many of the commuters witness different experiences aboard the bus.

An important reality of riding the bus involves significant differences in how students perceive Tom's Creek BT during the weather. Most sunny days bring out a heavier crowd of anxious students energized to reach their destination. When the weather is warm and humid, some passengers wave their notebooks as fans since the air conditioning is simply not enough. The most interesting trips involve how passengers act when it is raining. The bus becomes wet with water dripping from everyone's hair onto the floor. Conveniently, students are aware of the flooring to the bus which is surprisingly not slippery. The rigid floor of Tom's Creek BT is designed with vent-like levels which grip a passenger's shoes. It is interesting to witness how carefully every passenger maneuvers on the bus when they are wet. Their movements are carefully calculated to prevent from touching someone else who is soaked. Rainy days make many riders uneasy and anxious to get out of the saturated area. Cold mornings bring a unique quality to riding the bus. With Blacksburg's wind and chill, the bus provides a temporary source of warmth as the bus's heat is pleasing. Commuters rush to get on the bus as soon as they step out of their apartments on a chilly morning. With the cold conditions, the bus is appreciated in a special way as students step on the bus welcoming the immediate warmth. The weather influences passengers' reactions in how they approach the bus ride.

By the weekend, Tom's Creek BT becomes an entirely new form of transportation. Students no longer have to use the bus to reach their classes on time. The bus is now a vehicle used for traveling to parties and other apartments. With the bus, students can travel not only to campus but to their friend's house for free. The cars sit parked at the apartments and students rely on the bus for means of safe travel. The mood and atmosphere of Tom's Creek BT is highlighted by carefree voices and sociable attitudes. Saturday mornings bring an unmatched energy for Toms Creek BT as students happily join the ride to reach the football stadium. Orange and maroon blend the entire interior space of the bus as hats and shirts symbolize Virginia Tech. On Saturday nights, students such as Brandon Yates believe the bus provides many with a "designated driver" to travel legally and carefully. He says, "It is a great feeling to have a ride home when you need it late at night." The weekend periods provide a different reality for Tom's Creek BT compared to the campus travels of the weekdays.

The most experienced and proficient users of Tom's Creek BT include the bus drivers. Through their eyes, the ride is anything but short. Usually working five to six hour shifts, Daniel Smith thinks the bus route of Tom's Creek BT has become an "effortless routine." Working for two years as a bus operator of Tom's Creek BT, Smith finds the job fairly simple and relaxing. He remarks, "I find myself staring at my watch every five to ten minutes since timing is everything on the job." The bus drivers such as Smith make Tom's Creek BT incredibly dependable and reliant. "The afternoon shifts can be chaotic as I see all kinds of students crowding every stop." The bus drivers repeatedly encounter new students providing a little diversity for the working atmosphere. Smith enjoys the night hours as "the crowds have drifted away from the bus stops and I finally have some room up front without people hovering over my shoulder." Smith acknowledges that the students need the bus since many cannot afford to drive to school every day. He believes "Tom's Creek provides all students endless opportunities to get a ride to anywhere they wish." Smith says he picks up "familiar faces all the time," yet students rarely acknowledge him. It is typical to watch students casually pass the bus drivers without displaying a nod or smile. Smith understands several students feel "the bus is a continuation of school property and many would rather be somewhere else." Bus drivers of Tom's Creek BT are capable of observing the surroundings of the bus during a longer frame of time. Their direction and responsibility allows the bus to run.

Tom's Creek BT provides Virginia Tech students a quick and effective form of transportation. Student commuters use most of the routes throughout the periods of the day. These passengers are unique in the ways they behave and perceive the public place. Huddled together, shoulder to shoulder, some students cannot wait to escape while others stand patiently. The surroundings of Tom's Creek BT such as the weather and convenient interior features influence certain patterns in how students react and understand the public area. Many students share similar views and experiences when using the bus based upon the perspectives of people such as Kelly Harris, Anthony Davis, and Lindsey Jarrett. Several passengers share overwhelming feelings of congestion during the afternoon hours while single travelers such as Dean

Ferguson encounter calmer situations during the evening periods. The characteristics and realities of Tom's Creek BT are constant not only through the dependable timing of each ride but through the same bus drivers who operate the bus every day. Throughout the different periods of the day, numerous amounts of students use Tom's Creek BT expressing different opinions and behaviors. However, the riders of the bus demonstrate one continual belief that Tom's Creek BT is a place of necessity.

Works Cited

Davis, Anthony. Personal Interview. 15 September, 2006.

Ferguson, Dean. Personal Interview. 14 September, 2006.

Harris, Kelly. Personal Interview. 15 September, 2006.

Holloway, Ryan. Personal Interview. 12 September, 2006.

Jarrett, Lindsey. Personal Interview. 15 September, 2006.

Kroll, Amanda. Personal Interview. 18 September, 2006.

Smith, Daniel. Personal Interview. 21 September, 2006.

Williams, Keith. Personal Interview. 14 September, 2006.

Yates, Brandon. Personal Interview. 16 September, 2006

EXERCISE

6.g Using Interviews

1. Notice that each of the previous papers (Kristen's and Mike's) were written in the same class for the same assignment. Comment on the different ways each student approached the assignment.

2. How do the interviews contribute to this paper's analysis? Why do you think the author chose to include so many interviews?

3. What is gained by using third-person point of view? What is lost?

6.11 ■ "Library" Research Paper Example

In English 1106 you may be asked to write a research paper using only library and online resources. In the example below, students were asked to write a research paper that argues a perspective on an issue. Specifically, the assignment was to persuade an audience that the author's perspective on an issue was valid. The assignment required that the argument be supported by evidence found using the library and online resources.

6

Michael Mauceri
Instructor Katie Fallon
English 1106
15 November 2006

BALLPARKS

The crack of the bat sends a blast over the center field wall and the roaring crowd cheers with excitement. Over forty thousand fans scream with enthusiasm and relief as their team seals the win in the bottom of the ninth inning. One man turns towards his father with an overwhelming smile and thanks him for bringing him out to the ballpark today to witness this unparalleled flavor of entertainment. America's baseball stadiums have grown throughout the century and have earned the reputation of hosting "America's favorite pastime." The sport of major league baseball has developed in the nation's populous cities such as New York, Boston, and Chicago. These prominent cities have constructed and maintained the ballparks millions of fans flock to every year. The architectural designs, features, and surroundings of the thirty major league stadiums are inviting and offer a diverse sense of entertainment and enjoyment for all types of people. Evaluating the conditions that make baseball stadiums pleasing and attractive is essential in proving how more stadiums should be built in other American cities. States without ballparks can benefit from stadium additions when examining the positive realities a ballpark brings to a city.

Popular baseball stadiums throughout America such as Fenway Park in Boston and Yankee Stadium in New York City have flourished as the focal point for entertainment in the cities. These sites are attractive for the public based on the reputation of the winning teams. However, the baseball stadiums themselves are often indelible in their forms. The gigantic wall in Fenway Park offers an endless sense of imagination for the spectator. The small number of seats available in the park will surely sell out weeks ahead of time due to the town's commitment to pack the house for every game. Yankee Stadium, which was built in 1923, has evolved as the most prominent place of play for all of baseball (Smith 4). The stadium seats over fifty thousand people and has assured the fans of the city a place of valuable entertainment and success based upon a continual winning tradition. The monument park, which is decorated with golden plaques of historical players such as Babe Ruth and Mickey Mantle, is a breathtaking feature which makes the stadium even more captivating. The history of the stadium has captured the city and helped create a memorable feeling for the city's stadium. As Ira Rosen writes, "You cannot help but be awed by the majestic expanse, echoing greatness from decades past. No matter how often you walk through the gates, no matter where you sit, the feeling is there, thrilling yet humbling" (215). Yankee Stadium possesses a solid history of success and memorable moments of celebration many fans have experienced in the city's ballpark. Despite its popularity, the design and location of the ballpark has proven to have inadequate space for parking, chaotic traffic jams, and a surrounding area of high crime rates in the Bronx (Rosen 212). Utilizing the positive and negative realities of Yankee Stadium, America can construct new stadiums in other cities when analyzing how a stadium can lift the reputation of an area and how important it is to provide a safe means of access.

The thirty major league baseball stadiums are positioned sparsely throughout America, usually including the most populous states. These stadiums are commandingly present in northeastern states such as New York, Pennsylvania, Maryland, Ohio, Minnesota, Illinois, and Michigan. Other states such as Florida, Georgia, Texas, Arizona, and the most notorious state for stadiums, California, contain the remainder of the thirty ballparks. Midwestern states such as Wyoming, Idaho, North and South Dakota, and Montana lack a major league ballpark or even a minor league stadium (Noll and Zimbalist 114). Many southern states, including Louisiana, Arkansas, Mississippi, Alabama, South and North Carolina, Kentucky, Virginia and Tennessee, do not have a single major league ballpark (115). Many fans may suggest that thirty teams in major league baseball are more than enough. However, with the addition of nearly twenty other stadiums in the states without a ballpark, the popularity and demand of baseball would grow even more. The availability of ballparks in every state would allow fans to travel locally to their home stadium, and it would distributes baseball teams evenly throughout the nation. With stadiums in every state, the demand for professionals would increase, and the probability of turning pro would rise. It is certain that many will object to the proposition of constructing a ballpark in a scarcely populated state such as Montana. Regardless, it is possibly unfair for a major league ballpark to exist in Toronto, Canada when more than ten states in the United States do not include a professional baseball stadium.

A new wave of ballparks would most likely be subject to cost considerations and concerns. Some opponents may proclaim that a new stadium for a city will cost hundreds of millions of dollars of taxpayers' money. Accurately, based upon the latest stadium designs and developments such as Safeco Field in Seattle and Bank One Ballpark in Arizona, the costs of these projects exceed three hundred million per stadium (Rosen 17). These stadium designs do require hundreds of millions of dollars from mostly taxpayer money, due to the elaborate and excessive features of the stadiums. With highly decorated brick designs on the faces of the stadium, enormous steel girders supporting dome-like roof arrangements, limitless numbers of box seats, and a modernized style of expensive pillars surrounding a ball park, the costs of the new stadiums are overwhelming (15). However, evaluating the cost excessiveness of these stadiums through their advanced features will prove how new stadium designs can cost less by following traditional stadium layouts and still maintain the quality and beauty of a modern ball field. The millions of dollars of taxpayer money required for a new stadium in the other states can be avoided and cut drastically when the projects are modeled after famous ballparks such as Candlestick Park in San Francisco, Comiskey Park in Chicago, or Wrigley Field in Chicago, which each cost under a million dollars to build and renovate (204). The reputations of the cheap stadiums, ironically, are more popular and recognizable than the multi-million dollar stadiums in Seattle and Arizona. Wrigley Field is enriched by a simple design with ivy-covered walls and home-like garden fences surrounding the outfield bleachers. The field has been reno-vated and continues to be the least expensive baseball stadium amongst the thirty major league teams (204). Ira Rosen states, "For its combination of beauty, intimacy, and ambience, Wrigley stands out in a league of its own. Pubs, bookstores, and cloth-ing boutiques make this area of the big city the funkiest, most livable ballpark neigh-borhood in any major-league city" (203). The surroundings of this inspiring, simple ballpark bring the city's commitment to the field together as baseball develops as a way of life in the local downtown areas. New stadiums needed in states without a field can imitate Wrigley Field's inexpensive seating layout of fewer than forty thou-sand occupants and its elimination of the fancy glass-sheltered box seats which spoils the purity of having all outdoor seats.

The new stadiums that could be designed and constructed throughout the remaining states should mimic the open, outdoor style for a ballpark. The dome or covered roofs should not be considered for the new stadium additions throughout the country due to complex features that are expensive. An outrageously expensive example of a dome stadium is present in Montreal, Quebec, where Olympic Stadium is located (Smith 384). The features of this stadium include a retractable roof, carpet-styled turf, and seating positioned at heights difficult to view the game, and clearly present a ballpark trying to combine too many features (384-385). Some fans may argue that dome stadiums provide an exact sense of space which some people possi-bly enjoy. Nevertheless, the surroundings in Olympic Stadium diminish the meaning-ful themes that are special in traditional ballparks such as the inspiring sunshine and the rainy days which make the game unpredictable. The older-fashioned ballparks place simple settings in front of the crowds such as well-kept grass lines and sand that have been used by historic players throughout the decades. As Neil Sullivan illus-trates, "The old parks are vital to the middle-aged fan's memories because the parts are so distinctive. If we followed a club in those years, we can easily bring them to mind today because its field of play was so striking" (75). The ballparks that are used for the past fifty years such as Wrigley Field and Fenway Park have displayed a sense of familiarity and understanding throughout their small parameters. The surroundings that are present in the older ballparks need to be incorporated in the new designs that can be established in other cities. Their physical features are not extravagant or overwhelmingly advanced, rather it's the simplicity involved with ivy-coated walls and waste-basket fence lines that catch the balls above the wall. This simplicity mirrors the naturalness of the game of baseball and helps the city's fans relate to the stadiums with ease. Adversaries of older stadium designs can commit to expensive dome-like layouts to satisfy their uniform, sheltered intentions. The idea of a dome demonstrates a lack of creativity and imagination that overshadows the playing field and the ideals that are present in older stadiums.

The physical presence of a ballpark within a city enhances the flow of an urban area by drawing audiences in to the stadium. The growth of a city such as Cincinnati has radiated around Riverfront Stadium, which is located in the center or heart of the city (Shannon and Kalinsky 9). Neighborhoods can form in the midst of a city as people welcome an inner-city ballpark down the street from their homes. If stadiums are constructed in the middle of a city, key public transportation will be available and organized for fans. Likewise, ballparks located in the center of a city can serve as an easy indicator when traveling from any direction. When a stadium is built in a city, the possibility of a baseball community can penetrate through the neighborhoods. A sense of unity and tradition can form collectively as a whole if a ballpark exists in the heart of a city. Bringing traditional ballpark stadiums in states without ballparks can revitalize a city's development as people begin to live in a unified style, happy to be part of a baseball community.

Introducing stadium projects into states without fields can provide a fulfilling atmosphere in a city. The very presence of a stadium symbolizes a vision of unlimited possibilities within its walls. Observers understand how continual baseball games take place inside a ball park; yet, the situations that occur are always diverse, entertaining, and desirable for fans. "The shape of the playing area, spreading outward from home plate, suggests our ability to break out of the restraints of modern life, find a gap, and keep rolling forever" (Puhalla, Krans, and Goatley 11). The nature of the game expresses the fans' desire to be surprised and delighted by coming to the ballpark and rooting for their home team in an amazing surrounding. Audiences that come to any stadium can witness a feeling of excitement and amazement as they approach a ballpark. As one enters a ballpark, a sense of immensity can pump through a person's veins as they approach their seats and view the magnificent scenery of the field. The atmosphere brings confidence, anxiety, and a joyful taste of hope as fans await the opening pitch.

A stadium can be spectacular for a city and earn a valuable reputation for containing memorable circumstances within its walls. The experiences remembered in a single game at a professional stadium can last a lifetime for both the fan and player. Professional ballplayer Rich Delucia describes a moment entering Veterans Stadium in Philadelphia: "I walked down a dark tunnel and then came out and it was all light. That was a really neat feeling, and I guess that's the way in any stadium, it's kind of dark inside a tunnel, and then boom, you go in and it's like a big cathedral outside" (qtd. in Rosen 199). Rich Delucia compares his experience of Veterans Stadium to a cathedral which symbolizes a deep appreciation for this immense surrounding that

6

illuminates a ballpark. Stadiums provide situations that audiences willingly pay to experience and witness. Scattered across an immense green surface, players can be pinpointed with ease as a viewer observes and idolizes every slight move of a ballplayer (Angell 25). A baseball stadium supplies a scene of isolated players in which audiences pay attention to their favorite player and approve with admiration. The vividness that is maintained in baseball stadiums creates dynamic, memorable structures within a city. People from every state would be able to relate to a home stadium if every state contained a ballpark. The joy of competition which fuels the economy and culture of the country is overwhelmingly present in baseball stadiums. This spirit of competition that heightens a stadium is created by the fans and players. If stadiums are added to other American cities, the same spirit that lives in a ballpark can filter through nearby city surroundings.

Constructing a baseball stadium in states without ballparks will add a significant timeless dimension to a city. Since only a baseball game can be played inside a stadium, this new structure in a city provides scenes that are not measured by time. The game follows innings rather than hours and seconds. As Roger Angell explains, "Since baseball time is measured only in outs, all you have to do is succeed utterly; keep hitting, keep the rally alive, and you have defeated time. You remain forever young. Sitting in the stands, we sense this" (31). The significance of a timeless surrounding allows people of a city to enjoy this place of everlasting moments outside of a world that moves so quickly. This timeless existence adds a powerful aspect to a city by having a great building where time does not define the event taking place.

Opponents to new stadiums in states lacking fields might believe that the thirty stadiums in existence are enough for America. Where is the parity for the country and the sport of baseball if only the populous states contain stadiums in their major cities? States without ballparks should contain the same attractive and inviting sources of entertainment that these thirty stadiums demonstrate in cities. The sight of a beautiful ballpark can create confidence and meaning for a city and state. By balancing the number of baseball stadiums evenly throughout America, every state will contain a special aspect of creativity and tradition through its ballparks. Opponents are blind to the possibility of bringing new fans into the sport of baseball by building a stadium in their own home states. The first encounter with a major league ballpark can emotionally lift a person and open his or her mind to a different beginning of entertainment.

"It's capturing the wonderful memory of seeing a major league baseball stadium for the first time—emerging from the ramp into the brilliant sunshine, the vast expanse of green grass lined so carefully with white chalk; seeing the thousands of people, the scoreboard, the dugouts, the players. These are indelible images" (Rosen 9). People who have never been to a ballpark will embrace this boundless atmosphere, sparking a lifetime of memories.

Stadium additions to a city will provide not only memorable ball games but also other means of enjoyment and entertainment. These spectacular structures provide several sources of food and souvenir venders for the fans. The classic ballpark Comiskey Park is memorable for its former ideal surroundings: "Part of its charm is the culinary fare. There were none better than at Old Comiskey. On field level behind home plate a cook stood over a sizzling barbecue grill, sweat pouring down from under a huge chef's hat, grilling burgers, steaks, and hot dogs to perfection" (Rosen 42). Despite being replaced by Wrigley Field in Chicago, Comiskey Park magnified the adventure and enjoyment of a ball park with great foods made available to the fans throughout the entirety of the game. Concession stands and souvenir shops help enhance the memorable journey to a ballpark as people savor every bite and every dollar spent. Special features present in a stadium can also attract people to the ballparks in a city. It is exciting to witness a real-life classical train run across the top of left field wall at Enron Field in Houston when a homerun is hit by the home team! (80) The train serves as this sort of prize or present for the fans in an act of celebration for a homerun. Another inviting feature of a present major league field is the waterfalls located behind center field at Kauffman Stadium in Kansas City. This cascade of water is very pleasing and magical for an audience to witness during ball games. Ira Rosen states, "Spanning the distance from center field to right field, the waterfall measures 322 feet across and is said to be the world's largest privately funded fountain. The water spouts high into the air, an effect that is even more spectacular at night, when the falls are backlit by a multicolored display. There is nothing else quite like it in baseball" (102). The fans who come to the ballpark are amused by the presence of this magnificent feature. Ballparks provide more than just a baseball game; special features and food act as appealing accessories captivating audiences.

Some people may persist to add stadiums in states without ballparks in areas distant from a state's major city. These areas may include rural lands or regions virtually in the middle of nowhere. This rural setting proposal complicates the realistic chance of bringing success to a ballpark given these isolated sites (Smith 436). Stadium additions should be constructed in the cities of a state because more people will have a sense of connection with the ballparks rather than the limited number of people living in rural areas of a state. Bringing new stadiums into the cities of states lacking ballparks can easily attract people to the location. Cities could think highly of themselves by containing an exceptional, entertaining facility that only exists in one state. It is more difficult to have people pay attention and attend to a place that is located far away from a familiar city. Stadium additions constructed in cities can easily be recognized and sighted if they are positioned in an urban surrounding.

The features of a stadium and the experiences of the fans bring a ballpark to life. Ballparks contain a timeless dimension that provides an escape from our daily lives. The memories that are created in these spacious structures are unforgettable.

6

Adding stadiums to states without ballparks can be extremely beneficial for a city. Stadiums become part of a city's culture, revitalizing neighborhoods and communities. Audiences that visit their home stadiums form a connection between other fans based on the intimacy that a stadium surrounding creates. The bright blue sky and perfect green grass provide an irreversible sight of beauty within a ballpark. Constructing new stadiums in states without fields can be achieved cheaply by following the simple designs of the classical ballparks such as Wrigley Field. Following simple stadium creations such as Wrigley Field brings the purity and naturalness of baseball together as fans can easily relate to a ballpark containing the charm of ivy-coated walls and old-fashioned scoreboards. The simple ideas and designs of this world are the best and most durable parts of life. Bringing ballparks to every state in America will intensify the entertainment of a city and help provide a bit of fun and fulfillment for anyone willing to witness a ball game.

Works Cited

Angell, Roger. *This Great Game*. New York: Prentice-Hall, Inc., 1971.

Noll, Roger N., and Andrew Zimbalist. *Sports, Jobs, and Taxes: The Economic Impact of Sports Teams and Stadiums*. Washington: The Brookings Institution, 1997.

Puhalla, Jim, Jeff Krans, and Mike Goatley. *Baseball and Softball Fields: Design, Construction, Renovation, and Maintenance*. New Jersey: John Wiley and Sons, Inc., 2003.

Rosen, Ira. *Blue Skies Green Fields: A Celebration of 50 Major League Baseball Stadiums*. New York: Clarkson Potter, 2001.

Shannon, Bill, and George Kalinsky. *The Ballparks*. New York: Hawthorn Books, Inc., 1975.

Smith, Curt. *Storied Stadiums: Baseball's History Through Its Ballparks*. New York: Carroll and Graf Publishers, 2001.

EXERCISE

6.h Reading for Rhetorical Appeal

1. Describe the rhetorical situation. What point is the author arguing? Who is the audience for this argument? How would you describe the tone of this essay? How would you describe the point of view?

2. How does the author use logos, pathos, and ethos to appeal to his audience?

3. Where and how does the author address opposition to his argument?

4. Can you suggest another title for this essay?

5. What kinds of sources does the author use? Where might he look for additional sources? Does the author correctly cite his sources?

For a useful tutorial on how to cite and find sources using a database, please visit
www.ablongman.com/faigley211

To hear audio commentary on an annotated bibliography, please visit
www.ablongman.com/faigley212

To hear audio commentary on a sample informative research paper, please visit www.ablongman.com/faigley215

6.12 ■ Further Exercises for Exploring Writing from Research

EXERCISES

1. Find two legitimate or acceptable web sites and two that are neither for the topic you are researching. Write down the URLs, summarize the sites, and evaluate them, explaining why they will or won't work as good sources.

2. Use a database from the VT library and Addison to find two magazine or journal articles and two books on a topic you are researching. Explain the steps you took to find the sources.

3. Devise 10 interview questions you might ask someone about a topic you are researching.

4. Create a 10-question survey about a topic you are researching.

5. Look at the list of texts below and mark each as P (primary) or S (secondary) source.

   Waking Life (film)

   "Three Injured in Accident on Route 11"

   Freud for Dummies

   The Master: A Biography of Henry James

   An interview with Clint Eastwood

   Romeo and Juliet

6

PART IV

Visual Literacy and Oral Presentation

7

Visual Literacy

Ours is a world saturated with images. We read them every day without much thought. The visual — whether it is advertising, painting, film, photography, television, charts and graphs, or street signs — has become an increasingly important means of communication as globalization and digital technology continue to change the ways messages of all sorts are conveyed and received. That is why a primary goal of the first-year composition program — and of Virginia Tech — is to make you comfortable with and adept at working with a variety of texts, including visual texts.

7.1 ▌ Reading Your World Visually

In this chapter you will have an opportunity to work with several different kinds of visuals—photography, graphic design, film, advertising, and visual representations of information (charts, diagrams, etc.). To begin, consider the photograph below.

7

EXERCISE	**7.a Visual Expectations**

Before you read the photographer's statement about this image, look carefully at the photograph and answer the following questions.

1. Write down your first impression of this image. What do you think the men are doing? What makes you think that? Be specific.

2. What, if anything, (works of art, posters, murals, cd covers, etc.) does this photograph remind you of? Why?

3. How would you describe this image?

■ *The Photographer's Statement*

This image still haunts me. I was asked to photograph the marines of Delta Company, 4th LAR by their commander, Major Benjamin Busch, a good friend of mine. The marines were in the last stages of preparation for deployment to Iraq just prior to the start of the war in March 2003. There had been a frenzy of activity over the previous few days as the marines got down to business packing supplies and testing equipment. There were live firing practices and yards of paperwork. I took this photograph at the end of a long hard day where the marines trained in the snow. I returned to base to find some of the men filling in their paperwork. They were signing their wills and power of attorney forms. I took this shot very quickly, framing the men against the curve of the Quonset hut's wall. I was struck simply by the fact that these men were about to go to war and were filling in forms that would only be used in the event of their deaths. Many people first guess that the photograph shows a religious ceremony. They are unsettled when they find out the true story. In a sense, though, it is a religious ceremony.

EXERCISE | **7.b Looking Twice**

How does the photographer's statement change your initial response to the photograph? How does the added information shape the way you see the photo?

Below is a photograph of actor/director Benjamin Busch (*The Distance, Homicide: Life on the Streets, The Wire*) and his new-born daughter, Alexandra. Obviously, the more we know about

7

the people in a photograph or the circumstances under which it was taken, the more that knowledge shapes our response. How a photograph is used and where it appears will also influence the way an image is read. Look carefully at the close-up of Busch and his daughter. Now, with a group of your classmates or on your own, work through the exercise that follows.

EXERCISE

7.c Responding to Photos

1. What does this photograph of Benjamin Busch and his daughter make you think about? Why? Be specific.

2. As a photograph of a father with his infant daughter, this is clearly a touching image. What if this same photo were used in a new context? Create an advertising campaign using this photograph. Brainstorm with your classmates and write down at least three possible examples of appropriate products for an image like this one.

3. Choose one of your examples and create slogans and ad copy to complement the image. Present your ad campaign to the class.

Often, the way we respond to an image depends on our experience, the way the image is composed and lit, and what we know about the subject of the photo. If a photograph is part of a news story, the captions guide our reading. Camera angle, frame, and focus all influence the way we read any photograph. If the subject of the photograph is a famous person, our impressions of that person will also affect our reading.

When you are reading any image, the most important context is you. Everything about you—your age, gender, ethnicity, religion, family history, psychological makeup, political beliefs, and even your current mood determines how you respond to visual texts. Reading visually, like all reading, depends both on the subject being viewed and the viewer. Your feelings toward the war in Iraq, for example, will likely color how you respond to the photograph of the marines signing their wills. If you studied art history, you might see shades of Rembrandt in the lighting and composition. If someone close to you is serving in the military, you may be inspired by the marines' bravery and sense of service. You might think all or none of the above. Whatever the case, you always need to consider how you also contribute to meaning. We call this "reader participation."

EXERCISE

7.d The Images You Choose

Choose an image you have hanging on your wall or one that you have always liked—a poster, a painting, a photo, etc.—and write briefly about why you chose that image, what it means to you, what it reminds you of, or what associations you bring to it.

For more information on analyzing visual texts, see *The Brief Penguin Handbook,* Chapter 6, section e, and Chapter 7. Also, refer to the Composition Companion Website: www.pearsoncustom.com/vt_composition.

7.2 Visual Rhetoric — Design and Composition

You are probably used to encountering rhetoric in its more traditional forms — speaking and writing. For example, it is easy to *hear* an emphasis on certain words, or a change in voice in the speeches of politicians. It is easy to *see* rhetorical moves in body language (a speaker pointing sharply at the audience or bowing her head humbly), and it is often easy to *understand* a writer's rhetorical position as you read editorial pages and web logs. It is even obvious in much advertising that the picture conveys most of the rhetorical force of the sell. The message might not be as clear, however, in a painting, the design of a fast-food restaurant, a pie chart, or a family photograph. Yet these images, like all visuals, do carry rhetorical force.

Visual rhetoric might sound complicated, but it is actually just a formal term for something very simple: *the way the visual communicates meaning.* Meaning is communicated both in *the look* of the visual — what we call *graphic design* — and in *cultural codes* that allow readers to draw on what is familiar to them to make sense of what they see.

Graphic Design

When you bring color, images, and font choices together into a cohesive whole, you are starting to talk about design. You don't have to be a graphic artist to read the design of a visual image. Look for what draws the eye or captures the attention. In a shampoo ad, for example, what do you see first — the bottle of the product itself in the upper left corner or, in the bottom right, the semi-nude person laughing in sheer delight, head covered with shampoo bubbles, beneath a waterfall in an exotic landscape? What receives emphasis in the ad — the product or the sex appeal the ad promises the product will deliver? Is any word printed in larger or bolder or more eye-catching type? What is the interplay between image and text?

These are some of the details you'll need to pay attention to when you consider design. The list of terms below is not exhaustive, but it will provide a solid start as you think about how design contributes to meaning.

Color: Whether or not you have studied color for its symbolic significance, in the west we have become attuned culturally to certain traditional interpretations: **red** means danger (or, "pay attention!"); **black,** mystery; **white,** innocence; **purple,** royalty; and so on. Graphic designers routinely use color to reinforce meaning. For example, the Fall edition of any popular clothing catalog will rely on a color scheme that emphasizes oranges, golds, and browns — autumn colors. Similarly, the cover of the December edition of *Martha Stewart Living* probably features reds, greens, and other traditional "heartwarming" holiday colors.

Colors also lend images an emotional resonance. What are your associations with each? How, for example, would the mood of a landscape painting change if a light blue sky were darkened? What if, instead of wearing a black tuxedo to the Academy Awards, an actor chose bright yellow, instead?

The point is that we read colors in the same way we read other metaphors and symbols. We attach a meaning to them. That meaning is not always apparent and it might not always be the most important element of the visual, but it is one detail you should take into consideration when you read visuals. Look, for example, at the colors below. What meaning or mood do you typically attach to each?

Of course, even color is culturally coded. Where most U.S. Americans would identify white as the color of a bride's dress, in some other countries white is a symbol of mourning and would be more appropriate at a funeral service.

The associations we make with color are like all meaning: They depend on context and culture.

Fonts: Although it is easy and reasonable to consider written text one kind of message and visual another, it is also the case that written text is visual. The very look of the words — font style, size, and color — also contributes to the way a reader receives a text. Fonts can be formal or informal, futuristic or old-fashioned, happy or sad, even male or female. Beyond that, however, the font you choose can actually tell the viewer much about whether you — and therefore the message you are trying to impart — can be trusted.

Consider the fonts reprinted here. Which would you use in a formal invitation? A sign for a barbeque restaurant? A party announcement? Even when you choose a font style for the papers you write for college, you are sending a message about how you want that essay to be received.

Edwardian Script   Curlz MT

Braggadocio   BURNSTOWN DAM

Images: Although an advertisement, a magazine cover, or a book jacket is a visual in and of itself, when we use the term *images,* we generally mean photos, paintings, clip-art, drawings, diagrams, graphs, charts, and such. Like written text, images can also be read in terms of organization, focus, and point of view. Also, like font choices, the type of visual you choose to include says much about how you want your message to be received and who your audience is. Because of its general resemblance to cartoon drawings, much clip art, for example, is best saved for use in informal documents. Diagrams, graphs, and charts are common in technical documents, research essays, and news stories when the writer wants to visually present key facts, trends, or statistics, for example. Black-and-white photos often signify realism, documentary realism, or nostalgia. Pay attention, then, to what kind of an image it is and where you expect to see that kind of image.

White Space: While color and font are key elements of graphic design, the use of white space — what isn't there — can be just as crucial to conveying tone. Generally speaking, the more white space, the more formal, elegant, or upscale a design appears. Compare, for example, an ad for a very high-end product like *Rolex* watches in the *New Yorker* with an ad for *Swatch* watches in *Seventeen Magazine.*

Layout: Layout refers to how the elements of your message — words, pictures, shapes, etc. — are arranged on the page. An image that bleeds off the page (printed so that the edges of the pictures extend beyond the page) sends a very different message than one that is framed and carefully centered, for example.

EXERCISE **7.e Paying Attention to Design**

Choose a print ad currently running in popular magazines. Bring that ad to class with you for a discussion of the elements of visual design and how they contribute to the ad's message. Before class, write a brief explanation of how the ad works — how it attempts to persuade its audience. In preparation for your writing, study the ad carefully and take notes on the elements of graphic design we have outlined in this chapter.

EXERCISE **7.f Analyzing a Web Design**

Look carefully at the screenshot of the Virginia Tech Writing Center home page reprinted on the next page, or you can visit the site at http://www.composition.english.vt.edu/wc.

1. What is your first impression when you look at this site? What do you expect to see when you normally visit a university website? Does this site conform to or break with that expectation? In what ways?

2. Notice the font choices, layout, and color scheme for the site. What impression does the site designer convey about the Center with those choices?

3. One of the most important visual elements of a website is how well the design actually functions. Visit the site online and, after you have studied it, write a one-page report that answers the following questions:

   ▪ What does the Writing Center do?

   ▪ How do you get an appointment?

   ▪ Who can use the Center?

   ▪ Where is the Center?

   ▪ How easy is it to find that information from the design of this page?

   ▪ How and why might you re-design the page?

7

EXERCISE	**7.g Design and Audience**

Look carefully at the two wedding invitations reprinted below.

How does the design of each invitation convey personality or tone? What would you expect from each of these weddings? Why?

The photograph reprinted here is of jazz pianist Monty Alexander. It is a still photograph, yet the blurring gives it a sense of motion. One way of paying attention to design is to break down the details to isolate the key elements of the image.

Monty Alexander's expression draws our attention to his fingers on the keyboard. The white line of the piano keys and the face of his watch also draw our attention to the bottom left corner.

Vertical and horizontal lines play against the diagonal lines of the guitarist and keyboard.

The shirt's warm color complements the background.

7

The photographer used a longer than normal exposure with a single flash to capture the image in the XM Radio studio in Washington, DC. The flash froze one moment, whilst the longer exposure caught the movement of the pianist's whole body, especially his hands, lending them a ghostly quality.

EXERCISE

7.h Lines and Colors

1. Look carefully at the photograph below of jazz musician Tord Gustavsen. What does the photo seem to be about? How do the lines formed by the building and the lamppost contribute to the meaning? What is the effect of the man leaning against a tall building, head down, photographed at a distance? How does the predominant color contribute to meaning?

2. Find a photograph or poster that you consider interesting or exciting or beautiful because of its design. Use our example of the Monty Alexander photo to create a design diagram of your own pointing to specific design elements that are important in the look of the image.

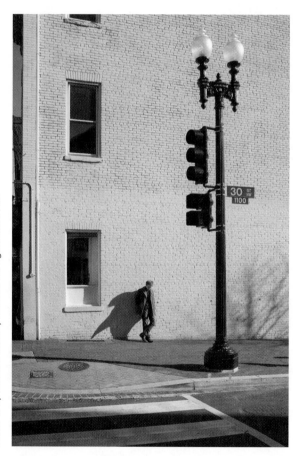

■ Visual Rhetoric— Composition

We have already introduced you to the term *layout.* That term to describe the arrangement of elements on a page usually refers to print or digital design. The layout editor of a newspaper, for example, determines how the paper will look—where photos will appear, the size of headlines, etc. When we talk about arrangement in pictures—either moving or still—we normally use the term *composition.* Even when a photographer or filmmaker is looking through the lens, composition is beginning to take place. How the image is framed (what is left in; what is left out); how the image is focused (and what is in the background), the distance of the figure to the camera—all of these constitute composition.

For more on visual rhetoric, see *The Brief Penguin Handbook,* Chapters 1 and 2. Also, refer to the Composition Companion Website: www.pearsoncustom.com/vt_composition.

EXERCISE | **7.i Reading the Visual Message**

All three of the photographs printed here of musician Branford Marsalis appeared in the magazine *Jazz Times*. Which one would you have put on the cover? Why? Where would you put the name of the magazine? The article titles? How do these three photographs reflect a different part of the subject's personality? How does the cropped image change our perception of the subject's face?

7.3 ■ Writing About the Image

Of course, design and composition alone do not constitute the meaning of a visual. When we are looking at pictures—family photos, for example—the design hardly accounts for what we see, how it makes us feel, and what it means to us. To understand more fully how visuals communicate meaning, you will have to think about what kind of an image it is, where it appears, what function it is meant to perform, what cultural norms or codes it draws on, how it was produced, the history of its form, and more.

In the section that follows, we take you through some of the steps of writing about photography, film—two types of visuals you are often asked to consider in college classes and that are common in your own experience.

■ *What's in a Picture? Reading Photography*

Ever since 1900 when Kodak introduced the Brownie—a small, easy-to-use snapshot camera that sold for $1—photographs have been a part of our lives. After all, anyone could suddenly do what it had taken a professional with large, heavy, expensive equipment to do. People took photos of just about anything that struck them, but they especially took photos of each other.

That is even more true today with the onset of digital imaging. Our cell phones have cameras in them. Our laptops are equipped with virtual photo booths. It doesn't take an expert today

to send a photo through email, use a photo manipulation program, or create greeting cards from the photos of our favorite people and places.

Take, for example, the photograph reprinted here. It was taken in October 2001, in Michigan's Upper Peninsula. This photo has been framed and placed on a shelf, used as a desktop wallpaper, and turned into a holiday greeting card.

What might a reader say about a photograph like this one? Virginia Tech instructor Jennifer Mooney began her writing by noting details that seemed important to her:

Placement of the figures in the middle of the composition and the calmness of their progress suggest control over the event. The forward, leisurely pace of their walk (notice the man's arms swinging gently at his sides) suggests that they are neither lost nor hurrying. This onward journey suggests hope and resiliency.

The scene's monochromatic colors (bright white and dark browns and blacks) and the muted colors of the man's clothing focus attention on the true subject of the shot: the pup, whose orange coat dominates the composition. As a result, we see the photo as being about the pup's relationship to the man.

The snowy landscape creates a cold, imposing scene. The jaggedness of the surrounding vegetation seems forbidding. However, the presence of the man and the pup shifts the connotations of the scene toward peace, happiness, and even warmth.

The proximity of the pup to the man suggests loyalty and affection. The pup is neither running ahead nor off on its own. Instead, it is barely a step behind, keeping up with its friend even in deep snow. Moreover, the pup's attention is focused on the figure in front of him, which also connotes loyalty and trust.

7

After Ms. Mooney had made her notes, she wrote the following brief analysis:

Visually, the snowy landscape creates a cold, imposing scene. The snow is deep, and the jaggedness of the surrounding vegetation seems forbidding. However, the presence of the man and the pup shifts the connotations of the scene toward peace, happiness, and even warmth.

Placement of the figures in the middle of the composition and the calmness of their progress suggest control over the event. The forward, leisurely pace of their walk (notice the man's arms swinging gently at his sides) suggests that they are neither lost nor fleeing. Literally in the middle of the shot, they are also in the middle of their walk, neither just beginning it nor retreating from it. This onward journey suggests hope and resiliency.

The somewhat monochromatic colors of the scenery (bright white and dark browns and blacks) and the muted colors of the man's clothing focus the eye of the viewer on the true subject of the shot: the pup, whose orange coat makes him dominate the composition.

The proximity of the pup to the man suggests loyalty and affection. The pup is neither running off on its own nor ahead of the man. Instead, it is barely a step behind, keeping up with its friend even in deep snow. Moreover, the pup's attention does not wander but is focused directly on the figure in front of him, which also connotes loyalty.

Notice that Ms. Mooney's analysis begins with formal features—the composition, color, subject—of the photograph and then moves to what the picture conveys: a sense of loyalty and affection.

There are other ways of writing about this same photograph, however. Professor Diana George, who took the photo of her dog Luca walking in the Michigan woods with her husband, wrote her own reflection:

I loved this picture from the second I saw it through the lens. Luca was barely three months old and really too small for the deep snow. He adored Chuck and would have followed him anywhere.

Look at how his ears are cocked and how determined he is to stay close on Chuck's heels even though he is up to his belly in new snow that would soon weigh him down.

Chuck didn't want another dog after our thirteen-year-old Golden Retriever died. He tried to ignore this new puppy who in turn ignored Chuck's disdain.

When I've taken other pictures of Luca (he's grown to an 80-pound, tall and lean Golden) the person in the picture with him is touching him, distracted by his affection.

Chuck, though, always walked straight ahead not looking back at him, and Luca, unfazed, fell right into place where he belonged in typical dog pecking order—right behind the leader.

EXERCISE

7.j Reflection and Analysis

Reread the two responses to this photograph. What does the analysis tell you that the reflection does not? How does the photographer's reflection differ from the analysis?

EXERCISE

7.k Images that Touch Our Lives

Read the following reflection written by first-year Virginia Tech student Christy Perry for H1204 in the Fall 2006 term. When you have finished, discuss with a group of your classmates what the image means to the writer and how she structures her reflection to move from a simple discussion of the photograph to the point she really wants to make. (*See Chapter 3 on reflection to read the original assignment.*)

Christy Perry is a Biology major at Virginia Tech.

Christy Perry
Instructor: Jennifer Mooney
English 1204H
September 10, 2006

A PICTURE WORTH 1,454 WORDS

For me it was right around the age of thirteen when I really started to get interested in photographs. Like most teenage girls, I covered the walls of my room with pictures of family and friends. In many ways, my picture-covered walls acted as a security blanket when my "typical teenage girl insecurities" decided to make a visit. As I got a little older, I became more selective with the pictures I allowed to hang on my wall. The newer ones had to meet stringent requirements: they had to possess deep meaning, had to be full of emotion, and had to be worth a minimum of a thousand words. Finding pictures worthy of my wall was a timely process, requiring hours of flipping through my mother's photo albums. Flipping through the albums over and over again allowed me to see things I had not seen the first time, though. However, there was always one photograph that always earned a second glance: a picture of my grandmother holding my brother, Mikey, asleep on her lap. The beauty of the picture was so stunning it consistently made me think, "If only I had a picture of Grandma and me as magnificent as this one." There were even times I envied the fact that my brother had been the one in my grandmother's lap that day. Perhaps if I had sat on her lap that day, I would have fallen asleep and this beautiful picture would have been of Grandma and me instead of Grandma and my brother, who couldn't care less about old family photographs. It just never seemed fair, until a few years ago when I realized the true meaning of the photograph, a moment of reflection that caused all envious thoughts to disappear.

This photograph clearly displays my grandmother's love for her grandson, making it very easy for one to make the mistake of calling it a "happy" picture. For years I made the mistake of assuming it was indeed taken in a "happy" environment until I

realized two things about the photo that I had never noticed before. One was the age of my brother, who looks to be about four or five years old, and second was recognition of the object in the top corner of the picture: an IV bag. After realizing that this picture must have been taken at the hospital in the final days of my grandfather's life, I could not help but view it with a completely new perspective.

While I can remember some very specific details from this time period, I have no recollection of this picture being taken. I remember I was six and just starting to read books with chapters. After waiting hours for Grandpa to wake up, Grandma would put me on Grandpa's left side, the side of his body that had become paralyzed from the brain tumor operation, so I could read to him. I never got that far in the book because there was seldom a period of twenty minutes when a nurse wouldn't have to interrupt to do some kind of medical check. Being so young, I did not grasp the gravity of the situation and liked the fact that we were visiting Grandma and Grandpa every weekend. Who cared if it smelled funny? I simply liked being there with Grandma and Grandpa, so I never was able to understand why Mom and Dad seemed to be having such an awful time.

Even better than my memory is this picture, which says so much about the time period of my grandfather's death, as well as the role of women in my family during a crisis. My grandmother resembles the ultimate woman in this picture, perhaps even Mary by the way that she is sitting with a young boy cradled in her arms. Grandma is not sad in this picture. In fact she looks almost happy. But how can this be when her husband is lying on his death bed? The caring and motherly quality inherent in most women caused my grandmother to put herself after us kids and make sure that our needs were met before hers. Grandma had to be as, if not more, exhausted than Mikey, yet she let her young, high-energy grandson take a nap instead of taking one herself.

Interestingly, the absence of other women in this photograph helps describe their roles. That day at least six people were at the hospital: Grandma, Grandpa, Mom, Dad, Mikey and me. I know where Grandpa was, as well as Grandma and Mikey, but where are the others? Dad was probably off getting food from the dining hall or some kind of "manly" task. Undoubtedly, my Mom was taking this picture. I never could understand why, in fact, she did so, until I grew older and put myself in her shoes.

Here is a woman undergoing one of the most stressful times of her life and has come down from Delaware to give my grandmother a two-day break from caring for my ailing grandfather. Most likely she has been running around the hospital all day, dealing with nurses and doctors. Finally she gets a break, takes a look around the room, and sees Mikey asleep on his grandmother's lap. After being physically and emotionally exhausted, she pauses for a moment, then reaches into her overnight bag for her camera. This sight is the best thing she has experienced all day and so she decides to capture it. She may have even gotten a little emotional after taking the picture, but the idea is that she possesses caring and emotional qualities: qualities of women. Because I don't even remember this picture being taken, I cannot say for sure where or what I was doing at the time. If I had to guess, I was probably sitting on Grandpa's left side reading to him and spending time with him. I was "the apple of his eye," as Grandma would and still tells me. Maybe I was just starting to understand the roles of women and saw Grandma caring for Mikey so I decided to care for Grandpa. I will never know, but I do remember those last and final times with Grandpa while Mikey does not, which is why I no longer envy him for being in this picture with Grandma.

This picture makes a strong argument for the role of women, but when it comes to the characteristics of men, it also suggests role reversals—some seen, some unseen. Although we commonly think of women as nurturing, and Grandma definitely is in this picture, we also commonly think of men as protective and strong, the ones to step in when those around them are tired and need aid. I understand that Mikey was only four at the time, but the fact that Grandma is taking care of the MAN and not the other way around seems reversed. In any case, my dad could have been holding Mikey instead of my grandmother, to give her a slight break from being the caregiver, but he is not. While my grandmother displays her mothering attributes, the men in my family seem to lack in strength, especially my grandfather. Words that would describe him in this situation would be helpless and innocent, words we

7

commonly associate with the feminine. In this setting, however, cancer had rendered my formerly strong Grandpa helpless, even child-like.

Based on what one sees in this picture, one could make the argument that although in everyday life men stereotypically are strong and brave, while women are weaker and more fragile, chance can change that quickly, especially when it comes to protecting those we love. Sometimes strong men become weak, unable to make decisions, innocent and in need of care, while women step up to become the protectors, the strong ones. Women are perfectly capable of adopting and even taking over these roles, particularly in times of crisis. After all, isn't it natural to protect those we care for?

Despite stereotypes and literary archetypes, this picture shows that gender roles are not black and white, that women are not always X and men are not always Y. The roles of women and men often blend or switch. Different circumstances demand different responses from us, and they defy stereotypes. Earlier, for example, I said my mom was emotional, a common characteristic of women, yet in her time of sorrow, my grandmother seems to be almost blissful, at peace. It is not that she lacks emotion; instead, she seems to possess an immense amount of strength, a fact that during this time kept the family together and allowed only the minimum amount of suffering for her children and grandchildren. Many may think strength is a masculine attribute, but the ability to keep a family together can be very feminine because it involves protection of those we love and care for. This is just another example of how gender roles intertwine to make us whole human beings.

Whatever characteristics my grandmother has developed over the years, whether they are feminine or perhaps even a bit masculine, I hope to gain these same qualities so that when a situation arises that has the power to destroy my family's world, I can care enough and have the strength to keep it (and them) together. This picture will always remind me that as a woman, particularly as my grandmother's granddaughter, I have such inner reserves of strength, hidden until needed. It will remain part of my wall of pictures until I am so strong that, like Grandma, I can provide a similar blanket of love and caring, the warmth of my protective arms, for others in need.

■ *Pictures that Tell Stories*

Although most of us think of moving images as the kinds of pictures that can tell stories—film and television, in particular—still images can also tell a story. *Life Magazine,* for example, pioneered and made popular what we now call the *photo essay*—a series of photographs that can be read as a story with almost no help from words.

Even a pair of pictures can suggest a narrative. Take, for example, the two photographs reprinted here of an adult Kodiak bear and two Kodiak cubs. The photographs were taken on Kodiak Island. What is the story in these two photos?

7

EXERCISE | **7.1 Seeing the Story**

Photographer Richard Mallory Allnutt took this pair of photos while on a photo shoot on Kodiak Island, Alaska. Below is his account of the "story" behind these pictures. How does it compare with the story you saw? How does your response to the photos change with this new knowledge?

■ *The Photographer's Statement*

I took these photographs on Kodiak Island, Alaska, on July 28th, 2006. I had flown out to Fraser Lake in a small float plane to photograph Kodiak bears fishing for salmon. The bears came as close as 30 feet to our viewing point, too close really. There were no barriers between us and no one was armed. The bears largely ignored us as they were used to the presence of humans at that location. At one point, however, a mother bear became separated from her cubs.

These two photographs are of those cubs and their mother. The one image shows the two cubs in a seeming Hallmark moment between siblings. It is terror rather than affection that I see in the photograph, however. The two were bawling their heads off. Their mother was nowhere to be seen and they were incredibly vulnerable to predators and other adult bears. Male Kodiak bears are cannibalistic and wouldn't hesitate to eat an unprotected cub if they felt hungry. This made for some anxious moments for my small party as well. We didn't know where the mother was either.

The mother appeared after some time, frantic, sniffing the air and grunting, her mouth frothing. While I was nervous, I did not see the real threat until I looked at my pictures later that evening. A camera can often seem like an impervious barrier to the danger of a situation. When I looked at the photograph of the mother, I could see that she was staring directly into the lens of my camera. I will be more careful next time!

7.4 ■ Reading and Writing About Film

While books and films both strive to tell us stories, inform us, and, hopefully, to entertain us, they are wholly different in both creation and final form. Literature uses words to tickle all five senses, while film can only engage sight and sound. Novels are usually the vision of one writer; film is collaborative, where hundreds, sometimes thousands, participate from initial concept to Hollywood premiere. That said, films can be read as literature. Films use both symbol and motif. They have tone, voice, point of view, and much more.

In his book *Adventures in the Screen Trade*, novelist and screenwriter William Goldman (e.g., *Butch Cassidy & the Sundance Kid, The Princess Bride, Marathon Man,* and *All the President's Men)*, identifies the seven elements of film that need to work for a film to succeed artistically. These elements are screenplay, production design, cinematography, acting, editing, sound design (effects and music), and direction. When analyzing film, it is important to examine how these elements work both separately and in concert with one another.

1. **Screenplay** — Look at the film *Pirates of the Caribbean: Curse of the Black Pearl.* Captain Jack Sparrow barely says a word in his introductory scene. We first see him standing proud atop the mast of his ship that turns out to be little more than a rowboat with a sail, that turns out to be sinking. The pirate blithely glides along into port as his "ship" swiftly sinks beneath him and comes to a halt not three feet from the dock. Captain Jack Sparrow steps from the top of his mast on to the jetty without a care in the world and without getting wet. After such an introduction, we know that

we're in safe hands. Everything will work out for this character, even in those moments of the greatest jeopardy. The scene plays without anyone saying a word up to this point, but it tells us everything we need to know about both his character and the nature of the film we are watching.

2. **Production Design** — While budget does not guarantee quality, there have been few films to rival the scale of production on the three *Pirates of the Caribbean* films. Put a copy of any of the three films into your DVD player and pause on any scene. Everything you see on camera was created and acquired especially for the production, from swords and pirate ships to stockings and corsets. Whole ships and houses and villages were built in the real and digital worlds just for the films. Production designers are, by necessity, a combination of artist, architect, engineer, and logistical wizard. Check out the DVD's special features to see for yourself.

3. **Cinematography** — The cinematographer "paints" with light. He or she controls lighting, lens, focus, framing, and whether to pan, tilt, track, or crane a specific shot.

   ◆ **Lighting** — The cinematographer plays with who and what is in or out of shadow. This can strongly affect the mood of a film and how we perceive a character.

   ◆ **Lens** — The choice of lens can radically shift the way we see. For example, a telephoto lens flattens the elements on a screen. A wide angle lens stretches subjects to the edge of its frame. There are many variations in between, including zoom lenses which can move between extremes in the same shot.

   ◆ **Focus** — The cinematographer decides who and what is in focus, and whether to shift focus within a shot. He or she can decide how to adjust the depth of focus (e.g., should everything be in focus, or just the foreground or background).

   ◆ **Pan, Tilt, Track, or Crane** — The cinematographer can move the camera itself within a shot. It can pan up, down, to the left and right. It can tilt at an angle. It can move on a track, or on the shoulder of the cameraman. It can even fly up into the air for a bird's-eye view.

   ◆ **Camera Angle** — The cinematographer chooses where to shoot from and how to frame it. He or she decides whether to shoot a close-up, medium shot, or long shot, etc.

   In Spielberg's film *Saving Private Ryan,* the sometimes blurred, shaky camera movements of the opening battle scene evoke more than the chaos and panic of the D-Day invasion. They purposely mimic the still photographs of Robert Capa, the only combat photographer present in that first wave on Omaha Beach. Look at Capa's photographs from that day and then watch the opening minutes of Spielberg's film and you will see more than a fleeting resemblance between the two.

4. **Acting** — An actor's performance can radically change a film. One of the keys to getting the right performance is choosing the right actor. Can you imagine what any of the *Pirates of the Caribbean* films would be like if Harrison Ford had been cast as Captain Jack Sparrow? It is highly unlikely the films would have had the same comedic tone, not intentionally at least. Had Johnny Depp been cast in Harrison Ford's signature roles of Indiana Jones and Han Solo (of the original *Star Wars* trilogy) it is likely that those films would also feel quite different in ways both subtle and significant.

5. **Editing** — Look at the introduction of Indiana Jones in *Raiders of the Lost Ark.* Count the number of times the camera changes what you see (shots per scene). Look at each

shot in slow motion. How does the editor juxtapose one shot with another shot to give the impression of action? When Indiana Jones whips the pistol out of the hand of his treacherous guide, we never actually see the whip wrap around the man's hand. We see Indy's head tilt to one side as he hears the gun cocking. We see a close-up of his hand grabbing the whip at his belt. We see his raised hand coming forward with the whip. We hear the whip crack. We see the gun fall to the ground and fire. We see the treacherous guide running away rubbing his wrist. Those elements cut together in our mind to give us the impression that Indy whipped the gun from the guide's hand. We never actually see whip strike hand.

6. **Sound Design** — Again, try one of your *Pirates of the Caribbean* DVDs and listen to it in French or Spanish. Whether you can speak the language or not, Johnny Depp's performance as Captain Jack Sparrow changes radically with someone else's voice. Imagine different sound effects. Turn the sound off completely and watch the visuals alone. Can you follow the story? You should be able to, but how does your experience of the film change without sound? Turn on the sound again, close your eyes, and listen to the film without the aid of the visuals. How does it change your film experience? If you've seen the film before can you revisit the images in your head?

7. **Direction** — A director oversees every element of the film from screenplay to sound design. They have veto power over every other department (see 1 through 6 above).

EXERCISE

7.m Rereading Film

Can you imagine *Romeo and Juliet* with a happy ending? What if Juliet wakes one minute earlier and stops Romeo from taking a swig of the apothecary's poison? That would very likely diminish the power of the story.

If you ever check out the special features on a DVD and look at the deleted scenes or alternate endings, you will find some surprises. Often the director adds his or her commentary to these scenes to reveal the decisions behind each change and cut. Listen in. Watch. Ask yourself if you would have made the same choices. If not, what would you have done? It's not as easy as it seems when you're first talking with you're friends after the lights come up in the movie theatre.

1. Choose a scene in one of your favorite films that you think either doesn't belong, doesn't work, that you don't like very much, or that you consider fundamentally flawed. If the film is an adaptation, choose an omitted scene from the source text (novel, short story, essay, etc.) that you think would improve the finished film.

2. Explain what is wrong with the scene in the film. Be specific. Dissect the scene to reveal its flaws in the context of the entire film. For example, to catch the nuances of the scene, you might produce a storyboard. Look at narrative and character as well as the technical aspects of the film like cinematography, production design, editing, etc.

3. Explain how you would fix the scene if you were the director and how you would fit the changed or additional scene back into the film. Using evidence from the film or source text, show why your version works better than the finished product. Again, be specific in terms of narrative and character as well as the technical aspects of the film.

■ Summary, Review and Analysis

When you work with film in your composition class, you might be asked to summarize it, review it, or analyze it—or maybe a combination of those tasks. What's the difference between the concepts? A single scene from *The Fellowship of the Ring* (2002) should illustrate the differences.

Summary

When you are asked to summarize something—an episode of *Grey's Anatomy*, a chapter from Charles Dickens's *A Tale of Two Cities,* the argument you had with your best friend over the weekend—you're being prompted to provide an encapsulation or abstract of the item or event. A summary answers the question, "What happened?"

As with any summary, your summary of a film should be brief; it should hit only the highlights. Also, in most cases (with the possible exception of that argument!), it should be objective. That is, if you are asked to summarize a film, you can't interject into it personal opinion. No, "and this was really boring." No, "I think this character is weird." Just the facts.

Consider this summary of a scene from *Fellowship of the Ring* depicting Boromir's death:

> To help Frodo escape, Merry and Pippin divert the attention of the Uruk-hai soldiers, who begin to chase them. As the battle continues elsewhere with Aragorn, Legolas, and Gimli, Merry and Pippin find themselves at the bottom of the hill, their escape cut off by approaching Uruk-hai. Boromir appears out of nowhere and single-handedly begins to defend the two Hobbits.
>
> Meanwhile, at the top of the hill, Aragorn, Legolas, and Gimli hear Boromir's distress call on the Horn of Gondor and move to help their comrade.
>
> As Boromir fights, the Uruk-hai's leader crests the hill and fires into him a single arrow. Boromir falls to his knees, then rises and continues to fight before being shot once more. He falls to his knees again.
>
> For a moment, he is on eye-level with Merry and Pippin, with whom he exchanges a meaningful look. He rises again, is shot again, and falls for the last time, wounded but not dead.
>
> The Uruk-hai soldiers swarm around him but pay him no mind; instead, they pick up Merry and Pippin and carry them away.
>
> The Uruk-hai leader makes his way down the hill, stands before the fallen Boromir, and prepares to deliver a final arrow. At that moment, however, Aragorn arrives, jumps onto the Uruk-hai leader, and begins to engage him in battle. Aragorn kills the leader, then returns to Boromir, who dies of his wounds.

Review

In order to clue in the potential viewer to the plot, but without giving away major surprises or details, most film reviews actually include some measure of summary. However, for a review to be a review, it must focus on critiquing or evaluating the film. In a limited amount of space, a review must answer, with evidence, questions like

7

- ◆ What are the best elements of this film (plot, acting, cinematography, etc.)?
- ◆ What are the worst elements of this film (see above list)?
- ◆ Is this a good film or bad film?
- ◆ Should one see it?

As this brief list of questions suggests, reviews begin to move away from objectivity. They become a bit more subjective. However, there is one rule to remember: if you are asked to review a film, you cannot let personal bias against the subject matter, director, actor, location, or anything else sway your evaluation. In that respect, your review must maintain some level of objectivity. Every judgment you make must be grounded in hard evidence.

The following passage from a review of *The Fellowship of the Ring* focuses on the use of music in Boromir's death scene:

> Masterful direction and acting, a script faithful to Tolkien's vision, amazingly inventive cinematography, and the latest innovations in computer-animated graphics provide only part of the secret to the success of Peter Jackson's *The Fellowship of the Ring*. Music—both instrumental and choral—helps the director realize his vision of Tolkien's cult classic. Howard Shore's original score shifts appropriately given the group or location with which we are to associate the music. For example, with the Hobbits, it is light, melodic and filled with happy flourishes, what one might call an "Elvish" quality; with the Black Riders, Mordor, Saruman, and Isengard, it is driving, marked by deeply resonating drums and horns, almost Wagnerian in its intensity. There is little doubt that music and sound flesh out the film.
>
> Jackson's masterful integration of music into the narrative is perhaps nowhere better evidenced than by Boromir's death scene. In this scene, Jackson artfully layers musical interludes with a chorus of voices in a manner that is both suspenseful and spiritual. As Merry and Pippin stand helpless, confronted by a tide of Uruk-hai, Boromir appears out of nowhere, his arrival marked by a musical flourish that is hopeful yet brief. From there, the music moves in concert with the sounds of swords clashing. Into this mix then enters a chorus of angelic voices that rises and falls as the fight progresses.
>
> In terms of technique, Jackson's ability to make music a vital part of his narrative is realized most effectively by the presence of this chorus, which reaches two crescendos, both of which identify significant events in the battle. The first crescendo occurs when the Uruk-hai leader crests the hill to begin his downward journey toward Boromir and the Hobbits. As he steps into view, the voices reach their peak, then are abruptly stilled. When they return, they re-intensify, reaching a second crescendo as the Uruk-hai leader fires an arrow into Boromir. A hush once more descends as Boromir falls to the ground. When he regains his footing, the chorus resumes, as does the music, but the tone of both now is mournful.
>
> At this point, Jackson introduces another technique that further illuminates his awareness of how music and sound can make or break a scene. When Boromir falls, we hear only three sounds distinctly: the sound of the arrow thudding into him, his gasps of pain, and the force of his knees hitting the ground. Momentarily, the battle noises are gone. From this point, sound becomes muffled. Pained gasps, battle-cries, the clink of swords, even the angelic chorus—all are present, but now they are hollow, filtered. The technique gives the scene a slightly unreal quality, but also lends it a measure of horrible gravity. Together, the mournful nature of the chorus and music and the muffling of the sound suggest in a way that the actions alone could note the winding down of Boromir's life.

7

Analysis

As with a review, a film analysis might also include plot or scene summary; however, a straight analysis rarely includes elements of review. Instead, a film analysis functions very much like a literary analysis: it breaks down the larger whole into smaller segments and generally focuses on analyzing or providing an in-depth interpretation or reading of one facet. It explains how the film works.

A film analysis might focus on some of the same elements that characterize an analysis of literature:

- **Structure:** How the whole is put together. If you focus on the structure of a film, you might consider how the separate scenes work together to create a coherent whole — or not.

- **Plot:** The action or story. Does it have a coherent beginning, middle, and ending, or is the story told out of sequence, using flashbacks or flash forwards? What effect does the plot have on the structure of the film?

- **Character:** Those involved with the action. Are they fully realized or one-dimensional? Do they act as one might expect or contrary to one's expectations? Do they ever seem false or unreal?

- **Point of View:** The frame of reference from which the story is told. Is the action seen through the eyes of a single viewer or more than one? How do those perspectives fit together cohesively — or do they?

- **Dialogue:** What is said. Is the dialogue natural? Stilted? Particularly if the film was adapted from a play, does the dialogue retain a "play-like" quality?

- **Setting:** Where the action takes place. Sometimes, the action of a film shifts constantly, from one setting to another; at other times, it might occur in a single location, such as the room of a house or a prison cell. What effect might setting have on the story that is being told?

- **Atmosphere:** The tone that comes through in the setting as a result of, for example, the lighting and elements within the setting. For example, horror movies are associated with darkness and often take place in old houses, while comedies are associated with brighter lighting and places where people gather.

- **Imagery and Symbolism:** Images appeal to the senses; symbols are images that have been repeated enough that they adopt a specific, widely-recognized meaning. For example, an image might appeal to one's sense of smell or taste, or it might be classified as kinetic (movement) or tactile (feeling), among other things. Symbols could include such things as colors (red=danger, white=purity), shape (round=womblike or feminine, long and straight=phallic), and other elements (bird=freedom, water=purification or rebirth).

The following example analyzes just one element—the symbolism—in Boromir's death scene:

7

Although its occurrence provides the focus and even the title for the opening chapter of *The Two Towers*, J.R.R. Tolkien's second installment in the *Lord of the Rings* trilogy, in print Boromir's death scene strikes one as anticlimactic: the fierce battle which precedes it, during which he single-handedly attempts to protect Merry and Pippin from the marauding Orcs, occurs off-stage and is recounted only briefly in a subsequent chapter as a part of Pippin's muddled memory. As if itself constrained by the limits of the written word, Boromir's unswerving valor against insurmountable odds is captured only by the description that when Aragorn discovers him, leaning nearly dead against a tree, he is "pierced by many black-feathered arrows . . . [with Orcs he has slain] piled all about him and at his feet" (Tolkien 4). The redemptive nature of his sacrifice likewise seems understated: "'I have tried to take the ring from Frodo. . . I am sorry. I have paid'" (Tolkien 4). Sacrifice and redemption—two of the key themes of Tolkien's narrative—thus occur, but in the case of Boromir they are neither stressed nor vividly brought to life.

When filmmaker Peter Jackson tackles Tolkien's novels for his own cinematic *Lord of the Rings* trilogy (2001–2003), he reenvisions "Boromir's Departure" in two vital ways. First, he wisely moves Boromir's death to the end of the first film—*The Fellowship of the Ring*—so it joins other scenes representative of the fellowship's disintegration: the capture of Merry and Pippin, the flight toward Mordor of Frodo and Sam, the pursuit of the kidnapped Hobbits by Aragorn, Legolas, and Gimli. More importantly, however, Jackson imbues the scene with a level of symbolism and imagery that literally envisions and thus underscores, in a way that Tolkien's version does not, the true level of Boromir's sacrifice and the measure of his redemption.

Boromir's death occurs in a location that is itself fraught with significance, in "the strange borderland of the Emyn Muil," where ruins dominate the landscape (Tolkien 452). The decaying "stone kings and the seats of Lhaw and Hen, and the great Stair beside the falls of Rauros" represent not just the "great works" of Gondor, Boromir's homeland, but also its encroaching destruction by successive invaders and time (452). The land of man is shrinking. Boromir's home, Minas Tirith, is at present under siege by the forces of Mordor, forsaken by others, and his desire to possess the ring is driven by his ardent hope that he can use its power to rescue his city. Both in the novel and in Jackson's film, his death is preceded by a scene in which he attempts to take the ring from Frodo by force, a scene that ends with his weeping in remorse at his actions.

Jackson's reenvisioning of Boromir's redemption begins as Merry and Pippin stand helpless before an advancing swarm of Uruk-hai. From out of nowhere, unbidden, Boromir appears and places himself and his sword between the Hobbits and the soldiers. Earlier scenes have revealed his strength and cunning as a fighter, but clearly as a lone warrior he is outmatched by Saruman's monstrous Orc creations. Yet, with his comrades elsewhere, he is all that stands between the soldiers and the young Hobbits. In the selfless nature of an act that must inevitably lead to his destruction, we see the first stage of Boromir's redemption.

The scene offers other measures of his sacrifice. As heir to the protectorate of Minas Tirith, Boromir carries the Horn of Gondor, a symbol not only of his position but also of his city and his people as a whole. Through the person who carries it and of itself, it thus embodies hope for mankind. Although it has been with him during the entire film, it is not until this scene that Boromir actually blows the horn in an effort to alert Aragorn, Legolas, and Gimli of his need for their assistance. Yet, as has been the case with his city itself, Boromir must also stand alone, for the others are too far away to arrive in time. The horn that represents Gondor is thus blown for the first and, significantly, last times in the moments preceding Boromir's death. As the battle progresses, we catch a glimpse of it swinging, broken in half, against his chest. Its cleaving neatly represents the potential destruction of Minas Tirith and the world of man.

In Jackson's hands, the symbolism of the broken horn, and what it represents for the future of mankind, is lent additional power in that portion of the scene when Boromir is first shot through by the arrows of Lurtz, the Uruk-hai leader. Until that moment, he appears invincible. As Boromir falls to his knees, though, he does so directly in front of a statue, a symbolic reminder that once in this now-barren landscape an entire civilization thrived before being destroyed by invaders. Jackson's juxtaposition of the stricken Boromir with the statue illuminates the depth of his sacrifice: in his selfless defense of the Hobbits against insurmountable odds, he knowingly has risked not only his own life but the future of his city and his people.

That Boromir is fully aware of the choice he has made Jackson makes clear at the end of the scene, which includes dialogue expanded from that found in Tolkien. As Aragorn attempts to remove the arrows from his chest, Boromir stops him. "It is finished," he tells Aragorn, and then confesses to his attempted theft of the ring from Frodo. "Forgive me. I did not see. I have failed you all. The world of men will fall, and all will come to darkness, and my city to ruin" (Jackson, Peter, Philippa Boyens, and Fran Walsh). Aragorn, of course, assures him that Minas Tirith will not fall, but this exchange reinforces our understanding of Boromir's actions. That he has sacrificed himself in order to protect Merry and Pippin while believing that the failure of his undertaking would end not only in his death but also in the destruction of his people articulates the selflessness that precedes true redemption. Jackson's reinterpretation of this crucial scene gives Boromir's sacrifice the honor it deserves.

Works Cited

Jackson, Peter, Philippa Boyens, and Fran Walsh. Screenplay for *The Fellowship of the Ring*. Special Extended DVD Edition. Dir. Peter Jackson. New Line Home Entertainment. 2002.

Tolkien, J.R.R. *The Two Towers*. New York: Ballantine, 1994.

EXERCISE | **7.n Writing About Film**

Choose a film that you can watch several times and consider carefully.

- Write a summary of a scene.

- Then write a review of the film. (Make sure you don't repeat what others have said.)

- Finally, write an analysis of the same film focusing on a specific aspect—the cinematography, the acting, the directing, the narrative structure, the soundtrack, etc.

7

■ *Try Isolating a Scene — Using a Storyboard*

Traditionally, storyboards — visual representations or sketches of scenes in a film — are produced before or during the process of filmmaking. In one respect, they are similar to the outlines or drafts you might produce for a composition course: they provide an opportunity for their creator(s) to put ideas on paper, to sketch (literally) a plan that will lead to a final, polished product. The scenes they imagine likely will find their way into the film.

Interestingly, though, storyboards could also prove useful to you as you study a film in preparation for writing about it in your composition course. For example, say you are asked to analyze a specific scene in a film. How do you go about studying that scene? Watch. Pause. Watch. Pause. All the while, take notes frantically. Unfortunately, there really isn't any way to avoid these steps. But due to its very nature, storyboarding forces you to zero in on specific details. If you storyboard the action, the images, the symbols, then you have a concrete, hands-on translation of that scene that you have created — one that, because it focuses on the important details, can provide the foundation for your entire essay.

EXERCISE   ### 7.0 Storyboarding a Scene

Choose a film that you really enjoy and one that you would like to be able to write about to explain how lighting or setting or camera angle help tell the story, for example. After watching the film, choose a scene that is very short but very important for the development of the story or the mood or the development of character. Now storyboard that scene.

Following is a storyboard from the film *Love, Actually*. It is an extremely short scene but one that tells us about Colin Firth's character Jamie, who is alone after finding his girlfriend in a compromising situation with his brother.

This kind of exercise will help you focus on the details of the film and explain how some scenes work and why they are important.

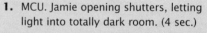
1. MCU. Jamie opening shutters, letting light into totally dark room. (4 sec.)

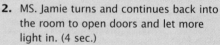
2. MS. Jamie turns and continues back into the room to open doors and let more light in. (4 sec.)

3. CU (POV) of angel cut-out in shutter. We can barely see hints of the green outside. Everything surrounding the cut-out is black. Only a slit of the shutter opening shows light as the shutter opens. (1 sec.)

3a. CU (POV) of window opening onto LS (POV) of sunlight on pond and trees outside. (1 sec.)

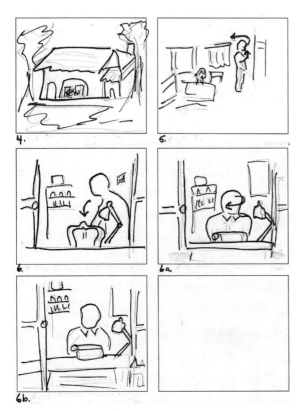

4. LS (Establishing shot) of country house. Jamie barely visible opening doors to the outside. (3 sec.)

5. MLS (Interior shot). Jamie stands looking out the door and then turns to walk behind desk. (4 sec.)

6. MS. Jamie slowly sitting down at his desk. (2 sec.)

6a. MS. Jamie seated at desk in front of type-writer. Turns head to look around and think. Camera has pulled back slightly. (5 sec.)

6b. MS Camera has pulled back more, reveal-ing more of the desk and the room. Jamie is behind the typewriter, settled, and, after a pause, says, "Alone again. [pause] Naturally." (5 sec.)

Storyboard by Diana George

Key to abbreviations

CU – close-up

MCU – Medium close-up

ECU – Extreme close-up

POV – Point of view (this means the audience is seeing the shot from the point of view of the character in the scene — in this case, from Jamie's point of view).

LS – Long shot

MLS – Medium long shot

ELS – Extreme long shot

CU (POV) – Close-up point of view shot.

Arrows drawn indicate movement.

7.5 ▪ Using Visuals in Your Writing

▪ *Diagrams, Graphs, and Pie Charts*

When logically designed and intelligently integrated, visual aids such as diagrams, graphs, and pie charts not only complement but also complete a written text: they help the reader visual-ize what the written word alone cannot. Additionally, good visual aids prove useful for con-densing difficult or complex information, often numerical or scientific data, into a form easily digested by a range of readers (and viewers). That said, it pays to know that such visual aids do not always work.

How do diagrams, graphs, and pie charts work in terms of extending the written word?

Say you are invited to a wedding in another part of the large city in which you live. You know the area fairly well, but you're not sure about street names and rules that might govern and even impede the route you take (Is Fairmont Avenue one way?). A written set of directions can be helpful, but words alone might not help you see the route:

1. Take the Main Street Exit from I-15 N.
2. Take a right onto Main Street. Keep on Main until you reach Harrodsburg Road.
3. Take a left onto Harrodsburg Road. Stay on Harrodsburg until just past Orange Street.
4. Take a left onto Nottingham Street. It's the first street after Orange.
5. Take a right onto Lane Road. Lane is the first street after Pierce Road.
6. Take a left onto Montgomery Place West. The church is located on the right, at 134 Montgomery Place West.

To enhance the written text and prevent potential traffic tickets for out-of-town and other directionally challenged wedding attendees, the invitation might include the sort of **diagram** with which most of us are familiar—a map. Even a basic one (nobody expects you to compete with MapQuest!) will suffice:

Likewise, if you are writing a research essay about water quality in the Virginia Tech Duck Pond, you might decide that while photographs—maybe a great shot of a floating island of cups and other trash—might grab the reader's attention, the most succinct way to show the types of pollution present and the volumes at which the effluents have changed over time is to **graph** your findings.

Although a program such as Microsoft Excel places graphs within the larger category of charts—along with a wide variety of others, such as pie, doughnut, radar, surface, and bubble—most of the time when we refer to graphs we mean the most basic types: line and bar. Both the simple line graph and the bar graph can be used effectively to plot alterations in X factor over a designated period of time:

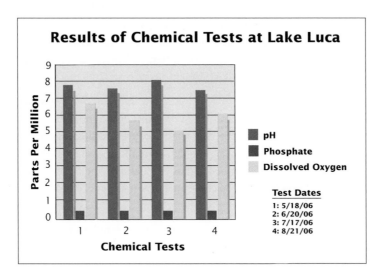

That other tried-and-true visual aid, the pie chart, is helpful when you need to illustrate a whole thing (for example, a Dutch Apple pie) broken down into parts (for example, who gets the bigger piece) at a certain point in time. When you create a pie chart, remember that you can't let the visual stand alone: you must include in it the relevant percentages. Otherwise, what you have is merely, well, a pie.

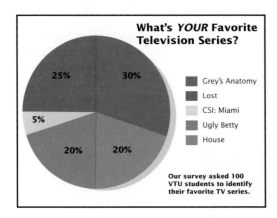

Some basic guidelines to keep in mind when you design your own visual aids:

Declutter (aka Divide and Conquer). Let's say you need to tell your readers about nationwide communication and travel statistics among businesspersons during 2006. You've got to include info on who traveled (or didn't), why, where they went, and how they kept in touch with the home office while they were away. Do you include all of this information in a single visual? Here's the thing: you can, but nobody who sees it will be able to grasp it easily. If you include in your visual too much material — particularly too much disparate material — it becomes indecipherable. So declutter, or divide and conquer: create as many different visuals as it takes to pass along the info clearly to readers.

Enlarge (aka Think like Goldilocks). Due to the fact that visual aids should be integrated with, rather than replace, the written word, most of them do not take up an entire page, as any textbook for, say, a Statistics or Western Civ course would indicate. As a result, you might be tempted to create ones that are smaller, as smaller ones are easier to embed within a page of text. Yet you must remember that any visual must be big enough so that readers can interpret its message clearly. So choose a happy medium: Not too big. Not too small. Just right.

Simplify. For your first big bar graph or pie chart, you might be tempted to go wild: Look at all of these color choices! I can use a different font for each slice of pie! Ambition is a great thing, but when you're designing a visual aid, you want to dial back the creativity. The key: a simplified visual is easier to decipher and easier on the eyes.

If you're not a graphic artist, or even if you're not particularly adept at the visuals program you have loaded onto your computer, don't be afraid to turn to a program like Microsoft Excel, which provides a large library of templates for an impressive variety of visual aids.

EXERCISE   **7.p Research and Visual Information**

Read the research essay below written by Virginia Tech student Alice Lee for her English 1106 class in the Spring of 2006. What do the visuals contribute to this paper?

Virginia Tech Geophysics major Alice Lee (left) with her instructor Lynette Moyer.

Alice Lee
Instructor: Lynette Moyer
English 1106 Research
April 11, 2006

HUMAN EFFECT ON GLOBAL WARMING
AND THE GREENHOUSE EFFECT

"We just got these results from our simulation model. They explain what's caus-ing this severe weather . . . Mr. Vice President . . . our climate is changing violently, and it's going to happen over the next six to eight weeks. I was wrong . . . it's not going to take a couple hundred years . . . it's happening now!" After viewing this scene in the film *The Day After Tomorrow,* I looked up at the sky and half expected to see hail the size of golf balls pouring out of the sky. Hollywood takes the issue of global warming and presents the consequences of it, in such a way that *The Day After Tomorrow* strikes fear into many hearts, as it did to mine. For many years now, scientists and citizens alike are debating whether or not global warming is a real issue. Some people believe that global warming is not a big deal, and that people are merely overreacting. They believe that this is all part of a natural process, and that these fluctuations in climate have occurred in the past, so we have nothing to worry about. Others believe that people really need to start doing something about the emission of greenhouse gases, and prevent the greenhouse effect from getting worse. Still others remain indifferent, and although they acknowledge the fact that global warming is happening, they feel that they do not need to worry about it because no serious effects will start until after they die. But the truth is that it is a problem that affects everyone, and everyone has an effect on it. The question at hand is, "Are humans doing something to accelerate the 'greenhouse effect' on earth, or is it just an act of history repeating itself?" As I will explain in detail later, most people do rec-ognize the fact that humans are putting more carbon dioxide and other greenhouse gases into the atmosphere, but still some believe that what humans are doing is not enough to have a major impact on the greenhouse effect as most scientists believe. But we should listen to those scientists because since the Industrial Revolution, humans have been increasing the amount of greenhouse gases that are excreted into the environment, which in turn leads to the worldwide debate on global warming and the greenhouse effect.

The temperature changes every day. Some winters may have warm, sunny days and have cold, snowy days in the same week. Some summers may be rainy and cold, while others could be hot and humid. These changes in temperature merely refer to the temperature changes of the area. But the issue at hand is not about temperature, per se, but rather climate, and climate is a totally different story. According to the Environmental Protection Agency website, "Climate is the long-term average of a

7

region's weather events...." Therefore, the issue of climate change becomes an important issue here. When the average climate increases or decreases as much as it has in the past century here on Earth (about one degree and increasing as we speak), everything from fauna to flora to human life becomes greatly affected by this change. The following graph, or Figure 1, shows the record of global average temperatures over the past century and a half. It was made by the Hadley Centre for Climate Prediction and Research of the UK Meteorological Office (Global warming: the Evidence). As Figure 1 shows, the average temperature, or climate, has fluctuated over the past years, but the trend indicates that the overall average temperature has been increasing.

An example of the consequences of climate change is the increasing frequency and strength of hurricanes. Since the time hurricane Katrina hit the United States, many scientists and citizens alike believe that hurricane Katrina is just the beginning of other major catastrophes that will hit the Earth because of global warming. According to Christoph Lumer, the author of the book *The Greenhouse: A Welfare Assessment and Some Morals,* "The amount of injuries and illnesses due to flood and storm

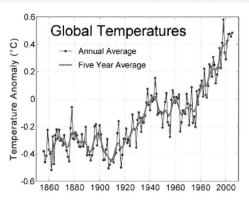

Figure 1

catastrophes, acute famines, exertions of migration and heat stress can be guessed," but he also warns that "Death is regarded here as the tip of an iceberg" (Lumer 32). He says this because he believes that although it is inevitable that death will result from catastrophes such as hurricanes and famines, it only accounts for a small group of people. That small number of deaths is not going to even compare to the number of injuries and illnesses resulting from these catastrophes, such as malaria or extreme poverty and hunger. Just like an iceberg, only the tip shows above the water, but under the surface, a massive amount, hundreds of times larger than the surface tip, is hiding. That is the "iceberg-hypothesis" (Lumer 32). From what I understand, what the Earth has experienced so far, with hurricanes and other natural disasters, is only the beginning of the series of catastrophes that are waiting to occur in the future.

Now that there is evidence shown that climate is changing, specifically, increasing temperatures, the question is, "What exactly are humans doing to accelerate the greenhouse effect which results in this increase in climate?" When some people hear "greenhouse gas," these words automatically carry a negative connotation because people believe that greenhouse gases are always bad, but in reality, greenhouse gases are necessary for Earth to maintain a climate suitable for humans and other life forms on Earth. From what I have learned from environmental science classes I have taken in the past, carbon dioxide, methane, water vapor and nitrous oxide are examples of greenhouse gases, and as Figure 2 depicts, the greenhouse gases carbon dioxide, methane, nitrous oxide, and CFCs, respectively, are increasing at dangerous rates, and show no sign of changing direction. In a natural state, these gases prevent heat from escaping into the vastness of space and keep the Earth warm. This is the greenhouse effect: the sun radiates energy towards the Earth in the form on UV rays, and the greenhouse gases listed above, "... and several very minor constituents (such as manmade chlorofluorocarbon [CFC] refrigerants) intercept a portion of this energy and then reradiate it... down (back toward the surface)" (Michaels and Balling 25). Yet as I stated before, the issue with the greenhouse gases does not lie within itself, but rather, it lies in the amount that is excreted into the atmosphere by humans.

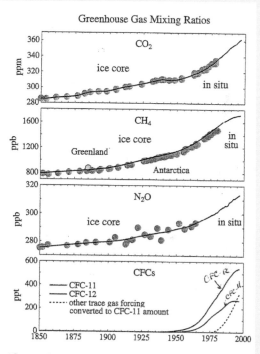

Figure 2

The Environmental Protection Agency states that, "According to the National Academy of Sciences, the Earth's surface temperature has risen by about 1 degree Fahrenheit in the past century, with accelerated warming during the past two decades" (www.epa.gov). One degree may not seem like much, but from what I have learned from my historical geology professor, professor Read, and the Environmental Protection Agency website is that this change in average surface temperature can alter many things such as sea level, crop yield, human health, animals and especially ecosystems. According to my geology professor at Virginia Tech, "99% of scientists believe global warming is occurring, and most of them, including me, believe that it is because of the burning of fossil fuels." Such fossil fuels include coal, oil, and natural gas.

For millions of years, the Earth has been able to keep this climate change under control until humans interfered with the natural processes. According to the

Environmental Protection Agency website, ". . . through population growth, fossil fuel burning, and deforestation..." humans are altering the greenhouse effect, and in turn, we are getting more heat than we need. From what I have learned from my historical geology class, in the past, before humans roamed the Earth, carbon dioxide was emitted into the atmosphere by natural processes. Volcanoes, for example and mid oceanic ridges or MORs under the ocean, which I will explain about in more detail later, spew out carbon dioxide. Therefore, with volcanoes and MORs giving off carbon dioxide naturally to control the Earth's temperature, and humans adding to the emissions by burning fossil fuels, and also by cutting off natural carbon dioxide users by deforestation, naturally, we'll have more greenhouse gases than we need, which in turn causes major problems when it comes to global warming.

Many people believe that there really is nothing to worry about, and that global warming is just a scare. As I have researched and learned from my historical geology lab, there have been many fluctuations in climate and temperature in the past. Professor Read of the Geology Department here at Virginia Tech explained to me through an interview, that the mid-Cretaceous period, which happened about 90 to 120 million years ago, was a time of world-wide warm climate. Professor Read states that this warm climate was "indeed, due to global warming and greenhouse gases in the atmosphere." However, in this case, there were no humans around to emit these greenhouse gases forcefully into the air, but rather, nature expelled these gases into the atmosphere. As most people that take a geology course would know, carbon dioxide is naturally put into the atmosphere by volcanoes above and below the ground. These "underground volcanoes" are also known as mid oceanic ridges or MORs. These MORs spew out igneous rocks, and cause spreading of the oceanic crust. Knowing this, critics of global warming believe that this new era of "global warming" or rising global temperature is all part of a natural process, and because it has been controlled in the past by rock weathering and other natural processes, there is nothing to worry about.

Here is where they are wrong. True, global warming has been controlled naturally in the past by trees and rock weathering, but that was before humans roamed the earth. Agriculture became a major way of life for humans. According to William F. Ruddiman, the author of the article "How did Humans First Alter Global Climate?," "...Human actions first began to have a warming effect on the earth's climate within the past century..." (Ruddiman 46). In this article, Ruddiman takes the global warming issue, and puts it into an agricultural perspective. Ruddiman sternly states that, ". . . our ancestors' farming practices kicked off global warming thousands of years before we started burning coal and driving cars" (46). As any environmental science student would know, and I have stated before, carbon dioxide is taken out of the air by processes such as rock weathering and by the chemical process of photosynthesis. Photosynthesis, as everyone may already know, is a process that trees perform to produce oxygen, which is essential for human beings. When farmers first began to farm, they cleared land to start their agriculture. Even today, more and more forests are being cleared or burned to make room for agriculture. When those trees are cut, the Earth is being deprived of resources that take carbon dioxide out of the air.

The Industrial Revolution marked an age where humans were becoming exponentially knowledgeable and coming up with ways to make life earlier for all human beings. This time period also marked an era of indescribable amounts of emissions of carbon dioxide and methane into the atmosphere. Most of the greenhouse gas, methane, as my geology professor explained to me through an interview, comes from raising cattle. Methane is excreted from the cattle, and although "Almost all of the natural greenhouse effect… comes from water vapor," adding

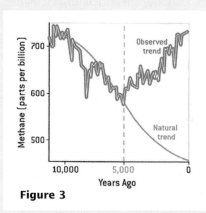

Figure 3

anything to the balanced natural process can have a huge impact on something as sensitive as the greenhouse effect (Michaels and Balling 25). As Figure 3 indicates, methane levels are unusually high, and are not following the natural trend. The natural trend is one of decreasing methane levels, yet the observed trend indicates that methane levels are rising rapidly.

As a conclusion from scientific studies, the Earth is supposed to be in a current cooling phase. Figure 4 indicates that the natural trend, that the Earth is supposed to follow, should have taken us into a global cooling phase, and eventually into a glacial

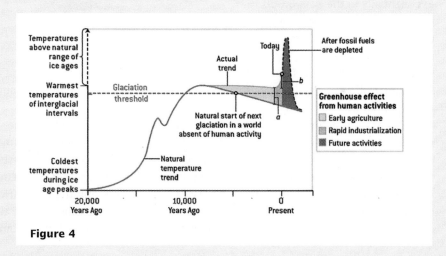

Figure 4

period. However, because of the greenhouse gases, and their heat trapping character-istics, our Earth is being driven into another warming phase. It also indicates that about 8,000 years ago, "human activities warded off a glaciation that otherwise would have begun about 5,000 years ago. Early human agricultural activities produced enough greenhouse gases to offset most of the natural cooling trend during the preindustrial times" (Ruddiman 53). Figure 4 also shows insight about what will happen once fos-sil fuels are depleted. As we can see, once the fossil fuels such as oil, coal and natural gas are gone, or are too expen-sive to extract from the earth, the car-bon dioxide levels will drop dramatically, sending the Earth into another age of global glaciation. Before industry and agriculture, nature had a natural balance of greenhouse gases, and had just enough to keep the Earth at a livable climate, until about 8,000 years ago when humans interrupted that stability. Both Figures 5 and 6 indicate that carbon dioxide levels have accelerated and increased exponentially in the past 8,000 years, and seem to continue to rise. Although these graphs indicate that the warming really

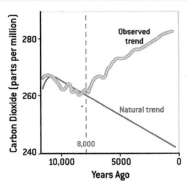

Figure 5

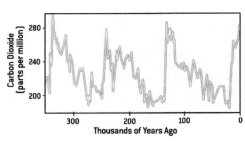

Figure 6

started about 8,000 years ago, way before the industrial revolution, the point here is that humans have started this warming phase. Humans have ultimately changed the course of nature.

There is no definite evidence, at least not enough to convince everyone on this planet, especially the American Association of Petroleum Geologists, that humans are totally at fault for this anomaly in climate. However, even if humans are not "totally at fault," as inhabitants of the Earth, we have a responsibility to try to do something to slow down the damage. For example, as Darcy Frey described in the essay "How Green is BP," BP is one of the largest oil companies in the world. But because they are an oil company, they have this stereotype of a company that doesn't really care about the environment, but rather focuses on their revenues. BP finally decided that it was about time that they change their image, to a more environment-friendly company (Frey 152). Frey explains that, "by cutting the emissions of carbon dioxide that it creates while producing oil and gas," they were planning on "shifting to cleaner fuels like natural gas, which emits about half the volume of CO2 generated from coal and ultimately... positioning itself as a producer of alternative and renewable energy: hydrogen, wind, solar" (Frey 153). It is important that all humans and especially other oil companies follow this example, and strive for a more sustainable future. According to Professor Read, these solutions may not be as pragmatic as one may believe them to be. In the interview I conducted with him, he states that, "even if we stop it [emitting greenhouse gases] today, there will be a long lag of about 10 years before we even see the slightest of progress." He believes that it will take a long time for the carbon dioxide level to get back to normal. However, these are estimations of carbon dioxide levels if we completely stop emitting all traces of it at this very moment, so basically, he thinks that these are not very practical solutions, but they are a start in the process of cleaning up the mess humans have made.

In my opinion, this is the most important issue humans are facing today. Issues like the war in Iraq and the oil crisis are all important, but they are temporary problems. Sooner or later, the war will cease, and humans will someday find an alternative source of energy besides the use of oil. Global warming and the greenhouse effect, on the other hand, are things that are permanent. They will stick with the Earth forever, and cause major lasting impacts. Sadly, this has already begun. Humans have two choices; we can either sit back, do nothing, and continue to pump out carbon dioxide and CFC's into the environment, or we can stand up for our earth and do something about it. This Earth is the only place we have to live on, and humans should not take this grace lightly.

This heated debate has even entered our entertainment world. For example, the movie *The Day After Tomorrow* was a small spark that ignited a flame in both the public and the scientific world. This movie showed what would happen if global warming got out of hand. According to Doctor George Philander from Princeton, global warming does create a problem with more heat, but that heat can then change the delicate water cycle that is crucial to the balance of the world. When there is more heat, there can be the problem of more condensation in the atmosphere, which then leads to more precipitation. This precipitation can be rain, but it can also lead to massive amounts of snow, ice and hail, as the movie portrayed. On the other hand, there are also still some people like Michael Crichton, who wrote the book *State of Fear*. This book indicated that there is nothing to fear, and that there is nothing to worry about. I have yet to read the novel, but according to Doctor George Philander, the novel was not just a fiction. Yes, Michael Crichton wrote *State of Fear* as a fiction, but he spent a few years to research the topic before he wrote the novel. And because of this,

7

many people took the fiction seriously, adding more fuel to the already massive fire.

The consequences of global warming may not be as extreme as *The Day After Tomorrow* portrayed, yet that does not mean that we should completely ignore the issue as Michael Crichton described in *State of Fear.* Global warming is a serious problem today. In a way, the greenhouse gases are doing more work than they should. Nature has its own way of keeping a balance of climate and temperature on Earth, and humans really should try not to do anything to imbalance this. Currently this delicate balance of nature has been modified, and now we are falling into a world of uncertainty: the uncertainty of a safe future. With the continuation of humans expelling carbon dioxide, methane and other greenhouse gases, humans can only anticipate the next consequence of our actions. But that doesn't mean we shouldn't do anything about it. Humans should take responsibility for their actions, and clean up their act.

Works Consulted

Budyko, M.I. *The Earth's Climate: Past and Future.* New York: Academic Press, Inc., 1982.

Day After Tomorrow, The. Dir. Roland Emmerich. Perf. Dennis Quaid, Jake Gyllenhaal, Emmy Rossum, Dash Mihok, Jay O. Sanders, TM and Fox, 2004.

Environmental Protection Agency. *Global Warming.* Last Modified on Monday, July 12, 2004. E.P.A. April 6, 2006. http://www.epa.gov/globalwarming/kids/gw.html

Environmental Protection Agency. *Global Warming.* Last Modified on Friday, January 7, 2000. E.P.A. April 4, 2006.
http://yosemite.epa.gov/oar/globalwarming.nsf/content/emissionsindividual.html

Environmental Protection Agency. *Global Warming.* Last Modified on Wednesday October 2, 2002.E.P.A. April 4, 2006.
http://yosemite.epa.gov/oar/globalwarming.nsf /content/index.html

Frey, Darcy. "How Green is BP?" New York: *The New York Times Magazine,* 2002.

"Glaciers' Melting in Greenland Accelerates." *The Roanoke Times.* 17 February 2006: 10A.

Ledley, Tamara S. "Climate Change and Greenhouse Gases" *American Geophysical Union* Vol. 89, No. 39, September 28, 1999, pages 453–454, 457–458.

Lumer, Christoph. *The Greenhouse: A Welfare Assessment and Some Morals.* Lanham, Maryland: University Press of America, 2002.

Michaels, Patrick J. and Balling, Robert C. Jr. *The Satanic Gases: Clearing the Air about Global Warming.* Washington D.C.: Cato Institute, 2000.

Philander, George. "A Geologic Perspective on Global Warming." Dr. Jim Spotila and the Virginia Tech Geoscience Department. Virginia Tech, Derring 4069. April 7 2006.

Read, Fred. Personal Interview. April 7, 2006.

Royer, Dana L. "CO2 as a primary driver of Phanerozoic climate." *GSA Today.* March 2004: 4-10.

Ruddiman, William F. "How did Humans First Alter Global Climate?" *Scientific American.* March 2005: 46–53. "Scientists urge steps against warming." *The Roanoke Times.* 3 April 2006: 4A.

7.6   Conclusion

To end this chapter, we provide one final student example of a kind of visual rhetoric that might seem very different but has become increasingly popular in the past decade: Comics. Marlon Guinto's comic tells his story and makes his argument with pictures and words. His introduction gives us a context for the comics. The comics themselves rely more on visual than verbal communication. As you read, pay attention to where the images carry the story and meaning and where we have to have words to follow Guinto's argument. Notice, also, the different kinds of visuals Guinto uses. How do the different types (photos, drawings) of visual affect the way you might read this story?

This paper was composed for Virginia Tech Instructor Matthew Vollmer's English 1105 class in Fall 2006. Read the assignment and notice what he has asked his students to do.

Illuminating Graphics:
Using Comics to Educate
Matthew Vollmer

Overview

It's probably safe to say that most people associate the word "comics" with superheroes and the Sunday funnies — and not, necessarily, with "serious" art. However, as we will discover, comics can be a complex, highly sophisticated print medium with the unique power to harness both words and images to reach its audience.

In your next assignment, we will focus our attention on comic books and graphic novels. We will examine comic art in class, while discussing the conventions of comic book artists and writers. We will also read Marjane Satrapi's *Persepolis*, a graphic novel about a girl growing up in Iran. Finally, you will write and create your own comic, not only for the purposes of entertaining your audience, but also, like Satrapi, to inform them about a stereotype that you feel is especially damaging, by illuminating the complicated, human realities that lie beneath that stereotype.

7

But Wait! I Can't Draw!

It doesn't matter whether you consider yourself an artist or not. Your drawings can be as detailed as Michelangelo, and as simple as stick figures. What matters is the story you have to tell, and how you tell it.

So, Um, What's a Stereotype, Anyway?

Here's a definition, from Microsoft Word Dictionary: "An oversimplified standardized image or idea held by one person or group of another." Here's another definition, from dictionary.com: "a simplified and standardized conception or image invested with special meaning and held in common by members of a group: *The cowboy and Indian are American stereotypes."*

These are good definitions, and we may come up with more in class. But you might also think about/recognize the fact that stereotypes are always reductive in nature; that is, they take someone—or a group of someones—and reduce them to a set of predetermined notions or ideas. Stereotypes can act, then, as blinders, preventing people from seeing others as whole people. Those affected are often robbed of their humanity.

In other words, it's pretty serious stuff.

Initial Questions to Consider

1. What comes to mind when you hear the word stereotype? What stereotypes are most prevalent in society? At Virginia Tech? Your home community? Your high school? Your family?

2. Have you ever been stereotyped? Under what conditions? How did it feel? How did you respond?

3. Have you ever stereotyped others? When? How? Did you understand that you were stereotyping someone? How did you feel about it then? How do you feel about it now?

4. What kinds of stereotypes make you uncomfortable? Why?

5. Have your friends or family perpetuated any stereotypes?

6. What stereotypes are most damaging? What stereotypes are the least damaging?

7. What stereotype are you most concerned about? What kinds of stereotypes do you find most disconcerting?

Summary of the Steps to Creating this Comic
(More detailed instructions to follow)

1. First, you will identify the stereotype that intrigues you/ infuriates you/ hurts you or people close to you. You may even choose to identify a stereotype that you yourself have helped to perpetuate. You will write a few paragraphs explaining why you have chosen this stereotype and why you want to explore it further and why you want to inform others about how the perpetuation of the stereotype may actually damage someone else.

2. Second, you will write down the story you want to tell. This could be the story of your experience, the story of someone else's experience. You will have to keep your scope manageable, since your final product will be only a few pages long.

3. Next, you will create two storyboards for your comic. Using lineless index cards as your cells (individual frames), you will first sketch a sequence of images in order to preview what your comic could look like. Then you will illustrate the same story, but drawing each cell from different angles.

4. After storyboarding, you will create your comic. You may draw your comic. You may trace images for your comic. You may lift images from the web or use photographic or magazine images. The decisions will be up to you—and, as you will find out, every decision you make will be important, as it will shape the way your story will be told.

5. Finally, you will compose a one to two page introduction for your comic and submit it to me.

EXERCISE

7.q Considering Comics

1. In the composition below, Virginia Tech student Marlon Guinto writes about issues of assimilation, cultural expectations, and stereotyping. After you have read his introduction and looked at his comic, write a brief response. Is Guinto's conclusion (comfort = assimilation) the same you would come to? What other ways might you write about this situation? What do the comics add to Marlon's story?

2. Look through the comics. How does Marlon convey emotion and other concepts with visuals alone? Which are the most effective? Would you change any? Which ones? How?

Marlon Guinto is in General Engineering at Virginia Tech.

7

Marlon Guinto
Instructor: Matthew Vollmer
English 1105, Fall 2006

ASIAN ASSIMILATION

Despite the fact that many Asians who immigrate to this country seem to be able to successfully integrate themselves into American society, they often experience alienation because of lingering stereotypes. These stereotypes, heavily perpetuated by various kinds of media, including movies, television, the internet, and magazines, often portray Asians with indecipherable accents, buck teeth, squinty eyes, big glasses and conical hats. The stereotypical image of an Asian may not be as extreme, but it certainly delivers the wrong message concerning Asian-American lifestyles. This false image strips Asians of individuality and unique personality, further limiting Asian and American communication and interaction.

As an Asian-American, I was the only non-white person within my group of friends. Race was always a joke between us; and naturally, my ethnicity would come up in conversation. My friends would jokingly make racist comments and it would not bother me at all. I did not take offense to the occasional comments referring me to rice patties and servant positions. My American upbringing made it easy for me to differentiate myself from foreigners. I almost felt like I was better than the stereotypical Asian, since I was able to integrate myself with American culture.

Because I felt superior to those Asians who had recently immigrated to America, I often made assumptions about the race without even thinking of how it could affect me. Every now and again, my parents would expose me to Filipino gatherings; I would not fit in at all. I noticed how the other Filipinos were different from me; they knew Tagalog (a Filipino native language), had plenty of Asian friends, and had an Asian accent when speaking English. I decided that they could not accept America's culture, only because they were so different. But then I met Tom; he was also a Filipino. Tom spoke fluent English, had Asian and American friends, and also appreciated the Filipino gatherings that I felt uncomfortable in. This new friendship made me realize how wrong I was in perpetuating this typical Asian stereotype.

I find it necessary to expose the truth behind the stereotype and show my friends that I was wrong in assuming that Asians are incapable of assimilating into American culture. Hopefully by reading and understanding this comic, my friends will be more open to assimilating with each other's cultures. Learning about each other is the best way to ensure comfort when socializing, and comfort is a large step towards acceptance. I hope that the message behind this comic will encourage others to explore the cultural diversity of their surroundings, and maybe make a few friends along the way.

7

GUINTO 3

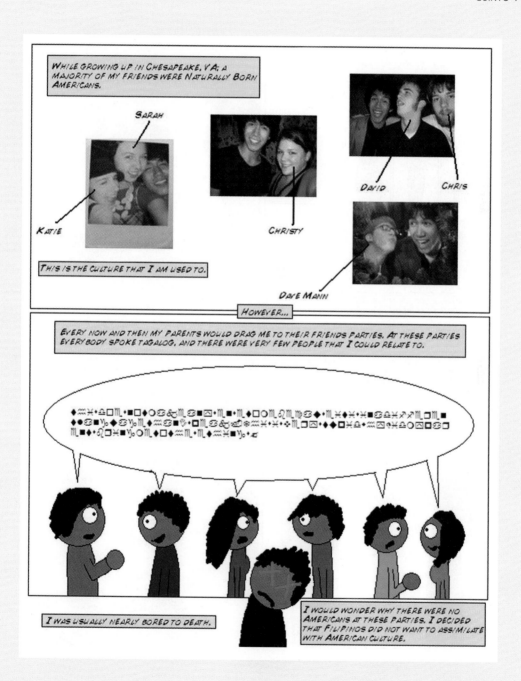

7

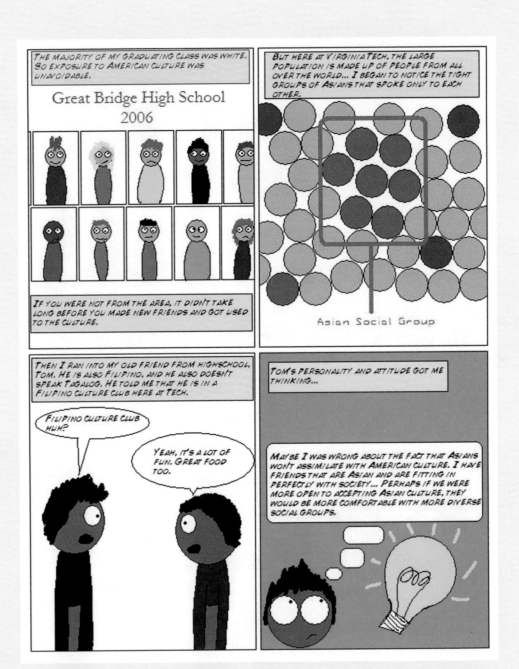

NOW, I'M NOT SAYING TO GO CRASH CULTURE CLUBS.

IDIOT.

WOO CULTURE! FREE FOOD!

(LAMPSHADE)

JUST TRY TO LEARN MORE ABOUT THEIR CULTURE, AND MAYBE THEY WILL BE MORE WILLING TO LEARN ABOUT YOURS.

HI!

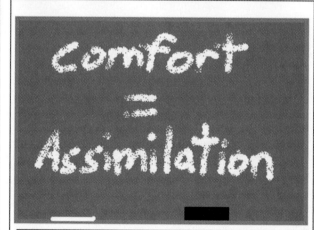

Comfort = Assimilation

I NOW KNOW THAT ASIANS ARE NOT UNWILLING TO ACCEPT AMERICAN CULTURE. IT IS ALL JUST A MATTER OF COMFORT AND KNOWLEDGE. IF WE KNEW MORE ABOUT THEIR CULTURE, THEY WOULD WANT TO KNOW MORE ABOUT OURS. IT WAS WRONG OF ME TO STEREOTYPE THEM AS SOCIALLY UNACCEPTING.

END.

7

The work you have done in this chapter constitutes a beginning. As you continue your work as a student at Virginia Tech, you will discover even more uses for visual communication. Your oral presentations, for example, should be complemented by strong visual material, and that material will depend on what you are presenting, to whom, and for what purpose. Keep in mind, though, that, like all language, visual language is complex and demands thoughtfulness and care.

7

Oral Presentation in First-Year English

According to Virginia Tech alumni, there are two kinds of speaking abilities in which college students need far more instruction and practice. The first of these skills is the ability to listen carefully to an ongoing conversation and respond and contribute in a cogent, meaningful, and appropriate way. Of course, this particular ability has long been fostered in the typical first-year composition classroom, through class discussion as a teaching method, small group work, conference teaching, and the like. The second of these skills, however—the ability to make a spoken presentation, to deliver content to an audience in a one-way flow of information from speaker to hearers—is no longer typically associated with writing courses but with public-speaking courses.

The separation of spoken and written composition into separate courses of study is a fairly recent development. For nearly 2,500 years, from the 5th century b.c.e. in Athens through the nineteenth century in America, spoken and written composition were taught side by side, synergistically, as students studied the art of rhetoric. But as S. Michael Halloran argues in *A Short History of Writing Instruction* (ed. James J. Murphy, Davis, CA: Hermagoras Press, 1990), a variety of cultural forces—literary, educational, political, economic, and technological—converged in the nineteenth century to transform the undergraduate course in neoclassical rhetoric into "English composition."

The resulting rift between instruction in spoken and written composition in American higher education widened quickly, and in the twentieth century, speaking and writing instruction became distinctly separate disciplines. Generally speaking, Communication Studies departments taught public-speaking courses while English departments taught writing courses. That gap has begun to close—and rapidly, too. University administrators across the country have come to understand that good speaking skills, like good writing abilities, are everybody's business and cannot be relegated to any one department, faculty, or course. Here at Virginia Tech, we are working hard to address the long-standing criticism of our graduates: that while they are very smart people and experts in their technical knowledge, they have not been strong communicators. Every program of study in every major must now work to ensure that its graduates are effective written, spoken, and visual communicators.

8.1 ◼ Strategies for Working Successfully in a Group

Elect a communication leader: Working in a group means that each individual member is working toward the greater good of the group. There are many ways to make a group work successfully. Take time to get to know each other, to recognize and understand each other's strengths and weaknesses. Then elect a communication leader—someone who is comfortable and experienced with presentations and has the confidence and organizational skills to keep everyone on track. This person will be in charge of sending out e-mails to the group and coordinating meetings.

Work for a single, unified presentation: A successful group presentation will be smooth and coherent. It's easy to spot a presentation by a group whose members have not worked well together: speakers repeat each other's information, offer conflicting ideas and data, and fail to develop a strong thesis. The creation of a purposeful and organic presentation requires more than simply meeting once and assigning each person an individual speech. Successful collaboration will depend upon your ability to communicate frequently with your group members (be sure you have everyone's phone numbers and email addresses), meet frequently, be open to revision when necessary, and practice the presentation several times, striving for unity and consistency between speakers.

Work through each member's strengths: To begin creating an effective group presentation, you should ask members to identify their own experiences, strengths, weaknesses, and con-

> *What we hear most from employers is the importance of being able to write and speak effectively. Your ideas and proposals may be wonderful, but if you can't communicate, you're just blowing smoke.*
>
> —Richard G. Oderwald,
> Associate Dean for
> Undergraduate Programs,
> College of Natural Resources

cerns as presenters. Then work with each person's strengths; for example, have a dynamic speaker present your introduction or conclusion, and have a nervous speaker present in the middle. While each member needs to speak and contribute equally, respecting each student's preferences will help you work as a whole and create a successful presentation.

◆ **Make the most of planning meetings:** Make sure you meet with your entire group several times before your presentation. Before the meeting ends, make sure everyone knows the next steps to be taken. When you meet again, make sure that you have completed your tasks. Be prompt, and always come to group meetings prepared.

◆ **Practice together:** Practicing as a group is essential. Make sure your group gets together and practices the presentation a few times before the day of the presentation. As you practice together, listen for repeated facts and unclear transitions. If your presentation includes a technological component, familiarize yourself with computer hookups in the classrooms, as well as remotes and projectors. Finally, time yourselves and make sure you do not go over the allowed time.

8.2 ■ Preparing for Your Presentation

8

■ *The Topic*

If your instructor has not given you a specific topic, remember that preparing a spoken composition is a lot like preparing any composition. Review the relevant texts. What did you find interesting? What parts would you or your classmates want to learn more about? How have your readings influenced your perception of the course theme? How have your perceptions of the course theme changed? What have you learned? What puzzled you? Freewriting on any of these questions may help you discover what you would like to speak about.

If your instructor has given you a specific topic, find a way to make it your own. What part of the topic interests you most? What might other students most want or need to know about the topic? If you were in the audience, what would make the topic most interesting or helpful? What would make you want to listen? What would make you want to learn? Again, freewriting on these questions may be beneficial.

■ Research

As you begin your research, you may find that your topic is too broad or that you are over-loaded with information. Remember the time limit for the presentation, and make sure you do not try to cram in too much information. Narrow your focus. For example, if you decide to speak about Appalachian coal mines, you might consider narrowing the topic and focusing on a significant historical event. *(See Chapter 6 for further information on narrowing and research-ing a topic.)*

■ Avoiding Plagiarism

As explained in Chapter 6, plagiarism is presenting someone else's work as though it is your own. It is a serious academic offense. Plagiarism comes in many forms, and learning what those are can help you avoid it. You must be careful to avoid plagiarism in all of your work, includ-ing oral presentations.

If your presentation requires research, remember to keep track of all of your sources. Refer to your *The Brief Penguin Handbook* to make sure you collect all the appropriate source infor-mation.

Your instructor may require you to turn in a Works Cited page with your presentation. Refer to *The Brief Penguin Handbook* (or to the companion website for this text) and follow MLA standards for creating a Works Cited page. Even if your instructor does not require a formal Works Cited page, it is important that you keep track of your sources in case someone has a question or concern about your facts.

While giving the presentation, you must credit your sources. Be sure to find out how your instructor wants you to credit sources, as particular assignments may require specific ways of acknowledging sources.

Use of exact quotations: If you are presenting an exact quotation, give the source's name and affiliation and then say "quote" and "end quote" before and after the quoted material. For example,

> Sarah Marshal from the Chicago News Tribune notes QUOTE "Women in the work place are finding new ways to break through the dreaded glass ceiling."
> END QUOTE.

Use of paraphrases: If you are paraphrasing a source, you still need to credit your source. For example,

> According to John Walsh, a journalist for the New York Times, genetic enhancement will change the face of our future.

■ *Analyzing Purpose & Audience*

Beyond the Composition Classroom: When giving a presentation to your employer or to your community, you will always have to consider your purpose and your audience. Your rhetorical strategies will depend on what you want to accomplish and what your audience needs. For example, imagine you are preparing a presentation on the rising crime problem in your neighborhood.

◆ **To analyze your purpose,** first you need to decide whether you want to persuade, inform, entertain, or motivate. You might ask questions like these: What outcome do you want from your presentation? Do you want the audience to be more informed, write a letter, join your group, believe that your new plan to fight crime will work? If your goal is simply to raise awareness, then you'll need to concentrate on presenting compelling evidence. If you want them to take action, you'll have to convince them that the action will benefit them in some way, as well as that the action they take will be effective. For instance, if you want them to write letters to the city council, your strategy should include evidence that letter-writing campaigns are an effective strategy, perhaps even supplying them with a template for the letter, as well as a handout with specific addresses.

◆ **To analyze your audience,** ask yourself the following questions: How much do other community members know about this problem? How does the problem affect them? What abilities do they have, individually or together, to change the situation? If you are speaking in a historically active community, you won't need to convince them that they can make a difference. However, if your community has never gotten together to take on the power structures, then you will need to start by showing that group action can be effective.

In the Composition Classroom: It may be less clear to you that you need to consider your purpose and audience in preparing your presentations for your composition class, since your purpose is to fulfill the assignment, of course. But you need to go beyond that generic purpose and develop goals of your own. Unless you know what outcome you want for the audience, you cannot plan your presentation.

You will be speaking to your fellow classmates and your instructor—at first glance a homogenous audience. Remember, however, that even your classmates are a diverse group of people. Each student has a different background, religious affiliation, political viewpoint, educational

8

history, and understanding of the topic. For any audience, you must ask yourself how you can address their backgrounds and meet their needs.

For example, imagine that you are a computer science major, and you are giving a presentation to your first-year composition class on internet security.

- ◆ **To analyze your purpose,** ask yourself what you want to accomplish. Do you want to scare your audience into updating their virus protection more often? Do you want to convince them to take the trouble to become even more knowledgeable? Do you want them to join you in a petition to get Virginia Tech to provide a particular security service? Or do you want simply to explain the security issues upon which some plot twist in a novel depends? You would develop a different strategy for each of these purposes.

- ◆ **To analyze your audience,** you should remember that your classmates do not have your background. You can assume that they know their way around a computer; however, you must remember to limit your use of technical jargon and make sure to explain concepts in everyday language, since some will know only enough about a computer to read e-mail, surf the internet, and type their papers. Any audience will respect expertise, but no audience will be able to act on terminology they don't understand. These examples of audience and purpose considerations can help you think about your own plans for your presentations. The principles apply to any situation.

■ *Organization*

Remember that a spoken presentation follows the same principles as a written composition. Try creating an outline to make sure that your material is organized logically. Consider the same elements that you would work on if you were organizing ideas in a written composition. Here are some questions to consider.

- ◆ Do you have a clear and focused point? Are you prepared to make the focus clear to the audience toward the beginning of the presentation?
- ◆ Do you plan to begin in a way that can generate interest by using wit, humor, anecdote, or surprise?
- ◆ Do your ideas flow logically? Are your points well supported?
- ◆ Does your planned conclusion bring your ideas together clearly?

■ *Practice*

Practicing is the single best way to prepare for and improve your presentation. Here are a few strategies.

- ◆ **DON'T MEMORIZE** the presentation! Reciting your presentation word for word can make your speech seem stilted and mechanical. Instead, try to speak as though you were delivering your speech spontaneously, using conversational language and fluid body language.

◆ **DON'T READ** the presentation! Reading long passages out loud will prevent you from establishing eye contact with your audience; plus, you'll risk losing their attention. Instead of writing or typing your entire speech on a piece of paper, limit your notes to key phrases; this will force you to improvise and create a more organic presentation.

◆ Practice by yourself, addressing and observing yourself in a mirror. Force yourself to look up and away from cards or outlines. Watch the mirror, make eye contact, and practice gestures that allow you to emphasize your main points.

◆ Practice handling your notes or outline — figure out the best way to hold cards or papers, how to advance through the cards or turn the pages, and how to make your notes really useful to you. Make sure the notes are printed in a size that you can read at a glance at arm's length — you don't want to have to hold the notes up in front of your face to read them. If you plan to dim the lights for a PowerPoint presentation, make sure that you can still read your notes.

◆ When using PowerPoint, don't overload your slides with words. A screen full of words almost always proves distracting, and can sometimes intimidate your audience. Since an audience's attention is naturally drawn to the screen, you don't want a towering paragraph to compete with what you're saying. Instead, try to limit the words on each slide to two to four key points or phrases. This way, your audience will have an easier time digesting and remembering information.

◆ You may be tempted to use PowerPoint merely because it's the easiest way to assemble a presentation. Keep in mind, however, that PowerPoint has its limitations, and in the long run, may inhibit your creativity. Think of the ways that information can be relayed to an audience, and consider experimenting with these options.

◆ Practice using different tones of voice for different parts of the presentation.

◆ Try to incorporate helpful hand gestures and then repeat them as you continue to practice. Some of the most effective gestures are the simplest. For example, count off points on your fingers. This simple technique helps the audience hold a multi-point argument in mind.

◆ Get your audience involved. Engage them. There's nothing wrong with giving your audience a task to do. Provide handouts. Ask them to interpret or analyze information, then lead them to a conclusion. Pose a question, and give them time to respond; if they fail to do so, ask the question again, in a different way. Also, don't be afraid to walk around the room as you speak — a speaker who is on the move often commands the attention of his/her audience.

8

EXERCISE   ## 8.a Thinking About Audience

Once you get an assignment, take time to examine your audience for the presentation. Write a note for yourself that identifies the ways you might appeal to this audience. Remember that your audience is mixed: your classmates and your instructor. That makes it a bit more tricky than you might at first imagine.

For more information on spoken composition, see *The Brief Penguin Handbook,* sections 13 a-b. Also, refer to the Composition Companion Website:: www.pearsoncustom.com/vt_composition.

8.3 █ Visual Aids

Visual aids often play vital roles in presenting information to an audience. Using visual aids allows you to provide multiple means of representation, while illustrating — and, often, serving as evidence to support — your main points. Because audiences are naturally drawn to and captivated by visual aids, you will encourage a higher level of audience participation and interaction by making use of them.

Visual aids can help you, the speaker, as well. They can not only help you focus; they can also provide prompts as you present, which can be helpful if you lose your place, or when you're fighting a bad case of nerves.

Use caution when choosing and preparing visual aids. If poorly chosen, visual aids can quickly become an unwanted distraction. By considering all of the conditions surrounding your spoken composition, you can successfully choose, create, and execute visual aids that will show you as a well-prepared and confident presenter. Here are some guidelines to consider.

◆ Consider your presentation topic. Be creative! Think beyond posters or PowerPoint slides, and consider using such alternatives as props, photographs, charts and graphs, models to illustrate examples, and film clips. While music doesn't qualify as a visual aid, short excerpts from songs relevant to your purposes—and appropriate for your audience — can, like all effective supplementary aids, further develop your presentation, and add support to your main claims.

◆ Keep your audience in mind at all times. What kinds of visual aids will they respond to? What images are most likely to entertain them? To persuade, inform and/or educate?

◆ All visuals should serve a clear, specific purpose. For example, if you use visuals merely as decoration—i.e., a generic clip art image on a PowerPoint slide—they won't accomplish much. Every image you use should play a substantial role in your presentation.

◆ Be familiar with your presentation venue, and plan according to its equipment and space limitations. Each classroom at Virginia Tech is different, and each building is equipped with its own technology. Before you make plans to use any technology, discuss the options with your teacher. Is there a projector in the room? Can you connect your own laptop to the projector? Is a key required to access the technology box? If there is no projector in your classroom and you feel that your presentation would benefit from one, discuss the options with your teacher.

◆ Be aware of the time constraints. Be mindful of the time required to set up photographs, overhead projectors, or laptop computers. Because these can be time-consuming, your teacher may limit the technology you may use, especially in the individual presentations. Arrive early on the day of your presentation so that you have time to set up equipment.

◆ When you are using visual aids that integrate text, like posters with lists or PowerPoint slides, choose the size, font, and color of the text carefully. Text should be large enough to read from the back of the room, in a color that contrasts strongly with its background, and in a font that is clear. Limit the number of words on a visual aid; your audience cannot read more than a few concise phrases without becoming distracted from what you are saying — nor will they remember large chunks of text.

◆ When working with a group, be sure to collaborate on the use of visual aids, in order to achieve uniformity of design and consistency in form. If one group member uses a poster, another uses a single PowerPoint slide, and another uses no visual aid, your presentation may appear inconsistent and reflect a lack of preparation and communication on the part of all group members.

◆ Always, *always* have a back-up plan. Technology can and often does fail. Postponing your presentation is probably not an option, so be prepared to move forward if anything and everything goes wrong. For example, you might want to have a few overhead projector transparencies prepared in case the computer fails and you can't use your PowerPoint presentation. Think ahead to what you might write or draw on the board if necessary.

◆ Be sure to integrate visual aids as you practice. Plan when you will use and refer to them, and how you will manage your body movements to avoid obscuring your aid.

◆ Since your audience will look at whatever you place in front of them, introduce your visual aid only when you are ready to refer to it. As soon as you finish discussing and/or analyzing the aid, remove it from the audience's view.

◆ Avoid reading directly from your visual aid. The aid is primarily for the benefit of your audience; you should be familiar enough with your material so that you don't need to read it. Think of it this way: the more attention you give your visual aid, the less you'll give your audience.

◆ Be aware of your body positioning. Avoid standing in front of the aid or in the path of the projector's light. If your audience is straining to see, you no longer have their full attention.

◆ Think carefully about the use of handouts. Will your presentation benefit from this kind of supplementary material? If so, how will you design them? What kinds of text

8

and images will you use, and at what time, during your presentation, will you distrubute them? While handouts are easy to create and simple to use, they can also become distracting, especially if they provide the audience with too much information and if you hand them out before you are ready to refer to them.

◆ If something goes wrong with your visual aid, go to your backup plan. If all else fails, simply move on. We have all been in presentations when the poster fell off the wall, the projector bulb blew, or the prop malfunctioned. Your audience will take its cue from you when reacting, so apply some humor, remain calm, and proceed with your presentation.

For more information on incorporating a visual aid in spoken compositions, see *The Brief Penguin Handbook,* section 13 c. Also, refer to the Composition Companion Website: www.pearsoncustom.com/vt_composition.

EXERCISE

8.b Using Your Experience To Prepare for a Successful Presentation

Step 1. Think back to some of the best and worst presentations you have seen. Think about political speeches or debates. Consider school presentations or acceptance speeches you have seen. Think back to any motivational speakers who may have visited your high school or consider some of your current teachers. Compile a list of characteristics that made a presentation either move you or lose you.

Step 2. Once you have the list, pick two or three characteristics of both successful and unsuccessful presentations and write a few sentences on why those characteristics helped or hurt the presentation.

Step 3. Once you have considered these positive and negative elements, write a paragraph about your fears or concerns. Then write down what you see as your main obstacles in delivering a presentation.

Step 4. Look at the obstacles you listed, and consider what you might do before or during the presentation to help you avoid those problems. Write a sentence or two for each one.

Once you have considered what you already know about what makes a presentation effective or ineffective, and once you've taken into account some of your fears and your specific struggles, you will be able to make some changes before the presentation that will help you make a better delivery. If you can overcome even one of your obstacles, you have succeeded in improving your communication skills.

8

8.4 ■ Critical Listening

Why be an effective critical listener? Who cares? It's not your turn. You're not in the spotlight. You get to sit back and watch others sweat! What advantage is there to being a critical listener?

The truth is that if you want to be a better public speaker yourself, critical listening skills will get you there a lot faster. During individual and group presentations, you will be watching and listening to your classmates. Based on some of the principles presented in this chapter, what are they doing well? Where do they need improvement? When you notice how distracting it is when that young woman snaps the edges of her note cards endlessly, or that young man flips his hair over and over, or someone chews gum while speaking, you have learned what not to do by simply paying attention. When you are impressed by a speaker's shocking statistic or vivid visual aid, you have learned what you can do well by simply paying close attention. Witnessing another person making mistakes or succeeding is a much more powerful influence on you than just reading something like this book. You can feel the mistake like electricity in the air. On the other hand, you can almost hear the cheers for a job well done.

So how do you do it? What are you looking for?

Content: Consider the composition of the presentation as you might read an article or an essay. What is the speaker's main idea? Is that main idea obvious? Does the rest of the presentation work to support that main idea? Are there enough detailed, fully-developed, and well-connected ideas to build a full picture of the issue or argument or analysis?

Form: Consider the composition of the presentation as you might experience an artistic visual and auditory composition. How is the presenter standing? Is she speaking loudly enough? Is the tone of voice appropriate to the content? Does he sound like he's reading from a script? Does the speech seem overly rehearsed or memorized? Is the visual aid visible and available to the whole audience? Does it have a direct and obvious connection to the topic?

Because we learn from both failure and success, you will turn yourself into a more effective speaker by carefully observing others. Critical listening skills require you to use your eyes and your ears and your intellect. Through listening critically, you can give valuable feedback to your classmates, and you can learn for yourself, for the next time you speak in front of an audience.

8

8.5 ■ Further Exercises for Exploring Oral Presentations

1. Spend 5 minutes interviewing a partner in class, with an eye toward presenting in 2–3 minutes a brief bio of that person.

2. Prepare a brief (2–3 minute) speech on your favorite song, film, poem, or other creative work. In this speech, identify the characteristics of the work that you find compelling.

3. Give a report on a comic book series or a graphic novel. Below are some questions you might want to ask yourself as you prepare your presentation. Remember, these are suggestions only. Please feel free to pursue the topic in your own style. Be sure to prepare appropriate visuals.

- What is the premise or overall aim of your comic book series?

- Describe your particular issue.

- Has the series been around long?

- What would you say is the primary audience for this comic? Age? Gender?

- Have you read or followed this series before?

- If this is your first encounter with the series, what attracted you to choose it? Or, if you are an ongoing reader, what is the appeal?

- Offer some analysis of your particular issue.

- What comments would you care to make on the art work and its relationship to the story?

- Is it film/movie/TV series worthy? Why or why not?

- Are there web sites, fan sites, and other places on the internet to research your comic book and its audience? Did you make use of them?

- Does your series make interesting implications about the real world, society, psychology, etc.? Is it set up as satire rather than anything we'd call "comic"?

- What is the attraction of comic books and graphic novels overall?

8

English 1105/1106/H1204: Oral Presentation

Peer Review Sheet

Speaker's Name _____

Listener's Name _____

$\boxed{1}$ **= Needs Improvement** $\boxed{4}$ **= Very Successful** _____

Comments / Suggestions

CONTENT		

Introduction $\boxed{1}$ $\boxed{2}$ $\boxed{3}$ $\boxed{4}$

Focus $\boxed{1}$ $\boxed{2}$ $\boxed{3}$ $\boxed{4}$

Argument /Analysis $\boxed{1}$ $\boxed{2}$ $\boxed{3}$ $\boxed{4}$

Organization of
Information $\boxed{1}$ $\boxed{2}$ $\boxed{3}$ $\boxed{4}$

Effective Use
of Support $\boxed{1}$ $\boxed{2}$ $\boxed{3}$ $\boxed{4}$

FORM AND DELIVERY		

Eye Contact $\boxed{1}$ $\boxed{2}$ $\boxed{3}$ $\boxed{4}$

Tone $\boxed{1}$ $\boxed{2}$ $\boxed{3}$ $\boxed{4}$

Volume $\boxed{1}$ $\boxed{2}$ $\boxed{3}$ $\boxed{4}$

Use of Hand
Gestures $\boxed{1}$ $\boxed{2}$ $\boxed{3}$ $\boxed{4}$

Movement $\boxed{1}$ $\boxed{2}$ $\boxed{3}$ $\boxed{4}$

USE OF VISUAL AID		

Graphic Clarity $\boxed{1}$ $\boxed{2}$ $\boxed{3}$ $\boxed{4}$

Incorporation $\boxed{1}$ $\boxed{2}$ $\boxed{3}$ $\boxed{4}$

Usefulness $\boxed{1}$ $\boxed{2}$ $\boxed{3}$ $\boxed{4}$

GROUP WORK (IF APPLICABLE)		

Flow $\boxed{1}$ $\boxed{2}$ $\boxed{3}$ $\boxed{4}$

Teamwork $\boxed{1}$ $\boxed{2}$ $\boxed{3}$ $\boxed{4}$

PART V

*Knowing
Your Resources*

9

Where Do You Go for Help?

At some point in your studies at Virginia Tech, you may need help with your writing. Even students who are used to being very successful in their writing courses find that they sometimes need help on a particular assignment. Because it is sometimes difficult to constructively respond to one's own work, another person's viewpoint is often indispensable.

The first person you should always see for help if you are confused about a particular assignment is your teacher, because your teacher knows the assignment and expectations best. If you need more one-on-one work with any piece of writing—in composition or beyond the composition class—check out the Writing Center.

Sandra Davis welcomes students to the Center.

9.1 The Role of the Writing Center

Whether you would like some assistance with thinking through an assignment, organizing an essay, revising for clarity or focus, or strengthening your editing skills, the Writing Center can help.

The Writing Center is a place where you can benefit from sharing your writing and writing-related concerns with someone else. The Writing Center provides undergraduate students, graduate students, faculty and staff writing support through one-on-one consultations with a trained writing coach.

The Writing Center's goal is not to simply focus on one assignment, but to help you develop successful strategies for all the types of writing situations you encounter. Many of its clients meet with the same coach weekly for friendly, ongoing support. The Writing Center can help with all types of writing, from lab reports to scholarship applications, starting with the very beginning stages to the final draft.

Appointments are free, but students are generally limited to one appointment per week. Appointments are recommended in the main Writing Center (Shanks 340), although walk-in appointments are often available.

> *Regular hours:* Monday – Friday: 9am – 5pm
> *Location:* 340 Shanks Hall
> *Telephone:* (540) 231-5436

There is also evening drop-in Writing Center service available in the Newman Library on Sunday, Monday and Tuesday evenings from 7pm to 9pm. You will find the Night OWL table set up on the Newman Library's fourth floor, near the elevators.

9

9.2 ■ Library and Technical Support

In the process of writing you may find that you need resources that are not available to you immediately on-line from your personal computer. While many students feel that the library looks somewhat intimidating, they offer a range of instructional opportunities designed to help students and faculty maximize their effectiveness in using library information resources.

To help you learn to use the resources available to you at Virginia Tech, you should take a 45-minute tour of the library. No pre-registration is required. Tour schedules can be found at http://www.lib.vt.edu/help/instruct/toursked.html. You will be given a quiz after the tour, which the library staff will grade and return to the instructor.

Through your Composition class you may also attend a library session in which a librarian will teach you how to navigate the library website, how to search Addison to find books and journal titles based on found article citations, and how to search article databases to locate articles on your topic.

> *Newman Library Hours and Reference/*
> *Information Desk Hours:*
> Monday – Thursday: 7:30 am – 12:00 midnight
> Friday: 7:30 am – 8:00 pm
> Saturday: 9:00 am – 8:00 pm
> Sunday: 12:00 noon – 12:00 midnight

■ *The New Media Center*

As you work with incorporating images and or other forms of media into your texts, you may find that you need assistance. The New Media Center offers members of the Virginia Tech community access to multimedia hardware and software. From help with digital video projects to website support, you can find the tools and assistance you need at The New Media Center. They have video editing bays, Macintosh and Windows-based computers, scanners, tutorials, classes, and knowledgeable staff to help you.

> *Regular hours:* Monday – Thursday: 10am – 9pm
>   Friday: 10am – 6pm
> *Location:* 1140 Torgerson Hall
> *Telephone:* (540) 231-4826

■ *Customer Support Center (4Help)*

While the New Media Center can assist you with your software and multimedia needs, you may also experience hardware or other computer problems throughout the semester. The Customer Support Center (4Help) provides fast, courteous, and comprehensive computer support to Virginia Tech faculty, staff, and students.

9

Customer Support Agents are available 24 hours a day, seven days a week to reset PID, Banner ID, and Hokies ID, to monitor system outages, and to take questions on a wide variety of computer problems. If you need assistance, contact 4Help by using the Help Request Form (http://4help.vt.edu) or by calling (540) 231-HELP (4357).

Areas of support include internet connectivity through on-campus Ethernet, the Virginia Tech Modem Pool, and wireless access, as well as central computing resources such as My VT, Hokie Spa, and VT Mail.

Please be aware that the Customer Support Center is not able to do some things, such as work on homework assignments for any student; install or repair hardware, including network cards; install or configure operating systems or third party software; or reinstall operating systems.

The Helpdesk is open 24 hours a day/7 days a week

Contact 4Help via one of the following methods:

- ◆ Use the Help Request Form
- ◆ Call (540) 231-HELP (4357)

9.3 Student Services/University Offices

Below is an abbreviated list of some useful phone numbers. While the following resources are not directly related to the work that you do in your composition classroom, they are helpful phone numbers to have for the many situations that may arise throughout the academic year.

Center for Academic Enrichment and Excellence	231-5499
Counseling Services/Cook Counseling Center	231-6554
Dean of Students Office	231-3787
Honor System	231-9876
Police, University	231-6411
Services for Students with Disabilities	231-3788
Schiffert Heath Center	231-6444
University Academic Advising Center	231-8840

9

Student Author Permission Form

Department of English
Virginia Tech
Blacksburg, VA 24061
540.231.6501

Pearson Custom Publishing
75 Arlington Street, Suite #300
Boston, MA 02116
800.428.4466

I grant my permission to the Virginia Tech Department of English and to Pearson Custom Publishing for reproduction and editing rights to my work submitted for this class.

ENGL _____

CRN _____

During the _____ Semester, 2007–2008.

This permission includes publication in any future edition of the English Department's composition text, in any format, along with my photograph and profile—

YES _____ NO _____

—and/or publication in a collection of anonymous student work that may be used as examples in future composition classes.

YES _____ NO _____

Signature: _____

Print name: _____

Date: _____

E-mail address: _____

Permanent address: _____

_____

_____